THE AGRICULTURAL AND FOOD SECTOR IN THE NEW GLOBAL ERA

By the same author:

SOCIOLOGY OF AGRICULTURE
Technology, Labour, Development and Social Classes in an International Perspective (Concept, 1989)

Alessandro Bonanno is Associate Professor of Rural Sociology at the University of Missouri-Columbia. He has researched among other topics, Sociology of Agriculture, Regional and International Development, the State and Aging. He is the author of numerous journal articles and books, among them Small Farms (1987), Sociology of Agriculture (1989), Agrarian Policies and Agricultural Systems (1990), Retirement and the Welfare State (1993). Dr. Bonanno is the editor of the *International Journal of Sociology of Agriculture and Food*. He received his Ph.D. in Sociology from the University of Kentucky.

THE AGRICULTURAL AND FOOD SECTOR IN THE NEW GLOBAL ERA

ALESSANDRO BONANNO
Department of Rural Sociology
University of Missouri
USA

CONCEPT PUBLISHING COMPANY, NEW DELHI-110059

ISBN 81-7022-464-0

First Published 1993

Alessandro **Bonanno** (*b* 1954)

Publishied and Printed by
Ashok Kumar Mittal
Concept Publishing Company
A/15-16, Commercial Block, Mohan Garden
NEW DELHI-110059 (India)

Lasertypeset by
Microtech Advance Printing Systems (Pvt.) Ltd.
H-13, Bali Nagar
NEW DELHI-110015

ACKNOWLEDGEMENTS

Editing a volume such as the present one requires cooperation between a number of individuals. In my endeavor I was very fortunate to be assisted by very talented people. I wish to thank all of them. In particular, I would like to express my gratitude to the authors of the chapters included in the book. They have been prompt to respond to my requests and diligent in the long and, at times, tedious process of revision of the manuscripts. Special thanks go to Julie Brandt and Mary Hendrickson who spent an inordinate amount of time editing and polishing the manuscripts. A part of their sociological talent is certainly reflected in the book. Many thanks to my secretary Pat Nelson for her cooperation in producing the final version of the book. Finally, I would like to thank the Mobay Corporation, Agricultural Chemical Division, for financial assistance to the project from which the papers included in this volume were generated.

ALESSANDRO BONANNO

CONTENTS

LIST OF TABLES

LIST OF FIGURES

LIST OF CONTRIBUTORS

Amy Angel is a doctoral candidate in the Department of Agricultural Economics at Texas A&M University, College Station, Texas, USA.

Paulo Ortiz Aragão is Professor of Sociology at the Federal University of Paraiba, Brazil.

Rosario Bello is Professor of Sociology at Grupo de Investigaciones Agrarias (GIA) in Santiago, Chile.

Artur Cristõvão is Associate Professor at the Universidade de Tras-os-Montes e Alto Douro, (UTAD)/Vila Real, Portugal.

Shripad D. Deo is Assistant Professor of Rural Sociology at Colorado State University, Fort Collins, Colorado, USA.

James Glecker is Professor of Agriculture and Forestry at Northeastern Oklahoma A&M College in Miami, Oklahoma, USA.

Lourdes Gouveia is Assistant Professor of Sociology at the University of Nebraska, Omaha, Nebraska, USA.

Rosalind P. Harris is Assistant Professor in the Department of Sociology at the University of Kentucky, Lexington, Kentucky, USA.

Don R. King is Professor of Agricultural Education at Iowa State University, Ames, Iowa, USA.

Timothy L. Koehnen is Assistant Professor at the Universidade de Tras-os-Montes e Alto Douro (UTAD)/Vila Real, Portugal.

Leila Lueschen is Assistant Professor of Agricultural Economics at the University of Kentucky, Lexington, Kentucky, USA.

Estanislao Gacitũa Mariõ is a doctoral candidate in Rural Sociology at Virginia Polytechnic Institute and State University, Blacksburg, Virginia, USA.

Robert A. Martin is Professor of Agricultural Education at Iowa State University, Ames, Iowa, USA.

Glenn E. McGee is DuPont Fellow in Environmental Studies at the Glasscock Institute for Environmental Studies at Baylor

University and Assisant, Center for Clinical and Research Ethics at Vanderbilt University, Nashville, Tennesse, USA.

José Portela is Associate Professor at the Universidade de Tras-os-Montes e Alto Douro (UTAD)/Vila Real, Portugal.

José Bolivar Rocha is Professor of Sociology at the Federal University of Paraiba, Brazil.

Parr Rosson, III, is Professor in the Department of Agricultural Economics at Texas A&M University, College Station, Texas, USA.

Luther Tweeten is the Anderson Professor of Agricultural Marketing, Policy and Trade in the Department of Agricultural Economics and Rural Sociology at Ohio State University, Columbus, Ohio, USA.

Gary A. White is Academic Adivsor in Agricultural Education at Iowa State University, Ames, Iowa, USA.

Alessandro Bonanno is Associate Professor of Rural Sociology at the University of Missouri-Columbia.

INTRODUCTION

The papers contained in this volume were originally read at the international multidisciplinary conference "The Globalization of the Agricultural and Food Order" held at the University of Missouri-Columbia, USA in June of 1991. The principal objective of that symposium was to examine current research on the transformation of the agricultural and food sector carried out within a global perspective. The need to discuss the relationship between the agricultural and food sector and changes at the global level stems from advances in the literature of both the sociology of agriculture and that of social change and development. The former has underscored complex alterations in the manners in which agricultural products are generated and then transformed into food, and the relationships between social and economic actors involved in these processes. The latter has emphasized the crisis of the Fordist regime of international division of labour and the emergence of new international arrangements. This literature maintains that a new transnational phase of development has been entered which differs markedly from the previous multinational phase of expansion of capitalism. This transformation, in turn, mandates a rethinking of the processes of change and of the manners in which strategies of development are to be conceptualized and then implemented.

A wealth of research has recently been published on the globalization of the socio-economic sphere. However, the present volume differs from previously published works in its attempt to address the "new" character of global change at both the conceptual and empirical levels. Though it is not claimed that this collection of papers fully addresses all aspects of the topic, it is hoped that through the illustration of selected issues some light will be shed on new trends and phenomena.

The new dimension of the global re-organization of socio-economic relations in the agricultural and food sector can be synthesized in terms of changes in the production process, institutions and social agents.

From the point of view of the production process, the new transnational phase has signified the shift of a significant portion of production to the global setting. This situation refers to alterations of previous patterns of production characterized by the generation of food products within specific locations. In the new transnational setting, production of agricultural and food commodities is increasingly carried out through the global recomposition of partial production processes set in various locations and within various economic contexts. The recomposition of production processes is controlled by a few transnational corporations (TNCs) and defined as "global sourcing" to indicate the ability of TNCs to select factors of production across national and/or regional boundaries. To be sure, the increased control attributed to TNCs should not be equated with their absolute power at the world level. In fact, the transnationalization of production processes has generated new contradictions for TNCs which cannot be addressed by traditional strategies. The inability of TNCs to count on institutions to regulate, mediate and organize economic activities and their inability to over come local resistance are among the new emerging issues facing transnational corporations.

Institutionally, the globalization of the production process outlined above involves an ever increasing gap between the polity and the socio-economic sphere. While the production process is increasingly transnational the political process remains domestically based. This situation entails a decreasing ability on the part of the State to assist economic activities in the new transnational context. Furthermore, it mandates the re-definition of existing institutional arrangements. In the agricultural and food sector, the distancing between the sphere of action of the economy and that of the polity signifies the emergence of issues such as the decreasing ability of national institutions to regulate production, protect the interests of consumers, address the overall question of food security and protect the environment.

From the point of view of social actors, the new global system signifies primarily a re-organization of the participation of groups in the process of satisfaction of their needs. More specifically, it involves a re-formulation of social arrangements which have guided national social formations through the decades of multinational capitalism. Indeed, channels of creation and distribution of wealth cemented at various levels through previous phases of capitalism have been altered by the above indicated shifts in the organization of production processes and the emergence of limits in the range of actions of political institutions. There has been a fragmentation of once very homogenous social groups, such as the working class, paralleled by an absence of alternative and effective aggregative strategies. In this respect, the demand for the satisfaction of social needs generated at the local level finds significant obstacles in its path toward fulfilment. Obstacles arise at the level of identification and targeting of counterparts. Due to their transnational nature and their ability to shift capital globally, TNCs have become decreasingly connected with the territory where labour is located. The result is growing difficulties in translating emerging needs into actions in the political sphere. Political institutions, such as national and local governments, are also unable to direct economic development and, consequently, to address socio-economic claims. Obstacles also arise at the organizational and mobilization levels. Established patterns of social mobilization and organization have been disrupted by the collapse of the Fordist division of labour. In the Post-Fordist regime labour relations has been reshaped in terms of unstable, precarious forms of employment. This situation, in turn, provides fertile ground for the fragmentation of the labour experience, the lack of development of workers' social identity, ultimately hampering the possibility of workers' social mobilization. Paradoxically, this situation refers to developed and developing countries alike.

The reorganization of production at the global level has been paralleled by the emergence of trade blocs. This phenomenon refers to the creation and consolidation of multi-national political entities which foster trade and economic activities within the territory of the member nations. The most relevant example of this trend is the consolidation of the European Community culminating with the proposed trade unification of January 1, 1993. Negotiations for the strengthening of the North American Trade Agreement (NAFTA), for the creation of a Pacific Rim Common Market, and an African Common Market are other cases in point.

The emergence of trade blocs has been interpreted in various manners. The sociological literature has emphasized the complementarity of trade blocs with global production and global socio-economic re-organization. In this context, trade blocs are viewed as partial attempts to recompose the distancing between the polity and the economy. Moreover, by focusing more on production rather than exchange, this literature has emphasized the rather permeable character of trade blocs. In the economic literature, trade blocs have been interpreted as entities which ultimately limit the possibility of unrestricted global trade. Accordingly, they stand counter to a true process of globalization. Furthermore, the economic literature has interpreted the consolidation of blocs in terms of bilateralism. In this context it is underscored that the creation of larger-than-nation trade zones allows the enhancement of economic activities and growth of participating countries. Nevertheless, trade blocs remain the outcome of negotiations among single nations and constitute barriers for commodities, capital and labour coming from other world regions.

The themes illustrated above constitute the scientific background of the present volume, which is divided into three parts. The first addresses the general issue of globalization of the agricultural and food sector through analyses of specific cases and theoretical considerations of the implication that globalization has on various aspects of society. The second part discusses the issue of bilateralism, trade and ethics in the new global order. The third and final part deals with the issue of the role that institutions of higher education and extension can play in the new global order.

The first section of the volume opens with a paper entitled "Globalization of the Agricultural and Food Sector The Crisis of Contradictory Convergence." In this paper it is argued that transformations in the international division of labour, reflected in the globalization of the agricultural and food sector, have motivated students of the field to argue the reduced ability of the State to control and organize activities in the socio-economic sphere. The crisis of the polity at the national level has opened up a debate on new forms of State action available at the international level. Adopting a political economy posture, this contribution investigates the issue of the role of the State in the new global order by arguing that State action is needed by both dominant and subordinate classes. This action is contradictory, however, as it is demanded for opposing reasons and entails contradictions for both social groups. Furthermore, the paper provides a synthesis of the most salient aspects of the process of globalization, including a review of the difference between the transnational and multinational phases of capitalism, changes in the characteristics of farm labour, the relationship between First and Third World regions in terms of agricultural production, and the phenomenon of global sourcing.

This section continues with a paper by Estanislao GacitÈa MariÂ and Rosario Bello entitled "Towards an Assessment of Disarticulation and its Consequences on Food Consumption in the Third World." In this contribution, the authors explore the relevance of the process of disarticulation of agricultural production in Third World countries in the context of the global economy. Disarticulation refers to the absence of a positive association between growth of agricultural production and changes in food consumption patterns in developing countries. It is maintained that disarticulation is related to decreasing levels of adequate nutritional standards in Third World nations as earnings from agricultural exports have not been translated into improved wages for workers and investments in the staple food sector. The chapter concludes with a discussion of the political connotation of attempts to diminish the disarticulated character of the economies of developing countries.

The paper by Leila Sfeir Lueschen addresses the question of the possible existence of a globalization of agricultural policies. Employing a market approach, the author underscores that current agricultural policies have created a globalization of agricultural distortion. Governments have failed to control both prices and trade in terms advantageous to the interests of both developed and developing countries. In this context, major agricultural world actors, such as the United States and the European Community, have introduced protectionist policies and have fostered the creation of trade blocs. The latter stand counter to the enhancement of free trade and, consequently, to a free flow of goods, services and labour worldwide. From this point of view, any movement toward trade globalization is unlikely to happene in the near future. Consumers and taxpayers, the author continues, have been paying the burden of this type of agricultural policy through higher agricultural and food prices and fiscal pressure aimed at maintaining agricultural support programmes. It is concluded that, despite the situation outlined above, efforts to liberalize economic activities in the agricultural and food sector have been multiplying due to significant changes in the conditions of agricultural labour markets and rural communities.

The section concludes with "Immigrant Labour in the Internationalization of Meat-Processing" by Lourdes Gouveia. This chapter explores aspects of global restructuring in one of the fast growing segments of the agricultural and food sector, meat-packing. Employing primary qualitative data, Gouveia illustrates the strategies adopted by a large yet domestically-confined meat processor to compete in the global market. Moreover, she underscores the consequences that these strategies have for the internationally available pool of cheap migrant labour and for local communities in regions of the "developed" world. She argues that meat-packing processors, located in the American Midwest, are dependent on docile and cheap migrant labour from Central and Latin America for their effective survival in the global economy. She also documents that the use of migrant labour poses a disadvantage for rural communities as jobs for local residents are not provided despite the financial commitment that these communities have made to attract industry and combat the farm crisis. Latino workers also face inadequate economic conditions as their wages are low and are accompanied by limited fringe benefits.

The second part of the volume opens with a contribution by Amy Angel and Parr Rosson, III, entitled "Bilateralism, Agriculture and LDCs: The Case of the Mexico-U.S. Free Trade Agreement." The chapter begins by reviewing the salient steps taken toward the creation of a free trade agreement between the U.S. and Mexico and the characteristics of the Mexican agricultural sector. The authors then provide an analysis of the potential impact of the trade agreement on Mexico and Mexican agriculture. It is argued that exports of labour-intensive crops, such as fruits and vegetables, will increase along with other exports, including livestock, beef, poultry, pork, dairy products and feed grains. Other sectors of the Mexican economy should also benefit from the free trade agreement. It is predicted that manufacturing will experience the largest gains as Mexican workers should expect higher wages and more employment opportunities. Consumers should experience lower prices triggered by the elimination of tariffs. The chapter continues with an analysis of potential constraints to trade expansion. It is noted that factors such as external debt, foreign investments, exchange rate policies and rural-to-urban migration might limit the benefits that the trade agreement would generate for Mexico. It is concluded that, from the point of view of trade, bilateralism is a more appropriate term to describe the global situation in agriculture.

The theme of the limits imposed on globalization by the existence of trade barriers is also discussed by James Gleckler and Luther Tweeten in their "Benefits to U.S. Agriculture From Terminating

European Oilseed Subsidies." The authors argue that as world markets integrate both consumers and producers are increasingly impacted by events occurring in other parts of the world. Employing the case of oilseeds, they discuss the possible implications that changes in European Community policies might have for U.S. producers. Their findings indicate that U.S. soybean farmers will benefit from the elimination of oilseed subsidies in the EC. However, the authors also indicate that negative consequences might be experienced by U.S. grain farmers in regions where oilseeds are not a commercial crop.

The issue of agricultural exports as related to the enhancement of economic well-being is further explored by Paulo Ortiz Aragao and JosÇ Bolivar Rocha in a chapter entitled "Limits to Agricultural Policy Liberalization in Brazil." The authors review changes in agricultural policy in Brazil to assess their impact on society. It is maintained that the Brazilian government has played a significant role in directing economic adjustments in the agricultural sector to respond to the impact of external forces. The export of fuel crops was promoted through direct and indirect subsidies. Conversely, food crops received much less protection. This situation generated a fiscal crisis which was dealt with through a reduction of subsidies and production diversification toward more competitive crops. In this context food self-sufficiency, which has been a characteristic of Brazilian agriculture, has been de-emphasized. The authors conclude by underscoring the difficulties that strategies of economic development based on exports encounter even in a globalized context such as the present one.

The concluding chapter of the second section of the book shifts the focus of analysis to the ethical implications of the globalization of production and consumption patterns in the agricultural and food sector. Highlighting food consumption patterns, in "Consumers, Land and Food: In Search of Food Ethics," by Glenn E. McGee emphasizes the often obscured connection between the convenience and availability of food in the First World and its socio-economic consequences for less developed countries. It is maintained that the creation of food commodities based on high levels of energy use and sophisticated technological procedures has established pernicious consumption models in advanced societies. Due to the hegemonic posture of developed countries, these models tend to be exported to developing countries. The ethical question lies in the consideration that in order to maximize individual convenience and lifestyle preferences, First World consumers become oblivious to the socio-economic consequences that their consumption habits have on the lives of people in various regions of the world. This is not as important, however, as the actual socio-economic consequences of the continuation and expansion of such consumption habits. The often observed negative outcomes associated with the introduction of mono-crop, export oriented production in some areas of developing regions and the diminished sustainability of agricultural practices in developing countries are all cases in point. The author warns us of the powerful role that advertising, the introduction of new technology and the reordering of consumer priorities have on the knowledge of consumers regarding the consequences of their habits. On these grounds, he concludes by calling for a greater awareness on the part of the First World community of the hidden dimensions associated with "convenient" food consumption habits.

The third and final section of the book opens with a contribution by Shripad Deo and Rosalind Harris entitled "Globalization, Dependence and Underdevelopment: Towards Understanding the Context of Agricultural Research Institutions in India and in the US." This comparative study between a developed and a developing countries explores the relationship between science and technology and production in agriculture. It compares the development of agricultural universities in India and black land-grant institutions in the United States, stressing the evolution of their fundamental aspects: research, instruction and extension. Furthermore, it scrutinizes the extent to which these institutions have contributed to the satisfaction of the needs of these societies and of disenfranchised farmers. The authors also illustrate the role that scientists and bureaucrats play in initiating, nurturing and legitimizing the land-grant system. The paper concludes with a review of the process of transfer of technology and institutions to developing countries in the context of globalization.

The next contribution focus more directly on the role of extension in the development of training programmes for Third World countries. In their "Bilateral Curriculum Development for Assistance in Food Security for Luso-phone Africa," by Timothy L. Koehnen, José Portela and Artur Cristõvão link the identification of levels of professional competency of agricultural extensionists in donor countries with new strategies for the development of agriculture in developing nations. Employing the case of Portugal and Portuguese-speaking Africa, they maintain that adequate training of extensionists in donor countries is a fundamental step for the creation and implementation of new developmental projects. They add that the implementation of new strategies should be based on bilateral and multilateral projects which take into consideration indigenous knowledge and maintain improved levels of communication. Finally, they stress that the primary objective of cooperation in extension should be the en hancement of food security.

Agricultural education is the topic of the third chapter in this section. Don King and Robert A. Martin discuss the importance of the internationalization of agricultural curricula in institutions of higher education. Employing the case of the United States, they indicate that Americans seem ill-prepared to operate in an increasingly interdependent world. The internationalization of the agricultural college programme, then, becomes a key instrument both to develop awareness of the global nature of agriculture and to overcome the lack of knowledge of other cultures and agricultural systems. In this respect, the internationalization of curricula is identified in terms of the introduction of activities which open students, faculty members and administrators to different world realities and the interrelated character of the new global era. It is concluded that the international dimension of agriculture needs to be fully integrated into course offerings and into the broader array of activities constituting the various aspects of post-secondary education.

Internationalization in the new global system is also the topic of the concluding chapter of the book. Gary A. White presents a study of opinions of rural youth leaders on the importance of international seminars. "The Role of International Seminars in the Globalization Process" investigates the opinions of participants in the "13th International Seminar for the Promotion of Rural Youth Work," which was held in Germany in 1986. The seminar was organized to improve the skills of rural youth leaders who are employed in programmes of rural revitalization. Findings indicate that rural youth seminars are effective tools to enhance understanding and communication among people from different cultures. Accordingly, participation in international seminars allows rural youth leaders to transfer to rural communities a greater understanding of the international interdependence characterizing the present world situation. In this respect, participation in international seminars is an integral part of the process of globalization.

ALESSANDRO BONANNO

PART ONE

AGRICULTURAL AND FOOD GLOBAL ORDER, DIVISION OF LABOUR, DISARTICULATION AND POLICY

1

GLOBALIZATION OF THE AGRICULTURAL AND FOOD SECTOR: The Crisis of Contradictory Convergence

ALESSANDRO BONANNO

Introduction

Recent changes in the socio-economic sphere have prompted an increasingly large number of observers to frame the evolution of these processes in terms of globalization.[1] Globalization has been employed as both a discourse within which to analyze new patterns of development as well as an umbrella concept referring to a complex of specific phenomena related to the international division of labour and emerging patterns of capital accumulation. In essence, globalization has been employed to underscore the changed organizational forms by which the processes of reproduction of labour and capital take place.

The agricultural and food sector has also been subject to these changes and to an overall process of reorganization of the mechanisms regulating its development. The present contribution addresses some of these changes, focusing on the role of the State in the agricultural and food sector and on emerging problems affecting various social groups. More specifically, it discusses the changed relationship between the State and the agricultural and food sector and the limitations that globalization has imposed on the action of the State vis-a-vis transnational corporations (TNCs) and subordinate classes.[2]

The study opens with a discussion of the concept of globalization, stressing some of its fundamental characteristics. The following section reviews relevant literature on the topic, addressing various interpretations of the relationship between the State and the agro-food sector. The third section introduces the concept of contradictory convergence. It is argued that in a situation in which the State is increasingly unable to assist TNCs as well as subordinate classes, both TNCs and subordinate classes are interested in recreating a State form which transcends national boundaries. The attempt to create a transnational State is, however, motivated by opposing reasons and contradicts the basic objectives of these groups. The final section reviews some items which occupy center stage in the agenda for the creation of a transnational State and which constitute important elements in the eventual development of such an institution.

The Transnationalization of the Agricultural and Food Sector

Scholarship in sociology of the economy in general and in sociology of agriculture in particular has underscored the dissolution of the Fordist[3] division of labour and the emergence of a Post-Fordist regime (Bonanno, 1988; Friedmann and McMichael, 1988; Kenney et al, 1989; Lipietz, 1987; Piore and Sabel, 1984). Despite the lack of a clear map of the Post-Fordist regime, the transnationalization of the economy is one of the most important characteristics of the new international division of labour (Bonanno, 1991a; Friedland, 1991a; Friedmann, 1991; McMichael, 1991). In essence, transnationalization of the economy refers to the recomposition of production processes across national boundaries in such a way that they transcend the locus determined by the physical limits of the nation-state. This definition calls for a number of corollaries which have been discussed in the recent literature.

(i) There is a qualitative difference between the multinational phase of capitalism and the transnational phase of capitalism (Bonanno, 1991b; Borrego, 1981; Friedland, 1991a; Picciotto, 1991). In th e multinational phase it was possible to identify corporations with countries of origin (Bonanno, 1991a; Sassen, 1988). In this context, international operations were treated as extensions of entrepreneurial activities designed and engineered in the home country and supported by the home State apparatus. In the transnational phase, the association of economic activities, identity and loyalty of conglomerates with a particular country is less visible (Reich, 1991). The large number of acquisitions of companies by international conglomerates, the decentralization of production and the transnationalization of the financial sector are all cases in point (Bonanno, 1991b; Friedmann and McMichael, 1989; Harrison and Bluestone, 1988; Heffernan, 1990; Pitelis, 1991).

(ii) The transnational phase of economic development has affected the internal organization of productive sectors, including the agricultural and food sector. This situation has generated an alteration of the known mechanisms by which wealth is produced and distributed (Constance and Heffernan, 1991; Friedland, 1991a; Friedmann and McMichael, 1989). In the case of the agricultural and food sector, transnationalization has signified integration at the spacial and sectorial levels (Bonanno, 1991b; 1991c; Constance and Heffernan, 1990; Friedmann and McMichael, 1989). Spatially, transnationalization indicates an intensification of agricultural specialization at both the regional and productive unit levels through the integration of specific crops and livestock into agro-food chains largely controlled by transnational corporations (TNCs). At the sectorial level, it implies the increasing transformation of agricultural products from items destined to immediate consumption into inputs for the greater food manufacture system (Constance and Heffernan, 1991; Friedmann, 1991; Friedmann and McMichael, 1989; Goodman et al, 1987; McMichael and Buttel, 1990).

(iii) Transnationalization has affected the use of labour in farming. Full time farmers and/or farm workers are no longer the dominant social figures characterizing the labour panorama of agriculture. In recent years, work in farming has been characterized by the emergence of the new social figure of the multiple job holder (Bonanno, 1989:120; Pugliese, 1991:141-142). Furthermore, the restructuring of the traditional manufacturing sector has paralleled transformations occurring in the farming sector. In this respect, the traditional figure of the full-time worker has been replaced by that of a worker whose employment is increasingly based on flexible time, whose remuneration is lower than in the past and whose fringe benefits have largely been eliminated (Calasanti and Bonanno, 1992, Bluestone and Harrison, 1982). As indicated by Pugliese (1991:148-149) the homogenization of labour typical of the Fordist period has been paradoxically reintroduced in a segmented labour market. In this case, the instability of employment typical of the agricultural labour structure is increasingly found in non-agricultural labour structures.

(iv) The production of cheap and abundant food has been paralleled by economic crisis in regions of developing countries and in some regions within developed countries and by an increasing differentiation of the production/consumption linkage. As research has indicated (Morett, 1991; Barkin, 1990; Gómez and Goldfrank, 1991; McMichael, 1991; Renard, 1990), the production of abundant and inexpensive food for the West would be impossible under present conditions without the contribution of developing countries to global production. Moreover, the same research indicates that the process of integration generates regional inequalities as the global terms of production and trade make economic growth in these regions increasingly difficult. In terms of the production/consumption linkage, the transnationalization chains of production create a divergence between local food demand and local production aimed at international circuits. More specifically, the development of production for the globally integrated market has often resulted in a decrease in food self-sufficiency, and food availability and an increased foreign debt for developing regions. Furthermore, this situation calls for a shifting of attention from problems associated with the sphere of production to problems associated with the sphere of consumption.

(v) Global sourcing has become a characteristic of enterprises in the agricultural and food sector (Heffernan and Constance, 1991). Enterprises are seeking less expensive factors of production at the global level. This action implies the re-location and/or delegation of production to areas where factors of production, particularly labour, are less costly and easy to use. For example, as Constance and Heffernan report in their work (1991), TNCs in the poultry sector find it more convenient to raise birds in the US but de-bone them in Mexico for export to Asian markets. Similarly, animal feed is manufactured in China, where labour costs are extremely low, under the control of transnational corporations for export to Western markets. Global sourcing has been interpreted as a response to domestically based limitations imposed on corporations (Bonanno, 1991b; Constance and Heffernan, 1991). These limitations include, among others, legislation for the protection of labour, production regulation, and legislation in defense of the environment. In essence, the more the domestic States introduce measures which protect labour, production processes and the environment, the more companies attempt to by-pass State actions through the transnationalization of their operations.[4] One observer synthesizes this process thusly, TNCs "escape those checks and balances built over the years, in the nation-state framework, by workers' movements and parties of the left" (Lambert, 1991:9).

The Changing Role of the State in the Global Order: A Review of the Recent Debate in the Sociology of Agriculture

The transnationalization of production processes has called into question the role that the State plays in capitalism. To be sure, the issue of the changing role of the State in regard to the globalization of the economic sphere is not a new item in the scientific debate as it was discussed in the seventies (Murray, 1971; Rowthorn, 1971) and again in the eighties (Borrego, 1981). Nevertheless, the evolving division of labour has re-proposed this issue in new terms. More specifically and with some exceptions (Aglietta, 1979; Gordon, 1988), the process of economic expansion is viewed as located in a transnational arena. This position is significantly different from that of those who see national social formations as the loci of confrontation and interaction among various social groups an d who view the nation as the unit of analysis for the explanation of patterns of socio-economic development (Aglietta, 1979, 1982; Poulantzas, 1978).[5]

The recent debate on the relationship between the transnationalization of the economic sphere and the State underscores the effects that changes in the former have generated for the latter. In previous socio-economic phases, i.e. the national and multinational phases (Bonanno, 1991a: 21-22, 1987), the primary roles of the State[6] were those in support of the accumulation of capital and social legitimation. The manners in which the State performs actions aimed at fostering accumulation and legitimation have been called into question now that the accumulation of capital has entered its multinational phase. While there is a wide consensus that the nation-state will continue to play an important role in the future (Pooley, 1991; McIntyre, 1991; Koc, 1991; McMichael, 1991), there are a number of analyses which point out both the limits of State action domestically and the emergence of a transnational State. For heuristic purposes and in regard to the agricultural and food sector, I have elected to illustrate three positions which exemplify various understandings of the role of the State in the transnational sector.[7]

The first position interprets the State in terms of class control. This position is adopted by the work of William H. Friedland. In recent articles (1991a; 1991b) Friedland has emphasized that transnationalization of the economy requires the emergence of a State apparatus which can assert its powers beyond the boundaries of the nation. Historically, the State has emerged to minimize uncertainties in the accumulation of capital. This process must be continued in the new transnational scenario if accumulation is to continue without unbearable contradictions. More specifically, given the continuation of conflict among various fractions of the bourgeoisie (particularly between the domestic and transnational bourgeoisies) and between the bourgeoisie as a whole and subordinate social groups (environmental movements, consumer movements, ethnic and minority groups, organized labour, etc.), the organizational, mediative and legitimative role must be performed in the new global scenario. Following Hechter and Brustein's (1980) historical analysis of the emergence of the capitalist State, Friedland argues that the emergence of the transnational State must be linked to the issue of control of social oppositions. In fact, it was through the action of controlling oppositions that the domestic State emerged in the early phase of the expansion of capitalism. The question of the State, then, is recast in terms of which oppositions are developing at the global level which, in turn, will shape the terms of the emergence of a transnational State. Despite the availability of a number of possible outcomes, Friedland concludes that the path for the emergence of a transnational State is unclear at best, though some embryonic forms of transnational State can be detected in the regulatory attempts of international organization in the agricultural and food sector such as FAO and OECD.

The second position maintains that the domestic State has already been transformed into a transnational State by economic forces. This posture is exemplified by the work of Philip McMichael and his associates (McMichael and Myhre, 1991; McMichael, 1991). McMichael criticizes the regulationist literature which argues that global arrangements stem out of negotiations among nation-States

(Aglietta, 1979; Gordon, 1988). His critique is centered on the fact that by assuming a nation-center system, regulationists (a) are unable to understand the recently established global mechanism of regulation and (b) reify the concept of nation-state. Conversely, he argues that the transnationalization of the economic sphere has already transformed the State and the State system. This process is based on the integration of the State into capital circuits which are increasingly transnational. First, the State is faced with diminishing control of the activities of transnational financial structures. This decreased control, in turn, affects the existence of the State by generating a shift of power within the State in favour of finance ministeries and to the detriment of programme oriented ministeries. Second, the establishment of a global agro-food system has diminished the State capacity to control the composition of local food and agricultural production. The latter is increasingly extroverted and oriented toward the production of inputs for livestock feeds and processed foods for affluent markets. The net result of this situation is that the State is no longer a "political mediator" between global capital and national bourgeoisies and the working class. Rather, it has assumed the role of "facilitator of the requirements of global capital."

The third position emphasizes the limitations to the emergence of a transnational State by underscoring the importance that the domestic State still retains in terms of processes of accumulation of capital and social legitimation. As illustrated by Koc (1991), the domestic State plays fundamental roles which are still unresolved transnationally. First, at the legitimative level the domestic State has historically been an agent which has homogenized and controlled ethnically, religiously and politically diverse groups. These groups have been brought together through processes of legitimation which have culminated in the establishment of the "nation" and the ideological and normative dimensions associated with it. In this respect, the identification of diverse social groups with a country has allowed the creation of more or less cohesive social formations. The existence of an entity which could mediate and eventually resolve the differences among these groups at the international level is embryonic and certainly does not have the same powers of the domestic State. Second and at the level of accumulation of capital, the domestic State has been able to organize and maintain con ditions amenable to capital accumulation within its territory by controlling labour and protecting capital. The globalization of production has altered these conditions so that protectionist measures are called for by various segments of capital while others advocate State action in opposing directions. In this respect, the ability of the domestic State to perform actions in protection of some se gments of capital has been somewhat eroded. As far as labour is concerned, the transnationalization of production processes has not been accompanied by the transnational mobility of labour. Despite some partial exceptions such the EC, the regulation of fluxes of labour at the transnational level is unresolved at best and could become the source of a resurgence of nationalist and racist sentiments among the working class.

Globalization and the State: Contradictory Convergence

The literature reviewed above indicates that there are a variety of reasons to argue for the continuous existence of the State at the domestic level. Simultaneously, there are numerous reasons to argue that a form of transnational State should also exist. These arguments echo positions developed in fields outside the sociology of agriculture (e.g. Pitelis, 1991; Picciotto, 1991; Fine and Harris, 1979; Borrego, 1981),[8] which conclude that the collapse of the international order typical of the Fordist regime requires the emergence of new transnational forms of the State.

Overall, these studies pay considerable attention to the attempts of TNCs to by-pass State action and/or to direct State action toward the fulfilment of their interests. In this context little discussion is provided on the interests that both TNCs and subordinate classes would have in the emergence of a transnational State and the implications and contradictions that this process would entail for both groups. Drawing from the observations made above, the remainder of the paper addresses some aspects of the relationship between TNCs and subordinated classes and the State in the new global system.

The TNCs

TNCs have historically counted on the support of the State to enhance accumulation of capital and legitimize this action to the rest of the population (Block, 1980; Offe, 1985; Poulantzas, 1978). Furthermore, the State has been instrumental in the control of labour and in generating the legal and social instruments for the availability of labour. In the historical implementation of these actions, the State has been forced to extend concessions to subordinate classes. In this respect, the action of the State in favour of subordinate classes has partially limited the ability of the State to assist corporations in their pursuit of capital accumulation (Bonanno, 1987; 1988). The contradictory dimension of the relationship between accumulation and legitimation at the domestic level has been partially resolved through the transnationalization of the economic sphere and the by-passing of State action (Bonanno, 1991c; Friedland, 1991a; Heffernan and Constance, 1991). By-passing of the domestic State has been directed toward the reduction in costs of labour and operations (global sourcing) and the reduction of limits imposed by State regulations (Heffernan and Constance, 1991; Friedmann and McMichael, 1989; McIntyre, 1991).

Though by-passing domestic State action partially resolves the contradictions embodied in the relationship between accumulation and legitimation, it opens up new contradictions for TNCs. In fact, the roles of organization and mediation among various fractions of the bourgeoisie performed by the State domestically remain unresolved at the international level (Picciotto, 1991:55). In this respect, TNCs find themselves *internationally without an entity which can reproduce the functions performed by the State. Furthermore, they find themselves with a State with diminished power to assist them domestically.*

Two relevant trends have emerged in this context. The first involves an attempt to re-direct State intervention domestically in order to overcome the limits imposed by previous State policies and regulations (McIntyre, 1991:194-195). The second involves the emergence of tendency toward the strengthening of supranational organizations, such as the EC, and the creation of new trade blocs, such as the North American Free Trade Agreement (NAFTA) between the US and Canada and in the near future Mexico (McNally, 1991; Picciotto, 1991).

As far as the first trend is concerned, a convergence of interests between the domestically oriented bourgeoisie and the transnationally oriented bourgeoisie has created a neo-liberal front which has directed its efforts to reshaping the domestic economic policy in many advanced societies, including the United States (Bluestone and Harrison, 1986; Clarke, 1988; Newman, 1988). In essence, these policies[9] have attempted to reduce welfare and/or social programmes oriented expenditures while promoting tax cuts and free market oriented legislation. This action is justified in that it results in an increased availability of funds for direct investments and a reduced intervention from the State. The net outcome of this strategy, it is argued, would be economic growth measured in terms of increases in both the rate of profit and employment. Research has pointed out, however, that while TNCs have profited from the redirection of State intervention (McMichael and Myhre, 1991; Newman, 1988), workers have witnessed an increased availability of jobs which are relatively less remunerative and stable than those available in previous years (Belous, 1991; Calasanti and Bonanno, 1992).

As far as the emergence of tendencies toward the strengthening of supranational organizations is concerned, this trend has been interpreted in terms of both the resurgence of protectionist measures across national boundaries and the re-proposition of international free trade (Ostry, 1990). Moreover, some analyses (McNally, 1991) have underscored that the strengthening of international trade blocs can be interpreted in terms of simultaneous efforts to develop protectionism and internationalism. Nevertheless, the rapid movement toward economic and political unification of the EC and the proliferation of trade blocs worldwide[10] can also be viewed as an attempt to extend State support to accumulation and legitimation at the supernational level. In this respect, the strengthening of supranational organizations can be considered the most advanced effort to establish political and legal elements of the States beyond national boundaries. More specifically, it can be considered a first step toward the creation of a transnational State. It is obvious that the EC with its thirty year history and its accelerating process of political and economic unification represents the most advanced and sophisticated case.

Despite these strides toward the creation of a supranational organization, both the EC and the various trade blocs which have recently been created embody a number of contradictions in themselves. First, they represent only embryonic attempts to create transnational State forms. Even in the case of the EC, supranational organizations are still based on negotiations among nations as they lack a unifying political authority. In the case of the EC, for instance, policies are still determined by negotiations among representatives of individual countries, and it is very unlikely that unified political bodies will be created within the decade of the nineties (Bonanno et al. 1990:231-39; Lambert, 1991). In the case of other trade blocs, such as the NAFTA, the creation of a unified political entity is not contemplated as a reduction in State intervention is actually sought (Koc, 1988; McNally, 1991).

Second, trade blocs are limited from their inception. The dislocation between State power and the arena of capital accumulation may very well continue since individual trade blocs incorporate only a limited number of nations and do not constitute global political entities.

Third and more importantly, trade blocs do not resolve the discrepancy between the loci of accumulative and legitimative processes which have emerged with the globalization of the economy (Bonanno, 1991b). In earlier phases of economic development, accumulation and legitimation could be addressed, albeit in a contradictory manner, by the State as they occurred within the State jurisdiction. The increased transnationalization of the economic sphere has limited the ability of the domestic State to legitimize economic processes which transcend the sphere of its jurisdiction. It is increasingly difficult, for instance, for the State to justify support of economic processes which may disadvantage workers and communities located within the nation-State boundaries. In this respect, the mobility of capital and productive structures characteristic of the new global order can generate unemployment among local workers and economic distress for local communities.

In response to this situation local communities and workers have historically advocated either protectionist measures and/or material assistance from the State (i.e. welfare oriented programmes). Both measures, however, are contradictory to the conditions established by the emerging global order which simultaneously call for the elimination of both protectionism (at least within the bloc boundaries) and State intervention. While it is possible to justify actual economic losses (jobs and enterprises) with possible future gains,[11] the discrepancy between the locale of labour displacement and community crisis, on the one hand, and socio-economic growth, on the other, will remain. More specifically, the locale where investments are channelled and possible growth occurs is not necessarily within the sphere of jurisdiction of a particular State apparatus. Accordingly, the ability of the State to legitimize the new global forms of economic expansion is diminished.[12]

It can be argued at this point that, theoretically, mobility of capital and structures can be accompanied by mobility of labour. In this case, the crisis created by the displacement of workers in one community can be overcome by migration to new developing regions. While it is possible to argue that migration might ease the negative consequences of global economic processes, there is evidence pointing to the limited mobility of labour (Koc, 1991; Mingione and Pugliese, 1991) and the existence of cultural and ideological components which make the mobility of labour quite difficult (Mingione and Pugliese, 1991). These latter include feelings of attachment to the community and land of origin and to the cultural practices of the region. (Bonanno, 1987). Multilateral trade agreements thus represent only a partial and contradictory solution to the limits imposed on the State by the actions of TNCs, as the issues of legitimation and the economic wellbeing of labour are still problematic.

Subordinate Classes

It has been demonstrated that the relationship between subordinate classes and the State has historically been a contradictory one. On the one hand, the State has been an agent of social control (Block, 1980; Poulantzas, 1978). Accordingly, it has constrained the actions of subordinate classes seeking the satisfaction of their needs. On the other hand, the State has allowed the incorporation into society of norms which represent gains for members of this class. The establishment of social programmes, consumer oriented programmes and programmes in defense of the environment are all cases in point. Furthermore, the State has maintained "free spaces" accessible to subordinate classes which allow the participation of the public in decision-making processes. More specifically, the State has allowed the establishment of democratic spaces which have been used historically by subordinated classes to exercise their participatory rights in public life.

To be sure, it would be erroneous to equate the establishment of "free spaces" with formal democracy. As illustrated by the voluminous literature in political sociology (e.g. Offe, 1985; Habermas, 1975; Marcuse, 1964), the availability of democratic spaces within the sphere of the State is the outcome of confrontations among various social groups which establish the separation between the State's formal and substantive dimensions.

In terms of the agricultural and food sector, the role of the State in favour of subordinate classes has been established both in the sphere of the supply of agricultural and food products and in that of demand. As far as the former is concerned, despite important historical and geographical differences, the State has established protectionist systems which have guaranteed minimum levels of income to farmers around the world (Bonanno et al., 1990). Notwithstanding the fact that protectionist systems have often benefited large farms, overall they have guaranteed relatively long periods of price stability and have ensured income to a significantly large portion of medium and small producers (De Benedictis et al., 1990). With respect to the demand for agricultural and food products, legislation imposed by the State has established rules for the protection of consumers, for the improvement of the quality of products and for the availability of food to needy segments of society. These measures have partially enhanced the overall quality of life for members of subordinate classes.

The transnationalization of the economy implies limits to the action of the State in the above discussed areas, hampering the ability of subordinate classes to exercise privileges gained in the past (Bonanno, 1991). For instance, the TNCs' tendency to seek less expensive labour abroad jeopardizes the State's effort to maintain adequate wage levels within the national territory. The implications for labour interests are manifold. For domestic labour, the result is a net loss of employment and/or the existence of lower paying jobs; for foreign labour, one implication is the creation of low wage employment. For the entire international labour community there is the constant a threat of job elimination through relocation and the decreased possibility of labour mobilization for economic claims. In terms of regional development, there is a decreased possibility of long and sustained economic growth, as local demand and the emergence of external economies are hampered by a system of low wages.

Globalization involves limitations to State action in favour of subordinate classes in other areas, as well. Among these are State action in favour of the protection of the health and safety of workers, the protection of consumers and the preservation of the environment. State implemented measures in these areas can be significantly diminished and/or eliminated by the simple relocating of production to regions where they do not exist or are less stringent than in the original country of operation. The well documented relocation of agricultural related production processes to Mexico is a case in point

(Barkin, 1990; Fernandez-Kelly, 1983; Wright, 1986). In Mexico the pressure to attract foreign investments has given a very low priority to environmental protection, as well as to practices which enhance the quality and safety of agricultural products and the safety and health of workers. As reported by numerous studies (e.g. Fernandez-Kelly, 1983; Restrepo and Franco, 1988; Wright, 1986) industrially polluted soil and water are used for the manufacture of agricultural products which are then exported world wide through TNCs including to the United States. Similarly, agricultural inputs banned in many advanced countries, such as DDT, are still permitted in agricultural production in Mexico. The international commercialization of products treated with these substances nullifies other countries' existing laws against their use.

The interest of subordinate classes in maintaining some form of State action in their favour is not restricted to substantive issues such as those discussed above, but is extended to the overall process of participation of these classes in the democratic life of society. More specifically, globalization has activated processes which jeopardize the availability of "free spaces" for public participation in decision making processes. In the event that these spaces are closed the possibility of participation on the part of subordinate classes is severely compromised. Consumer protection, product quality, and the protection of labour and the environment pertain to this issue as well. Indeed, they all represent instances in which the political forum, where the interests of subordinate classes have customarily been articulated, is greatly devalued of its function. The inability of public institutions to enforce measures which directly affect these sectors of socio-economic life represents, then, a shift of decision-making processes from the public domain to the private sphere. In the public domain the possibility of participation in the decision-making process is available, at least in principle, to all segments of society. In the private domain, however, this possibility does not exist. It follows that such a change jeopardizes the continuous existence of effective spaces in which the subordinate classes can exercise their right to participation in the management of society.

The convergence of interests to construct a transnational State is paralleled by the emergence of other issues which are of concern to both TNCs and subordinate classes and which are also contradictory to the patterns characterizing the evolution of globalization. In this context, it is important to discuss two of these.

First is the issue of overcoming the limits imposed by globalization on domestic developmental strategies. Both TNCs and subordinate classes are interested in domestic socio-economic development. In the case of TNCs this implies the desire to maintain political stability, markets which can absorb production and control of the labour force. For subordinate classes, domestic socio-economic development affects the general socio-economic well being of class members. If both groups have an interest in domestic development, attempts by dominant and subordinate classes to forward their interests exclusively in domestic terms encounter significant obstacles in the inability of national institutions to control and direct them. Protectionist strategies, which have recently been demanded from both corporations and labour organizations, are made less effective by the ability of transnational organizations to penetrate domestic barriers, by the decreasing ability of labour to maintain adequate levels of compensation and job security, by the diminished ability of consumers to exercise their right to product control and by other limits resulting from the decreasing capacity for control of various segments of the State. Furthermore, the overall ability of a nation to address its domestic needs is hampered by the emerging limitations of the domestic State. The issue of national food security in an agro-food system which transcends the domestic State is a relevant example of this particular problem.

Second, the transposition of the political terrain at the international level appears as a fundamental aspect of the global system in terms of both addressing current problems and creating future developmental strategies. It is obvious that if some of the tendencies discussed above continue, the decision-making power of the domestic State will be increasingly limited by elements which can be addressed exclusively at the international level. As illustrated above, however, the formation of transnational political organizations as well as transnational institutions is embryonic and encounters significant resistance. It is embrionic due to the limited development achieved by emerging transnational organizations such the EC and the multination blocs of the various trade agreement zones discussed above. Resistance to the emergence of transnational political organizations and institutions refers to the various aspects associated with the existence of the nation as a social, political and economic entity. In this regard, nationally located interests and social relations represent obstacles to the internationalization of the political agenda.

Conclusions

The Agenda for the Creation of a Transnational State

If the scenario presented above is correct, the questions to be faced by both TNCs and subordinate classes are those related to the development and implementation of strategies for the creation of a transnational State and the attempt to overcome the contradictions embodied in their relationships with the State. A number of considerations should be made in this regard.

First, despite common interests in building a transnational State, TNCs and subordinate classes enter this phase in a position of conflict rather than cooperation. The contradictory dimension of the convergence of interests involves contrasting goals which are at the core of the agendas of both groups. In this respect, the organizational capacity and political strength of each of these two groups and their fractions can significantly affect the actual shape of the global system in the years to come.

Second, the confrontation between TNCs and subordinate classes takes place in the context of a globalization process which is in its initial stage. Despite the significant amount of information available, it is quite difficult to speculate on the future trajectories that globalization will take and the implications that it will have for various segments of society. Indeed, as an evolving phenomenon globalization is open to a number of possible and diverging outcomes. This situation leaves the possibility of debating and scrutinizing possible outcomes in light of desirable and equitable solutions. More importantly, it provides social groups with an opportunity to generate actual changes. The newness of the phenomenon and the possibility of correcting some of its most evident shortcomings are compelling arguments to work for the identification of desirable developmental patterns.

Third, the fact that social groups can consciously affect the evolution of globalization and that both TNCs and subordinate classes have interests in the creation of a trasnational State does not imply that these groups have the same historical possibility of affecting the creation of such a transnational organization. Through the years, TNCs have developed transnational networks which have enabled them to partially fulfil the process of coordination and organization provided by the State domestically. Numerous studies (e.g. Friedland,

1991a; Heffernan and Constance, 1991; McMichael and Myher, 1991) have pointed out that in the case of the agricultural and food sector the organizational and coordinating ability of transnational corporations is quite developed and their capacity to influence political decision is greater than ever. Busch and his associates (Busch et al. 1991) have also underscored this point examining the case of the development of new biotechnologies and the influence exercised by TNCs in shaping the legal framework within which such innovations are generated. In essence, the ability of TNCs to address some of the function performed by the State is empirically traceable in their ability to make use of their own economic structures (i.e. their ability to organize and control economic systems), their ability to influence emerging political entities such as the EC, OECD, etc., and their attempts to create and maintain transnational coordinating entities such as the Trilateral Commission.

As far as subordinated classes are concerned, they have established a presence in some of the emerging transnational political institutions such as the European Community. Simultaneously, new movements have emerged world wide with regard to issues such as the protection of the environment, food security and safety, and consumer rights along with the development of international labour solidarity (McNally, 1991:244-245). Despite the fact that the presence of subordinate classes is occasionally quite significant politically, they generally retain the status of political minority that they have at the domestic level. Moreover, a retreat of western labour organizations at the domestic and international levels has also been reported in terms of both the overall labour movement and labour in the agricultural and food sector (Bluestone and Harrison, 1986; Pugliese, 1991). The crisis of labour organizations is, indeed, one of the major characteristics of the new Post-Fordist regime.

Finally, and perhaps more importantly, the emergence of a transnational State must address the spacial distancing between production (i.e., global investment, global allocation of production tasks, re-allocation of employment opportunities across national boundaries, etc.) and social demands (i.e. employment opportunities, availability of consumer items, social services, etc.). More specifically, both TNCs and subordinate classes must confront the issue of the discrepancy between the needs of people and regional economic development, which remain local, and the economic and political processes which can address them, which tend to be increasingly located in the trasnational arena. In terms of TNCs, this situation mandates the existence and availability of instruments of social control and social legitimation which might minimize the emergence of social instability. Moreover, it mandates the creation of instruments which can maintain and/or expand the productive and consumption capacities essential for continuous capital accumulation. For subordinate classes this process involves the increasing inability to resort to traditional channels of actions for the satisfaction of economic and social needs. In terms of employment possibilities, the attraction of new jobs is often a function of discounted wages and community investments in favour of incoming enterprises. The maintenance of existing jobs is threatened by economic claims and by the very process of attracting new investments, which demands the taxing of existing activities. In terms of social services, the distancing of the economic sphere from the socio-political sphere has emerged as one of the most relevant factors exacerbating the fiscal crisis of the local State. Declining possibilities for local States to provide for social services coupled with the declining individual possibility of affording privately such services constitute the present scenario of many rural as well as urban regions around the world.

The contradictory convergence of interests for the creation of a transnational State in an international theater which is not under full control of any social group mandates the reformulation of social and political strategies by all parties. It is on these grounds and on the ability of TNCs and subordinate classes to mobilize that the future shape of the global system will be determined.

NOTES

1. The terms globalization and transnationalization will be used interchangeably throughout the paper. For the purpose of this study, they should be considered as synonyms.
2. The concept of subordinate classes is employed here in its most general sense. It refers to social and economic groups which do not occupy a dominant position in society. Moreover, it does not imply homogeneity in terms of political goals or action. On the contrary, it refers to heterogeneous groups which have and can be at odds in the political arena.
3. In a nut shell, Fordism refers to a system of mass production and mass consumption based on a stably employed and well paid labour force in core countries and sectors, intensive exploitation of labour and resources in the Third World and relatively large and concentrated production units (see Lipietz, 1987; Piore and Sabel, 1984).

4. It is not argued here that globalization has been generated by the action of the State. It is maintained, however, that State action in favour of subordinate classes has been one of the reasons for the attempt by transnational corporations to seek factors of production, including a less expensive and docile labour force, beyond the national boundaries.
5. The changing role of the State in the new global setting requires important specifications. It has been argued recently, particularly in the specialized media (e.g. *Business Week*, 1990), that transnationalization has initiated a trend toward the weakening and eventual disappearance of the State as an element of coordination and regulation of economic activities. This position has been based upon arguments first discussed by scholars who view the TNCs as more capable of coordinating the allocation of resources worldwide in terms of both market failure (i.e. the inability of market mechanisms to avoid socio-economic contradictions) and inefficiency of the State apparatus (Bullock, 1991; Kindleberger, 1986). The thesis of the weakening and disappearance of the State has also been proposed by writers within the political economy camp (Ross and Trachte, 1990). The action of TNCs has been viewed as "rendering the nation-State obsolete as the basic unit of economic decision-making for capitalist accumulation" (Borrego, 1981:727).

   Despite the importance of these arguments, caution should be exercised in regard to the conclusions reached. Recent research has pointed out that the organizational, coordinating and legitimative roles performed by the State are still fundamental for overall economic growth and for the interests of transnational corporations (Pitelis, 1991:143; Gamble, 1988). In this regard, there is no conclusive evidence to support the existence of trends toward the disappearance of the State. Similar considerations should be made in regard to the thesis of the weakening of the State. It has been pointed out that the transnationalization of the economic sphere has affected the internal composition of the State through the weakening of some of its apparati, and through the strengthening of others. More specifically, social programme oriented sectors of the State have been weakened, while finance oriented sectors have been strengthened (Murray, 1991; McMichael and Myher, 1991; Koc, 1991; Pitelis, 1991). In this respect, the weakening of the State is only relative, as it refers to the role of the State in support of subordinate classes.
6. As underscored by McMichael (1991:72-74, see also Bonanno, 1991a:18-22), in much of the literature on the State there is a tendency to identify the nation-State with the State. Nation-State refers to the historical State, which represents the emergence of relations of production in early phases of the development of capitalism. The concept of the State, on the other hand, transcends the domestic dimension that the relations of production may assume, as it is a part of the process of reproduction of capital and labour which is both domestic and international. In this respect, the crisis of the nation-state should not be equated with the crisis of the State as an historical component of capitalism.
7. The classification of these authors into three groups should be viewed exclusively as a heuristic simplification of a much more complex and differentiated debate.
8. Pitelis argues that capital needs both the nation-state and international organization on the grounds that, domestically, it needs to control and exploit

labour through the existence of some form of local State. Internationally, capital needs international organizational forms, particularly in relation to the crisis of the American hegemony world wide. Furthermore, Fine and Harris argue that transnational organizations better serve transnational capital.

9. They are commonly known as Reaganism and/or Thatcherism in reference to the economic postures introduced during the administrations of former President Ronald Reagan in the US and former British Prime Minister Margaret Thatcher.
10. Recently, the proposal to created an African Trade Agreement has been made. Currently, there are no major regions in the world which do not have some form of trade agreement which is already in place or is under study for possible future implementation.
11. This is, for instance, one of the legitimative strategies employed in North America and Mexico to justify the NAFTA. For the case of the agricultural and food sector, see Angel and Rosson, 1991; Morrett, 1991.
12 It could be objected at this point that in macro-economic terms the loss of investments and jobs across one national territory can be compensated for by the influx of investments coming from other regions. The benefits of incoming investments can compensate for the loss of existing jobs and economic activities. Two objections can be raised to this reasoning. First, global sourcing has been one of the most important characteristics of the transnationalization of economic activities. Accordingly, if investments are to be made in the region, in question they must provide factors of production (including labour) which are offered at costs as low as or lower than those available in other regions. Moreover, the receiving region must also guarantee desirable levels of socio-economic stability which include low levels of labour claims, legislation which favours the interests of TNCs, an overall climate favourable to business, etc. Second, if low labour costs and overall production costs are establised, it is very likly that the level of economic well being of the region will also be low.

REFERENCES

Aglietta, Michel, (1982), "World capitalism in the eighties." *New Left Review* (136): 5-42.

Aglietta, Michel, (1979), A Theory of Capitalist Regulation. London: New Left Books.

Angel, Amy and Parr Rosson, III, (1991), "Bilateralism, Agriculture, and LDC's: the case of the Mexico-U.S. free trade negotiations." Paper presented at the International Conference on the Globalization of the Agricultural and Food Order. Columbia, Missouri, June.

Barkin, David, (1990), *Distorted Development. Boulder*, Westview Press.

Belous, Richard, (1990), "Flexible Employment: The Employer's Point of View." Pp. 111-129 in Peter B. Doeringer, (ed.) *Bridges to Retirement: Older Workers in a Changing Labour Market*. Ithaca: Industrial Labour Relation Press.

Block, Fred, (1980), "Beyond relative autonomy: state managers as historical subjects." Pp. 227-240 in R. Miliband and J. Seville, (Eds.), *Socialist Register*. London: Merlin Press.

Bluestone, Barry and Bennett Harrison, (1986), "The great American job machine: The proliferation of low wage employment in the U.S. economy." Study prepared for the Joint Economic Committee, U.S. Congress, December.

Bluestone, Barry and Bennett Harrison, (1982), *The Deindustrialization of America: Plant Closing, Community Abandonment and the Dismantling of Basic Industry*. New York: Basic Books.

Bonanno, Alessandro, (1991a), "The Globalization of the agricultural and food system and theories of the State." *International Journal of Sociology of Agriculture and Food*, Vol. (1): 15-30.

Bonanno, Alessandro, (1991b), "The policy setting in the restructuring of the agricultural and food system." Testimony prepared for the Parliamentarian Groups of PDS of Italy. Rome, Italy, Chamber of Deputies, April.

Bonanno, Alessandro, (1991c), "Globalization of the agricultural and food order: A critique of the locus of policy action in a transnational setting." Paper presented at the International Conference on the Globalization of the Agricultural and Food Order. Columbia, Missouri, June.

Bonanno, Alessandro, (1989), "Decentralization, informalization and the agricultural labour market." Pp. 119-132 in A. Bonanno, (ed.) *Sociology of Agriculture*. New Delhi: Concept.

Bonanno, Alessandro, (1988), "Theories of the state: The case of the land reform in Italy, 1944-1961." *The Sociological Quarterly*, Vol. 29 (1):131-147.

Bonanno, Alessandro, (1987), "Agricultural policies and the capitalist state. Agriculture and Human Values, Vol. 4 (2,3):40-46.

Bonanno, Alessandro, Donato Fernandez and Jere L. Gilles, (1990), "Agrarian policies in the US and EC: A comparative analysis." Pp. 227-251 in A. Bonanno, (ed.), *Agrarian Policies and Agricultural Systems*. Boulder: Westview Press.

Borrego, John, (1981), "Metanational capitalist accumulation and the emerging paradigm of revolutionist accumulation." *Review*, Vol. IV (4): 713-777.

Bullock, Bruce, (1991), "Research Challenges for Social Scientists Generated by Globalization." Paper presented at the international conference on "The Globalization of the Agricultural and Food Order." University of Missouri, Columbia, MO. June.

Busch, Lawrence, William B. Lacy, Jeffrey Burkhardt and Laura Lacy, (1991), *Plants, Power, and Profit*. Oxford: Basil Blackwell.

Business Week, (1990), "The stateless corporation." *Business Week*, May 14:98-105.

Calasanti, Toni M. and Alessandro Bonanno, (1992), "Working 'over-time': Economic restructuring and retirement of a class." *The Sociological Quarterly*, Vol.33 (1):135-152.

Clarke, Simon, (1988), "Overaccumulation, class struggle and the regulation approach." *Capital and Class*, Vol. 36 (2):59-104.

Constance, Douglas H. and William D. Heffernan, (1991), "The global poultry agro/food complex." *International Journal of Sociology of Agriculture and Food*, Vol. (1):126-142.

DeBenedictis, Michele, Fabrizio de Filippis and Luca Salvatici, (1990), "Social and economic consequences of the EC agricultural policy." Pp. 151-179 in A. Bonanno, (ed.), *Agrarian Policies and Agricultural Systems*. Boulder: Westview Press.

Fine, Ben and Laurence Harris, (1979), *Rereading Capital*. London: MacMillan.

Fernandez-Kelly, MarÀa Patricia, (1983), *For Me Are Sold: I and My People-Women and Industry in Mexico's Frontier*. Albany:SUNY Press.

Friedland, William H., (1991a), "The transnationalization of agricultural production: Palimpsest of the transnational state." *International Journal of Sociology of Agriculture and Food*, Vol. (1):48-58.

Friedland, William B., (1991b), "The new globalization: the case of fresh foods." Paper presented at the International Conference on the Globalization of the Agricultural and Food Order. Columbia, Missouri, June.

Friedmann, Harriet, (1991), "Changes in the international division of labour: Agri-food complexes and export agriculture." Pp. 65-93 in William H. Friedland et al., (eds.), *Towards a New Political Economy of Agriculture*. Boulder: Westview Press.

Friedmann, Harriet and Philip McMichael, (1989), "Agriculture and the state system." *Sociologia Ruralis*, Vol. 29 (2):93-117.

Gamble, Andrew, (1988), *The Free Economy and the Strong State: The Politics of Thatcherism*. Basingstoke: MacMillan.

Gómez, Sergio and Walter Goldfrank, (1991), "World market and agricultural transformation: The case of neo-liberal Chile." *International Journal of Sociology of Agriculture and Food*, Vol. (1):143-150.

Goodman, David, Bernardo Sorj and John Wilkinson, (1987), *From Farming to Biotechnology: A Theory of Agro-Industrial Development*. Oxford: Basil Bleckwell.

Gordon, David, (1988), "The global economy: new edifice or crumbling foundations?" *New Left Review*, 168:24-65.

Habermas, Jurgen, (1975), *Legitimation Crisis*. Boston: Beacon Press.

Harrison, Bennett and Barry Bluestone, (1988), *The Great U-Turn: Corporate Restructuring and the Polarizing of America*. New Your: Basic Books.

Hechter, Michael and William Brustein, (1980), "Regional modes of production patterns of state formation in Western Europe." *American Journal of Sociology*, Vol. 85 (5):1061-1094.

Heffernan, William D., (1990), "Internationalization of the poultry industry." Paper Presented at the XII World Congress of Sociology. Madrid, Spain, July.

Heffernan, William D., and Douglas Cantance, (1991), "The limitations of the commodity system approach." Paper presented at the international conference on "The Globalization of the Agricultural and Food Order." University of Missouri, Columbia, M O., June.

Kenney, Martin, Linda M. Lobao, James Curry and Richard Coe, (1989), "Midwest agriculture and US fordism." *Sociologia Ruralis*, Vol. 29 (2): 131-148.

Kindleberger, Charles P., (1986), "International public goods without international government." *American Economic Review*, Vol 76 (1):1-13.

Koc, Mustafa, (1991), "Globalization, compartmentalization and the new world order." Paper presented at the international conference on "The Globalization of the Agricultural and Food Order." University of Missouri, Columbia, Missouri, June.

Koc, Mustafa, (1988), "Towards a North American Continental Market." *The Rural Sociologists*, Vol. 8 (2):164-172.

Lambert, John, (1991), "Europe: the nation-state dies hard." *Capital and Class*, Vol. 43 (2):9-23.

Lipietz, Alain, (1987), *Mirages and Miracles*. London: Verso.

McIntyre, Richard, (1991), "The political economy and class analytics of international capital flows: US industrial capital in the 1970s and 1980s." *Capital and Class*, 43 (2):179-201.

McMichael, Philip, (1991), "Food, the State and the world economy." *International Journal of Sociology of Agriculture and Food*, Vol. (1):71-85.

McMichael, Philip and Frederick H. Buttel, (1990), "New directions in the political economy of agriculture." *Sociological Perspectives*, Vol. 33 (1):89-109.

McMichael, Philip and David Myhre, (1991), "Global regulation vs. the nation state: Agro-food systems and the new politics of capital." *Capital and Class*, 43 (2):83-106.

McNally, David, (1991), "Beyond Nationalism, Beyond Protectionism: Labour and the Canada-US Free Trade Agreement." *Capital and Class*, 43 (2):233-252.

Marcuse, Herbert, (1964), *One Dimensional Man*. Boston: Beacon Press.

Mingione, Enzo and Enrico Pugliese, (1991), "The attack on rural subsistence, urbanization and food regimes: The current terms of an old question." Paper presented at the international conference on "The Globalization of the Agricultural and Food Order." University of Missouri, Columbia, MO. June.

Morett, Jorge, (1991), "Nuevas modalidades de control de las empresa transnacionales en la agricultura mexicana: el caso de la fresa." *Agriculturay Sociedad*, Vol. 60 (3):29-46.

Murray, Robin, (1991), "The state after Henry." *Marxism Today*, May:32-45.

Murray, Robin, (1971), "The internationalization of capital and the nation state." *New Left Review*, 67:84-109.

Newman, Katherine, (1988), *Falling From Grace*. New York: The Free Press.

Offe, Claus, (1985), *Disorganized Capitalism*. Cambridge: MIT Press.

Ostry Sylvia, (1990), Governments and Corporations in a Shrinking World. New York: US Council of Foreign Relations.

Picciotto, Sol, (1991), "The internationalisation of the state." *Capital and Class*, (43):43-63.

Piore, Michael J., and Charles F. Sabel, (1984), *The Second Industrial Divide: Possibilities for Prosperity*. New York: Basic Books.

Pitelis, Christos, (1991), "Beyond the nation-state?: The transnational firm and the nation-state." *Capital and Class*, (43):131-152.

Pooley, Sam, (1991), "The state rules, OK? The continuing political economy of nation-states." *Capital and Class*, (43):65-79.

Poulantzas, Nicos, (1978), *State, Power, Socialism*. London: New Left Books.

Pugliese, Enrico, (1991), "Agriculture and the new division of labour." Pp.137-150 in William H. Friedland et al., (eds.), *Towards a New Political Economy of Agriculture*. Boulder: Westview Press.

Reich, Robert B., (1991), The Work of Nations. New Your: Alferd A. Knopf.

Renard, Marie-Christine, (1990), "The world market and the production of coffee in the Soconusco, Chiapas, Mexico." Paper presented at the XII World Congress of Sociology. Madrid, Spain, July.

Restrepo, Ivan and Susana Franco, (1988), *Naturaleza Muerta*. Mexico City: Centro de Ecodesarrollo.

Ross, Robert J.S. and Kent C. Trachte, (1990), *Global Capitalism*: The New Leviathan. Albany: SUNY Press.

Rowthorn, Bob, (1971), "Imperialism in the 1970's — unity or rivalry." *New Left Review*, 69:31-54.

Sassen, Saskia, (1988), *The Mobility of Labour and Capital*. New York: Cambridge University Press.

Wright, Angus, (1986), "Rethinking the circle of poison: the politics of pesticide poisoning among mexican farm workers." *Latin American Perspectives*, Vol. 13 (4):341-361.

2

TOWARDS AN ASSESSMENT OF DISARTICULATION AND ITS CONSEQUENCES ON FOOD CONSUMPTION IN THIRD WORLD COUNTRIES

ESTANISLAO GACITŪA MARIŌ and ROSARIO BELLO

Introduction

After World War II, and the consolidation of the modern economic system, financial capital increasingly determined where productive capacities ought to be expanded, reproduced or simply abandoned. Third world economies have became more labile and subordinated to world economic powers. Within this framework, various strategies for third world development have been implemented achieving some industrial development and economic growth (Gereffi, 1990; Lal, 1985; Todaro, 1989). However, poverty continues to flagellate most of the third world population (World Bank, 1990).

The consequences of these processes have been various. First, there has been a polarization of productive forces and labour processes, creating specific chains of production and unequal exchange that feed the world economy (Castells and Laserna, 1990; Evans, 1985; Furtado, 1972; Frank, 1966, 1984; Gereffi, 1990; Griffin and Gurley, 1985; Timberlake and Williams, 1984). As a result of the above, sectoral disparities increased. The trickle down of industrial-based growth did not occur and the gap between classes increased. Foreign capital tended to favour only certain firms and industries, which were able to develop, increasing the technological distance and deteriorating the terms of trade between third world nations and the world economy. Second, a particular type of social political and economic structures characterized by disarticulation developed (Amin, 1974, 1976; de Janvry, 1985; de Janvry and Garramon, 1977; de Janvry and Sadoulet, 1983, 1985; Stokes and Anderson, 1990; Touraine, 1990). At the political level, disarticulation implies the exclusion of significant social actors from civil society and the constitution of a fragmented state. While popular participation is insignificant, different capitalist fractions advance exclusive accumulation patterns which lead to various degrees of disarticulation over time. Following de Janvry (1981), disarticulated growth could be defined as the lack of relationships between the growth in production and consumption potential. In other words, sectoral disarticulation is given by weak or null, forward and backward linkages between the various sectors of the economy, while social disarticulation implies an uneven development of the productive forces. Analogous to political disarticulation, social disarticulation represents the co-existence of high rates of absolute surplus with low retribution to the labour force and, therefore, stagnant local markets for wage goods.

Third, in the agricultural and food sector, the trends described before resulted in an increasing integration of production and agribusiness at the international level. For the third world, this resulted in a productive differentiation vis-a-vis developed nations and subordinated integration of the former nations to complex chains of agro-industrial production and, therefore, to international markets with decreasing terms of trade (Drucker, 1986; Friedmann and McMichael, 1989). This integration of agribusiness at the national and international level, rather than decreasing the disarticulation of third world economies, has either sustained it or contributed to worsen it. The increasing influence of foreign capital to reshape policy priorities at the national level such as exchange rates, agricultural pricing policies, fiscal and monetary policies (and others included lately under the heading of structural adjustment), contributed to the uneven development of the economies of middle and low income countries, therefore, to their disarticulation. At the same time policy priorities by third world states have changed, decreasing the weight of social policies. The above explain why the agro-industrial sector experienced a sustained growth, while at the same time food security has been threatened (Barraclough and Utting, 1987), "particularly in Latin America and Africa, [where] rapid economic growth has been accompanied by a worsening pattern of income distribution and a growing incidence of poverty and undernutrition" (Aziz, 1990, p.10).

This paper explores the impact of sectoral disarticulation on food consumption, a measurement of population well being. This issue has particular relevance, particularly in the current political context. Multinational agencies, as well as third world governments, tend to underscore economic performance and aggregate indicators of growth over issues of income distribution and food security, for example. However, it is increasingly clear that having healthy national accounts and positive trade balances would not necessarily result in a better quality of life for the poorest sectors of the population. Countries such as Chile, Mexico, Nigeria or the Philippines are examples of the pervading effects of disarticulation among countries at different levels of economic growth.

Previous research have tested that disarticulation has a negative impact on social well-being because it generates highly uneven social and economic structures, inhibiting the positive effects that economic growth could have for the quality of life of the poorest sectors. Disarticulated growth is assumed to have a negative impact on income distribution because the retribution that labour gets is, in absolute and relative terms, inferior. At the same time, there is a diversion of capital from internal "wage-goods markets" towards markets highly specialized and selective. That is, profits do not depend on the income and demand of popular sectors, and the earnings generated from exports are not redistributed to expand internal wage-goods consumption (de Janvry, 1985; de Janvry and Garramon, 1977; de Janvry and Sadoulet, 1983, 1985; Manale, 1991; Stokes and Anderson 1990). In summary, disarticulation is functional to the expansion of the dominant accumulation pattern, rather than a vitiated form of development.

Assessing disarticulation has singular importance for the formulation of policy alternatives aimed at achieving growth with equity in third world countries. The concept of disarticulation needs to be comprehended in its multidimensional character. This study contributes to having a better knowledge of these dimensions and to the understanding of the consequences of disarticulated growth. Also, the approach taken in this paper may contribute to calling into attention the urgent need for third world policy makers to design and target specific policy instruments aimed at decreasing economic and social disarticulation.

Disarticulation and Capital Accumulation in the Third World

National development strategies implemented by third world countries respond both to the internal economic crisis and class conflicts, and to the contradictions of the core economies (de Janvry, 1981; Marini, 1973). The interaction of these two levels have generated a global economy in which developed countries have progressively moved away from an accumulation pattern based on the extraction of absolute surplus to one based on relative surplus. That is, taking advantage of technological and capital intensive work processes, augmenting the overall productivity of the labour force. At the same time, labour intensive processes are moving into third world countries in the form of "maquiladoras", assembly plants, and other production processes characterized by the extraction of absolute surplus from cheap labour force (Amin, 1974, 1976; de Janvry 1981; Marini 1973; Portes and Kincaid, 1990).

The contradiction between these two strategies involves more than an international productive specialization. Rather, they are an expression of the structural character that disarticulated growth has for third world economies. State policies, although constrained by international macroeconomic conditions and international markets (Friedmann and McMichael, 1989), have the potential for modifying this structural situation either through fiscal and monetary policy or distributive adjustments, among others. In doing this, government intervention could change the specific set of relations that maintain disarticulation, shifting the degree of disarticulation of the economy (de Janvry, 1981; Marini, 1973).

Within that framework, each one of the development strategies implemented in the third world (neo-classical, import substitution, and export promotion) can be understood as processes of reorientation of the accumulation pattern of each particular economic period. For neoclassic economic theory, industrialization was the result of the overall process of economic growth and modernization of the economy based on the net addition of capital stock, thus, of external financial support and, transfer of resources from the traditional sector of the economy (rural/agricultural) to the modern (Todaro, 1989). However, the "trickle down" of economic growth associated with classical economic theory did not happen.

Import substitution emerged as an alternative aimed at creating internal markets for specific goods based on the assumption of replacing imported commodities with domestic sources of supply and demand. Import substitution generated a process of industrial development, although plenty of contradictions. Manufacture industries tended to be concentrated either in the production of exports goods or luxury commodities for the local elites. Consequently, sectorial disparities increased, favouring both the development of certain industrial sectors and firms, and foreign control over newly created industrial sectors (Grindle, 1986; Lipton, 1984; Todaro, 1989). In the 80s', export oriented policies guided development strategies. Based on the neoliberal principles of international trade and comparative advantages, development was seen as the outcome of productive specialization due to availability of natural resources, cheap labour force, and political conditions granting the industrial sector economies of scale and less costs of production and commercialization. While the export sector could become the key sector of an articulated economy, if the earnings generated are redistributed for internal consumption (de Janvry and Sadoulet, 1985, p.3), the export promotion strategy advanced by several third world countries during the 1980s, increased their disarticulation levels and vulnerability to international economic crises. Aggravated by the constraints created by the foreign debt, negative terms of trade, low income elasticity, overproduction, and other macroeconomic phenomena, third world economies mortgaged the achievement of growth with equity for healing their national accounts and increasing their foreign exchange earnings (de Janvry, 1987; Drucker, 1986; Love, 1989; Todaro, 1989).

Food security and basic needs satisfaction have become increasingly more problematic. Achieving growth with equity has become increasingly problematic for third world economies (CEPAL, 1990). Various factors intervene in the generation of the above situation. Among them, it is important to underscore: (a) the progressive budget cuts and fiscal restrictions that undermine the implementation of social policies; (b) the increasingly unequal income distributions; and (c) the shift of productive resources from internal wage goods consumption to either external or internal luxury markets (Barraclough and Utting, 1987; de Janvry and Sadoulet, 1983; de Janvry, 1985; Diakosavvas, 1989; Dore and Weeks, 1982; Todaro, 1989; Wei Yuan, 1989; World Bank, 1990). This phenomena can be partly explained by the disarticulation of Third World Economies (de Janvry 1985; de Janvry and Sadoulet 1983; Stokes and Anderson 1990).

There are various mechanisms through which disarticulation shapes the outcomes of economic growth and, thus, of human welfare. Disarticulation vitiates the relationship between productivity and wage levels. In disarticulated economies the retribution the labour force gets for its productive work tends to be depressed (Amsden, 1981; Breedlove, 1991; de Janvry, 1991; de Janvry and Sadoulet, 1985). As a consequence, circulation tends to be separated from production because labour's income does not have a significant participation in expanding the market for the key economic sector and, therefore, worker's consumption represents a small proportion of the accumulated demand for the goods produced in the economy (de Janvry, 1981; Marini, 1973). Also, disarticulation and associated productive transformations, tend to produce an excessive and disproportionate growth of the service and informal sectors (Portes, Castells and Benton, 1989; Stokes and Anderson 1990, p.67). Disarticulation implies the existence of one economy in which different economic sectors, disarticulated in terms of growth, are consolidated into one predominant accumulation pattern.

Specifically, disarticulation has an impact upon food consumption via two mechanisms. First, it is a problem of unequal income distribution between the different segments of the population, thus, of unequal access to food (Wise, 1987). In a disarticulated economy the growth of the economy does not require an expansion of the demand of staple foods (and wage goods in general) because the demand of the commodities produced does not depend on workers' demand potential. A second mechanism is what Lappe and Collins (1977, 1986) describe as the shift of governmental policies from the support of internal food production to the promotion of exports crops, with the subsequent shift in the use of land and other productive resources. These two processes partially explain why third world countries having experienced economic growth have not achieve real improvements in basic needs satisfaction (Aziz, 1990; Barraclough and Utting, 1987;Dore and Weeks, 1982; Wise, 1987).

Subsequently, it is hypothesized that the level of disarticulation of the economy has a significative negative impact on the levels of food consumption of low and middle income third world countries.

The problem is not a technical one (i.e. not enough food production), but it should be understood as a political problem derived from the disarticulation of third world economies (de Janvry, 1981; Rao and Caballero, 1990). Food security, understood as the capacity of a country to meet both the actual demand and the potential requirements for food of the whole population, is a major political problem that requires urgent solutions. Achieving sustainable development and growth with equity have become "buzz-word", but few third world governments, even those experiencing sustained economic growth and that have succeeded in reducing the debt burden, have really embraced the political agenda of equity. Brazil, Chile and Mexico are clear examples of this contradiction (Adelman and Taylor, 1990; Goldin and Castro de Rezende, 1990; Hojman, 1990a, 1990b).

Data and Methods

Variable Description and Measurement

Food Consumption (ZFOOD): The dependent variable is a composite measurement developed by adding the z-scores of total protein and total calories on a per capita basis (from animal and vegetable sources) in the diet for each country in 1986. Although appropriated caloric intake is, by and large, matched by proper protein intake, adding calories and protein results in a more appropriate measurement because of the different income elasticity that calories and proteins have. In this way it is possible to approach, at least tangentially, the effect of income differentials into the measurement. This proxy, though conservative (Gacitúa and Bello, 1991; Wimberley 1989), represents an aggregate estimate of the population's food consumption.

Disarticulation (DISAR): Previous research (Breedlove, 1991; de Janvry and Sadoulet, 1985; Manale, 1991; Stokes and Anderson, 1990) had measured sectoral disarticulation as the ratio of labour productivity across economic sectors. Such an approach incorporates only one dimension of the concept of disarticulation, disregarding other possible component of a disarticulated economy. Recent attempts have been made to measure different dimensions of disarticulation. Breedlove (1991) measures social and sectorial disarticulation, as two independent and distinct phenomena. While such a distinction at the conceptual level is possible, it is problematic because it artificially divides the multidimensional character the concept has. A better measure of disarticulation should include, as a composite indicator, the capacity for internal consumption of wage goods, or a measure of income distribution. Also, it should include the geographical location of the market, or the impacts of exports on the overall economy (de Janvry 1981).

The estimate of sectoral disarticulation developed in this paper seeks to incorporate both a measurement of labour productivity across sectors, similar to that of Stokes and Anderson (1990), and a measurement of the outward orientation of production. This measurement still is incomplete since it does not incorporate a measurement of export earnings use, or an estimate of consumption, such as income distribution, (there is no available data for income distribution). However, it represents an step forward in the assessment of disarticulation.

Labour productivity was measured as the log-ratio between labour productivity in the manufacture-industrial sector and the labour productivity in the agricultural and service sectors. The outward orientation of primary production was measured as the log-ratio of industrial/manufactured and non-fuel primary exports as a percentage of total exports. This measurement estimates the country's dependence on primary exports and, therefore, of the outward orientation of the country's economy (de Janvry 1981; Gacitúa and Bello, 1991). The higher the score in any of the two, the higher the level of disarticulation, which is computed by the addition of the two partial scores (see Appendix I). By adding both measures one gets a more comprehensive indicator that accounts for the productivity of the labour force and the processing capabilities of the economy (i.e. the relative importance of value-adding activities within the economy, which are in direct relation to the ratio between absolute and relative surplus).

Both estimates, as well as all three control variable were measured for 1980, while the dependent variable, food consumption was measured in 1986. This lag resembles the five years (1978-1983) lag taken by Stokes and Anderson, or Breedlove (1977-1982), or Manale (1978-1983).

Log Gross National Product per Capita (LGNP): GNP per capita represents an aggregate measurement of economic performance. Likewise the previous indicator, a log transformation, was necessary to correct for skewness and to approach a linear model. GNP, incorporated as a control variable allows to assess the net impact of disarticulation holding constant different levels of GNP. However, as any other aggregate measurement, it conceals the question of income distribution mentioned before (Dore and Weeks, 1982; Hicks and Streeten, 1979).

Debt Service as Percentage of GNP (DBGNP): It is a standard estimate of the actual payments made by third world countries. As such, it represents an approximation to the transfers made from third world economies to the developed world. Since it is related to the concept of disarticulation, it is important to control for it when measuring disarticulation.

Agricultural Output Percapita (AGOUT): This measurement represents an estimate of the country's agricultural production per capita between 1980 (base year) and 1986. It includes various products intended for human consumption. However, it is neither adjusted for exports nor for industrial use, therefore, it does not indicate necessarily the actual food availability in the country (Gacitúa and Bello, 1991; Wilkie and Moreno, 1985).

Sample and Data Sources

A subset of sixty-five low and middle income third world countries were selected (see Appendix-I). Eastern-European countries, as well as other socialist countries, were excluded from the sample because their political and economic system create another set of problems that the concept of disarticulation does not properly address. South Africa, Lesotho and Botswana, were also excluded due to their economic integration and the lack of independent data. Also, countries with less than one million population were not considered. Similarly, countries for which reliable or complete data was not available were excluded. After the examination of residual plots, Greece, Israel, Korea and Portugal were dropped from the sample due to their extreme and misleading statistical influence. The data for caloric and protein consumption, as well as the data for Agricultural Output was taken from the FAO (1981, 1987) Production Yearbooks. The data for GNP, GDP, Labour Force, Debt, and Exports was taken from the World Bank Annual Report Tables (1981, 1987).

Results

Bivariate relationships indicate a moderate association in the expected direction between food consumption and disarticulation (Table 2.1). The relationship between food consumption and the control variables are also in the expected direction, though the coefficients range from a fairly weak to strong association. Similarly, the relationship between disarticulation and control variables indicate the negative character of each association.

TABLE 2.1: Correlation Matrix For Complete Model (N = 65)

	ZFOOD	DISAR	LGNP	DBGNP	AGOUT
ZFOOD	1.000				
DISAR	−.446	1.000			
LGNP	.601	−.397	1.000		
DBGNP	.203	−.278	.344	1.000	
AGOUT	.192	−.107	.044	−.104	1.000
X	.000	6.692	2.793	3.720	99.477
S.D.	1.878	2.733	.379	3.065	8.504

Multiple regression (OLS) analysis indicates that the model explains 39.5 per cent of the total variance in food consumption, supporting the initial hypothesis that disarticulation has a negative impact on the aggregate levels of food consumption ($p<.05$). The unstandardized coefficient for disarticulation indicates that, holding constant all other variables, as disarticulation increases by one unit in the composite measure, the standardized indicator of food consumption decreases by.161 units (Table 2.2). Succinctly, countries with high disarticulation scores tend to present significantly lower levels of food consumption. On the other hand, the standardized B coefficient for LGNP indicates that higher levels of GNP are associated with higher levels of food consumption. Agricultural output per capita has no significance in the model, a result that concurs with the argument previously advanced that the food problem is not primarily a matter of food scarcity but, rather, of distribution and, thus associated with the disarticulated character of third world economies.

Discussion and Conclusions

The larger B coefficient for GNP (in comparison with the coefficient for disarticulation) should not overshadow the interpretation of the effects of disarticulation. GNP per capita as an aggregated measurement of development does not reflect the quality of life, or the differential access to goods and services that various segments of the population may have due to income inequalities (Dore and Weeks, 1982; Hicks and Streeten, 1979). There is an increasing criticism to the use and value of GNP as an indicator of development. The trends observed in third world economies clearly indicate that economic growth does not necessarily imply an improvement of the poorest people's quality of life. The bottom line of this issue is that development cannot be conceived simply as economic growth.

TABLE 2.2: Standardized Regression Coefficients for the Model ZFOOD = DISAR LGNP DBGNP AGOUT (N = 65)

	ZFOOD
DISAR	−.161 (−.234)**
LGNP	2.524 (.509)***
DBGNP	−.013 (−.022)
AGOUT	.031 (.142)
r2 Adj. r2	.433 .395

Note: Values in parenthesis are the standardized Betas.
Significance level ** = .05;
*** = .01 in a two tail *T*-test.

By the end of the 1970s, Hicks and Streeten (1979) stated a methodological critique of the various alternatives used for assessing development. Briefly, based on their experience and the review of the literature, they proved that various alternative indicators for development, such as literacy rate, infant mortality, food consumption, housing, access to potable water, et cetera had various degrees of association with GNP. Further, that according to the countries' GNP (above or below of US$ 500) these correlations changed and even disappeared. The basic explanation they proposed was that the relationship between GNP and the above mentioned indicators is not a linear one, and that by doing linear transformations of the variables, the relations obtained for the different countries were clearly misleading.

Economic growth under disarticulation not always brings about benefits for the population (Stokes and Anderson, 1990). In fact, it is possible to have economic growth (in aggregate terms) but not improvement in the quality of life (Dore and Weeks 1982). Sustained economic growth can go along with increasing income inequality (CEPAL, 1990).

There may be a positive and significant relation between GNP and food consumption levels, but that reading neglects the issue of growth with equity, which the notion of disarticulation attempts to tap. Disarticulation is a structural condition that promotes regressive income distributions and asymmetrical flows of surplus between economic sectors and productive forces. As such, one should not overlook the importance of economic growth, but economic growth would not resolve the consequences of disarticulation. Poor nations do not have a low quality of life because they are poor (e.g. they would need only to expand their rate of economic growth). Rather, poverty, is an indicator of a structural condition: disarticulation. Further, it is possible to experience slightly lower rates of economic growth and improve the quality of life of the poorest segments of the population (Burki and Ul Haq, 1981; Hicks, 1980; Lisk, 1977). The issue here is that policies aimed at improving the quality of life may have a positive impact on economic growth and, contrarily, policies which are not directly targeted to improve the quality of life, may have a negative impact on it, as in the case of food consumption.

Several mechanisms influence the effect of disarticulation on food consumption. In disarticulated economies, there is a shift of resources (capital, land, technology) favouring export crops over food production. However, the effects of disarticulation are not even across productive systems. In fact, Breedlove (1991) and Rhyne (1991) have found that the effects of disarticulation may change according to world region and type of productive structure. Under disarticulated growth, low wages tend to pervade the labour market depressing the potential food demand and consumption of the poorest sectors. While the exportoriented sector of the economy receives incentives and state support, experiencing growth, the staplefood sector does not receive the same support (either through internal demand or state policies).

The globalization and integration of the agricultural and food system within countries and across national boundaries, instead of decreasing the levels of disarticulation in low and middle income countries, has been based on it. This phenomenon has two expressions. First, the earnings generated through agricultural exports have not been redistributed with equity within the agricultural sector, therefore, reinvestment has been highly differentiated. Productive specialization and differentiation between rich and poor regions have contributed to the generation of a vicious cycle in which export-agriculture is increasingly integrated, while the earnings generated are not redistributed within agriculture, increasing the gap between subsectors (Aziz, 1990; Mann; 1990). Second, increasing substitution of raw material from productive processes by developed economies, increasing technological disparity between developed and developing nations, stagnant demand for third world agricultural commodities, decreasing terms of trade, and the debt burden, forced third world economies to elevate even more in their export strategy, curtailing social expenditures and internal consumption and deepening the disarticulation of their economies, and, certainly, of the agricultural sector.

Disarticulation is not a deceived or anomalous path of economic growth. Rather, it is an inherent component of capitalist development in third world nations. However, disarticulation is not dictated by external forces or transnational processes.

To conclude, third world economies move along a continuum from articulation to disarticulation, depending on the national development strategies implemented by the state, the class dynamics and other political factors that affect the definition of state policy. The state, in its relation to the various socioeconomic and productive sectors, plays a fundamental role either ameliorating or exacerbating the contradictions which a disarticulated economy presents. The expression of this tension in the agricultural sector is given by the different rates of capitalist penetration in various agricultural activities (Mann, 1990), being the export sector the one that nowadays concentrates the highest rate of capital investments and integration to transnational markets. But this is a dynamic situation that can be modified by state and private intervention through research activities, development of new markets, fiscal policies, and so on.

Future research should attempt to devise a more comprehensive measurement of disarticulation incorporating indicators of income distribution and consumption. Also, an improved measurement of disarticulation should include an indicator of public expenditures in social programs vis-a-vis export earnings as percentage of GNP. Another important issue to assess is the relationship between labour force in different productive sectors and share of GDP/GNP by sector. The issue here is that it has been assumed that this relationship is linear while in fact it may be curvilinear, especially if we incorporate high income countries, where an increasing amount of the labour force is located in the service sector, though a very different service sector than the one we find in low income countries. Also, it would be necessary to complement the analysis with longitudinal data, to assess change in time and across countries. Case studies and time series analysis would bring new insights that one point in time cross-national studies would not be able to grasp. Of particular importance, for assessing the relationship between disarticulation and the agricultural sector, would be incorporating other control variables, such as estimates of change in landuse patterns and use of capital and technology in agriculture. It is possible that a significant amount of variation on the levels of food consumption could be explained by the different levels of intensification of agricultural production across sub-sectors.

Finally, we have to confront the political issue at stake. The case is that growth with equity has been incorporated with the development discourse but no real policy instruments have been devised to achieve it. It seems like if, in the name of political realism and pragmatism, policy-makers would not be willing to assume that the current situation of poverty would not change unless specific measures tending to decrease the disarticulated character of third world economies are taken. We already discussed that economic growth in itself would not necessarily bring about an improvement in the quality of life of the poorest sectors. Achieving food security requires political determination to decrease poverty and to re-direct resources so that export earnings would be available to further internal consumption either through increasing production or imports. Specific policies stimulating investment in wage-goods industries and value-add industries must be in place. The development and integration of the agro-industrial sector should not be based only in the international markets but also on the need to expand internal demand, that is, the purchasing power of the poorest sectors of the population.

Appendix-I

Country	Disarticulation Scores	Country	Disarticulation Scores
Nepal	6.51	Algeria	2.58
Bangladesh	6.26	Burundi	4.62
Haiti	6.07	Mauritius	4.61
Guinea	5.88	Tunisia	4.51
India	5.87	Zaire	4.51
Sierra leone	5.61	Brazil	4.51
Yemen arab rep	5.55	Rwanda	4.50
Burkina faso	5.47	Colombia	4.47
Pakistan	5.43	Morocco	4.44
Zimbabwe	5.40	Burma	4.41
Central africa	5.31	Liberia	4.39
Thailand	5.29	Mexico	4.38
Benin	5.21	Paraguay	4.36
Philippines	5.21	Egypt	4.36
Kenya	5.17	Congo	4.27
Senegal	5.13	Peru	4.19
Turkey	5.10	Cameroon	4.16
Malawi	5.05	Sudan	4.16
Jamaica	4.99	Zambia	4.11
Tanzania	4.98	Mozambique	4.02
Mali	4.92	Indonesia	3.96
Guatemala	4.88	Uruguay	3.95
Sri lanka	4.84	Uganda	3.81
Malasya	4.83	Mauritania	3.72
Togo	4.72	Syrian arab rep	3.71
Madagascar	4.70	Somalia	3.70
Domenican rep	4.67	Nigeria	3.69
Costa rica	4.65	Ghana	3.66
Cote d ivory	4.64	Chile	3.62
Niger	4.64	Argentina	3.59
Honduras	4.62	Panama	3.57
Ecuador	3.44	Bolivia	3.54
Venezuela	2.68		

REFERENCES

Adelman, Irma and J. Edward Taylor, (1990), Changing Comparative Advantage in Food and Agriculture: Lessons From Mexico. Development Centre Studies, OCDE. Paris: OCDE.

Amin, Samir, (1974), Accumulation on a World Scale. New York: Monthly Review Press.

——, (1976), Unequal Development. New York: Monthly Review Press.

Amsden, Alice, (1981), "An International Comparison of the Rate of Surplus Value in Manufacturing Industry." *Cambridge Journal of Economics*, Vol. 5:229-249.

Aziz, Sartaj, (1990), Agricultural Policies for the 1990s. Development Centre Studies. Development Centre of the Organization for Economic Co-operation and Development (OECD). Paris: OECD

Barraclough, Solon and Peter Utting, (1987), "Food Security Trends and Prospects in Latin America." Working Paper No 99. The Hellen Kellogg Institute for International Studies, University of Notre Dame. Notre Dame, in: University of Notre Dame.

Breedlove, William L., (1991), "Disarticulation, Dependency, Techno-Economic Heritage and Human Welfare." Paper presented at the Annual Meeting of the Southern Sociological Society, Atlanta, April 1991.

Burki, Shahid J. and Mahbub Ul Haq, (1981), "Meeting Basic Needs: An Overview." *World Development*, Vol. 9:167-182.

Castells, Manuel y Roberto Laserna, (1990), "La Nueva Dependencia. Cambio Tecnológico y Restructuración socio-económica en Latinoamérica." Pp.97-131 in A. Portes and A.D. Kincaid (eds.), Teorías del Desarrollo Nacional. Costa Rica: EDUCA.

Comisión Económica para América Latinay el Caribe, CEPAL, (1990), Transformación Productiva con Equidad. La Tarea Prioritaria del Desarrollo en Amórica Latina y el Caribe en los Años Noventa. LC/G.1601 (SES.23/4). Santiago: CEPAL

de Janvry, Alain, (1981), *The Agrarian Question and Reformism in Latin America*. Baltimore, MD: The John Hopkins University Press.

——, (1985), "Social Disarticulation in Latin American History." Pp. 32-73 in K.S. Kim and D.F. Ruccio (eds.), *Debt and Development in Latin America*. Notre Dame: University of Notre Dame Press.

de Janvry, Alain and Carlos Garramon, (1977), "The Dynamics of Real Poverty in Latin America." *Journal of Peasant Studies*, Vol. 4:135-164.

de Janvry, Alain and Elizabeth Sadoulet, (1983), "Social Articulation as a Condition for Equitable Growth." *Journal of Development Economics*, Vol. 13:275-303.

——, (1985), "Disarticulation as a Theory of Inequitable Growth: Articulation as a Strategy for Equitable Growth (or Why Countries Should Beware of Jumping the Stages of Consumption)." Working Paper No 352, University of California Berkeley, Giannini Foundation of Agricultural Economics.

Diakosavvas, Dimitris, (1989), "On the Causes of Food Insecurity in Less Developed Countries: An Empirical Evaluation." *World Development*, Vol. 17:223-235.

Dore, Elizabeth W. and John F. Weeks, (1982), "Economic Performance and Basic Needs: The Examples of Brazil, Chile, Mexico, Nicaragua, Peru and Venezuela". Pp. 150-161 in M.E. Crahan (ed.), *Human Rights and Basic Needs in the Americas*. Washington: Georgetown University Press.

Drucker, Peter F., (1986), "The Changed World Economy". *Foreign Affairs*, Vol. 64:768-791.

Evans, Peter, (1985), "Transnational Linkages and the Economic Role of the State: An analysis of Developing and Industrialized Nations in the Post World War II Period." Pp. 192-226 in P. Evans et al. (eds.), *Bringing the State Back*. Cambridge: Cambridge University Press.

Food And Agriculture Organization (FAO), (1981), *Food Production Yearbook 1981*. Rome: FAO

——, (1987), *Food Production Yearbook 1987*. Rome: FAO

Frank, Andre Gunder, (1969), "The Development of Underdevelopment." Pp. 96-104 in C. Wilber (ed.), *The Political Economy of Development and Underdevelopment*. New York: Random House.

——, (1984), "The Unequal and Uneven Historical Development of the World Economy." *Contemporary Marxism*, Vol. 9:71-98.

Friedmann, Harriet and Philip McMichael, (1989), "Agriculture and the State System. The Rise and Decline of National Agricultures, 1870 to the Present." *Sociologia Ruralis*, Vol. 29 (2):93-117.

Furtado, Celso, (1972), "The Brazilian Model of Development." Pp. 297-306 in C. Wilber (ed.), *The Political Economy of Development and Underdevelopment*. New York: Random House.

GacitÈa, Estanislao and Rosario Bello, (1991), "Agricultural Exports, Food Consumption and Food Security in Latin America." *Rural Sociology*, Vol. 56 (3):391-405.

Gereffi, Gary, (1990), "Repensando la Teoría del Desarrollo: Visión desde el Asia Oriental y Latinoamérica." Pp.49-96 in A. Portes and A.D. Kincaid (eds.), *Teorías del Desarrollo Nacional*. Costa Rica: EDUCA.

Goldin, Ian and Gervasio Castro de Rezende, (1990), Agriculture and Economic Crisis: Lessons from Brazil. Development Centre Studies, OCDE. Paris: OCDE.

Griffin, Keith and John Gurley, (1985), "Radical Analyses of Imperialism, The Third World and the Transition to Socialism: A survey Article." *Journal of Economic Literature*, Vol. 23: 1089-1143.

Grindle, Merilee, (1984), State and the Countryside. Development Policy and Agrarian Policies in Latin America. Baltimore, MD: The John Hopkins University Press.

Hicks, Norman, (1980), "Is There a Tradeoff Between Growth and Basic Human Needs." *Finance and Development*, 17:17-20.

Hicks, Norman and Paul Streeten, (1979), "Indicators of Development: The Search for a Basic Needs Yardstick." *World Development*, Vol. 7:567-580.

Hojman, David E., (1990a), "Chile After Pinochet: Aylwin's Christian Democrat Economic Policies for the 1990s." *Bulletin of Latin American Research*, Vol. 9 (1):25-47.

——, (1990b), *Neo-liberal Agriculture in Rural Chile*. St. Martin's Press: Hong Kong.

Jaffee, Dav[illegible], (1985), "Export Dependence and Economic Growth: A Reformulation and Respecification." *Social Forces*, Vol. 64:102-118.

Lal, Deepak, (1985), *The Poverty of 'Development Economics'*. Cambridge: Harvard University Press.

Lappe, Frances and Joseph Collins, (1977), *Food First: Beyond the Myth of Scarcity*. Boston: Houghton.

——, (1986), World Hunger: *Twelve Myths. London*: Earthscan Publications Limited.

Lipton, Michael, (1984), "Urban Bias Revisited." Pp. 126-158 in J. Harris and M. Moore (eds.), *Development and the Rural Urban Divide*. London: Frank Cass. Lisk, Franklin

——, (1977), "Conventional Development Strategies and Basic Needs Fulfillment." *International Labour Review*, Vol. 11:175-191.

Love, James, (1989), "Export Instability, Imports and Investments in Developing Countries." *The Journal of Development Studies*, Vol. 25:183-191.

Manale, Jodie, (1991), "Disarticulation and Population Growth: A Test of Competing Theories about their Impact on Development in Less Developed Countries." Paper presented at the Annual Meeting of the Southern Sociological Society, Atlanta, April 1991.

Mann, Susan Archer, (1990), *Agrarian Capitalism in Theory and Practice*. Chapel Hill, NC: The University of North Carolina Press.

Marini, Ruy Mauro, (1973), Dialéctica de la Dependencia. México: Serie Popular Era.

Portes, Alejandro, M. Castells and L. A. Benton (eds.), (1989), *The Informal Economy: Studies in Advanced and Less Developed Countries*. Baltimore, MD: The John Hopkins University Press.

Portes, Alejandro and A. Douglas Kincaid, (1990), "Sociología y Desarrollo en los Años 90. Desafíos Críticos y Tendencias Empíricas." Pp.13-48 in A. Portes and A.D. Kincaid (eds.), *Teorías del Desarrollo Nacional*. Costa Rica: EDUCA.

Rao, J. Mohan and Jose M. Caballero, (1990), "Agricultural Performance and Development Strategy: Retrospect and Prospect." *World Development*, Vol. 18 (6):899-913.

Rhyne, Edwin H., (1991), "Disarticulation and World Regions: A Critique of Stokes and Anderson and a Reformulation." Paper presented at the Annual Meeting of the Southern Sociological Society, Atlanta, April 1991.

Stokes, Randal G. and Andy B. Anderson, (1990), "Disarticulation and Human Welfare in Less Developed Countries." *American Sociological Review*, Vol. 55 (1):63-74.

Timberlake, Michael and Kirk Williams, (1984), "Dependence, Political Exclusion and Government Repression: Some Cross-National Evidence." *American Sociological Review*, Vol 49 (1):141-147.

Todaro, Michael P., (1989), Economic Development in the Third World. 4th ed. New York: Longman Press.

Touraine, Alain, (1989), "Los Problemas de una Sociología Propia en América Latina." *Revista Mexicana de Sociología* Vol. 51 (1):3-22.

Wei-Yuan, Chen, (1989), "Testing the Food-First Hypothesis: A Cross-National Study of Dependency, Sectoral Growth and Food Intake in Less Developed Countries." *World Development*, Vol. 17:17-29

Wilkie, James W. and Manuel Moreno Ibáñez, (1985), "Latin American Food Production and Population in the Era of Land reform Since the 1950s." Pp. 65-105 in J. Super and T. Wright (eds.), *Foods, Politics, and Society in Latin America*. Lincoln, NE: University of Nebraska Press.

Wimberley, Dale W., (1989), "Investment Dependence and Food Consumption in the Third World: A Cross-National Study." Paper presented at the Annual Meeting of the Rural Sociological Society, Seattle, August 1989.

Wise, Timothy, (1987), "The Current Food Crisis in Latin America. A Discussion of de Janvry's The Agrarian Question." *Latin American Perspectives*, Vol. 54:289-315.

World Bank, (1981), World Development Report 1981. New York: Oxford University Press.

——, (1987), World Development Report 1987. New York: Oxford University Press.

——, (1990), World Development Report 1990. New York: Oxford University Press.

3

TOWARDS GLOBALIZATION OF AGRICULTURAL POLICIES?

LEILA SFEIR LUESCHEN

Introduction

This paper questions the issue whether globalization is occurring in agricultural policies. This is a difficult task due to the fact that many policies are formulated and implemented by economically powerful countries such as the United States and some European Community (EC) countries. The term globalization itself poses more problems than one could anticipate. Would it be possible to define globalization of agricultural policies as a set of policies applicable to the whole world independent from government intervention and domestic interests of the developed countries? Is globalization the ability to harmonize, integrate and coordinate agricultural policies? Would it be possible to talk about globalization in agriculture when essentially the EC and the United States are the major players?

This paper explores the contribution of developed countries, in particular the United States and the EC, to the widening disequilibrium and distortions in world agriculture resulting from domestic intervention and protectionism; assesses the reality of world agricultural trade and the destabilization in world agricultural production and trade; and evaluates the efforts for liberalizing agriculture through the General Agreement on Tariffs and Trade (GATT) negotiations, the EC 1992 Single Market, attempts to reform the Common Agricultural Policy (CAP) and the creation of free-trade zones.

The current GATT negotiations have accelerated studies on the effects of trade liberalization. Some studies deal with the issue of policy coordination and integration in world agriculture (Von Witzke, Runge and Job, 1989). Most of these studies are of economic nature. Yet the major difficulty in analyzing agricultural policies is that such studies require both economic and political disciplines. Most of these studies have focussed only on one perspective.[1] This might explain why economists have failed to understand the importance and political power of the farm pressure groups. This has limited economists' ability to analyze agricultural policy. Any attempt to understand agricultural policy needs to acknowledge the interplay of economic, social and political influence. This paper emphasizes the political and socio-economic components, in particular in analyzing the EC and the power of the farm lobby in shaping agricultural policy.

Agriculture in a Global Environment

The economic environment of international agriculture has changed significantly and there are now concerns over the environment and rural development, increased international competition, decreasing number of farmers, declining prices and farm incomes, and increased government intervention. Agriculture has become increasingly dependent on foreign markets, capital flow, exchange rate, monetary and fiscal policy and trade policy.

Other political events are changing the face of the international market and might promise greater cooperation and globalization. The integration of Europe is going fast. The EC might expand to in clude the European Free Trade Association (EFTA) countries (Austria, Finland, Iceland, Norway, Sweden and Switzerland). With the fall of Communism, all the new democracies in Eastern Europe are also eager to join the EC. Integration is also occurring on the other side of the Atlantic. The United States is completing a free trade agreement with Canada and Mexico. Latin American countries are discovering the disciplines of the market; they are pressing for structural reforms of their economies. An attempt is under way to resurrect the Central American common market. The Asia-Pacific int egration is occurring as economic relations are intensifying in the region. These changes will affect agriculture in many ways. They will reshape the global monetary environment of agriculture, the y will affect agricultural production and consumption and they will affect international agriculture and policy.

Increased Government Intervention

The agricultural sector is characterized by a massive and pervasive intervention of governments (both in developed and developing countries) into agricultural production and markets.

Agricultural Protectionism: Mechanisms and Costs

Agricultural protectionism has been the rule in developed countries, rather than the exception. The subsidization of agriculture is quite striking and paradoxical; governments in democratic countries have adopted agricultural protection to the point of "greenhouse agriculture" (Schultz, 1978:1; Olson, 1985:930). Typically the developed countries have endorsed policies that shield farming from market forces and protect domestic agriculture by supporting agricultural prices and limiting agricultural imports.

The EC and the U.S. share many common objectives and interests to protect their agricultural sector. These include supporting farm income, ensuring adequate supplies of food, and protecting the rural environment. Although many objectives are the same, the policies employed to implement and the rationale to adopt them are quite different. The United States uses a system of price and income su pports including loans, deficiency payments and other payments. The CAP uses a variety of mechanisms including price supports, variable levies (duty on imported commodities equal to the difference between world prices and internal prices), and export subsidies.[2]

The United States and the EC are overspending in agriculture to retain or conquer world markets. In the U.S., the federal government spending for farming support in 1986 reached a peak of $25.8 billion (a 46 per cent increase over 1985) although U.S. farm subsidies have fallen by over half since 1986. CAP spending on agriculture (including export refunds and intervention) is sharply rising (from $16 billion in 1985 to $36 billion in 1990 (Table 3.1) absorbing more than 57 per cent of the EC total budget. In addition, there are subsidies that do not show in the government budget. Such overs pending has resulted in overproduction and accumulation of "mountains" of food in some developed countries.[3]

Agricultural policies provide support to producers through monetary transfers from taxpayers (government budgets) and from consumers (high prices for agricultural products).[4] The Organization for Economic Cooperation and Development (OECD) has estimated total transfers associated with agricultural policies.[5] Total transfers are the sum of all transfers from taxpayers (federal and state expenditure for the U.S.; Community and member states expenditures for the EC) plus all transfers from consumers (implicit tax due to market price support) minus the budget revenues (receipts from tariffs). Total transfers reached $133.4 billion for the EC, $74.1 billion for the U.S. and $59 billion for Japan in 1990 (Table 3.2). It cost taxpayers and consumers in the world's 24 richest countries $299 billion in 1990 in farm subsidies to protect their farmers from competition (OECD, 1991:138).

TABLE 3.1: U.S. and EC Agricultural Expenditure

Year	U.S.*	EC**	EC	Exchange rate ($/ECU)
	Million dollars		ECU	
1980***	2,751	16,635	11,948	1.3923
1981	4,036	12,902	11,556	1.1165
1982	11,652	12,789	13,055	0.9797
1983	18,850	14,723	16,539	0.8902
1984	7,315	15,008	19,022	0.7890
1985	17,683	15,615	20,463	0.7631
1986	25,841	22,536	22,910	0.9837
1987	22,407	27,562	23,876	1.1544
1988	12,460	34,134	28,866	1.1825
1989	10,523	32,699	29,681	1.1017
1990	6,742	36,310	30,111	1.2059

* Total Commodity Credit Corporation (CCC), net budgetary expenditures. Budget expenditure for Public Law 480, Export Enhancement Programme (EEP), and Food Stamp Programme are not included.

** Total European Agricultural Guidance and Guarantee Fund (EAGGF), including export refunds and intervention.

*** EC-10 for 1980-85, and EC-12 for 1986-90.

Sources: USDA, Agricultural Outlook, various issues; and EC Commission, The Agricultural Situation in the Community 1984 to 1990 Reports.

Government Intervention in Developing Countries[6]

Government intervention in the agricultural sector has been a persistent characteristic of agricultural policies in developing countries. Such intervention became a major source of exploitation, corruption

TABLE 3.2: Total Transfers Associated with Agricultural Policies

(in billion U.S. dollars)

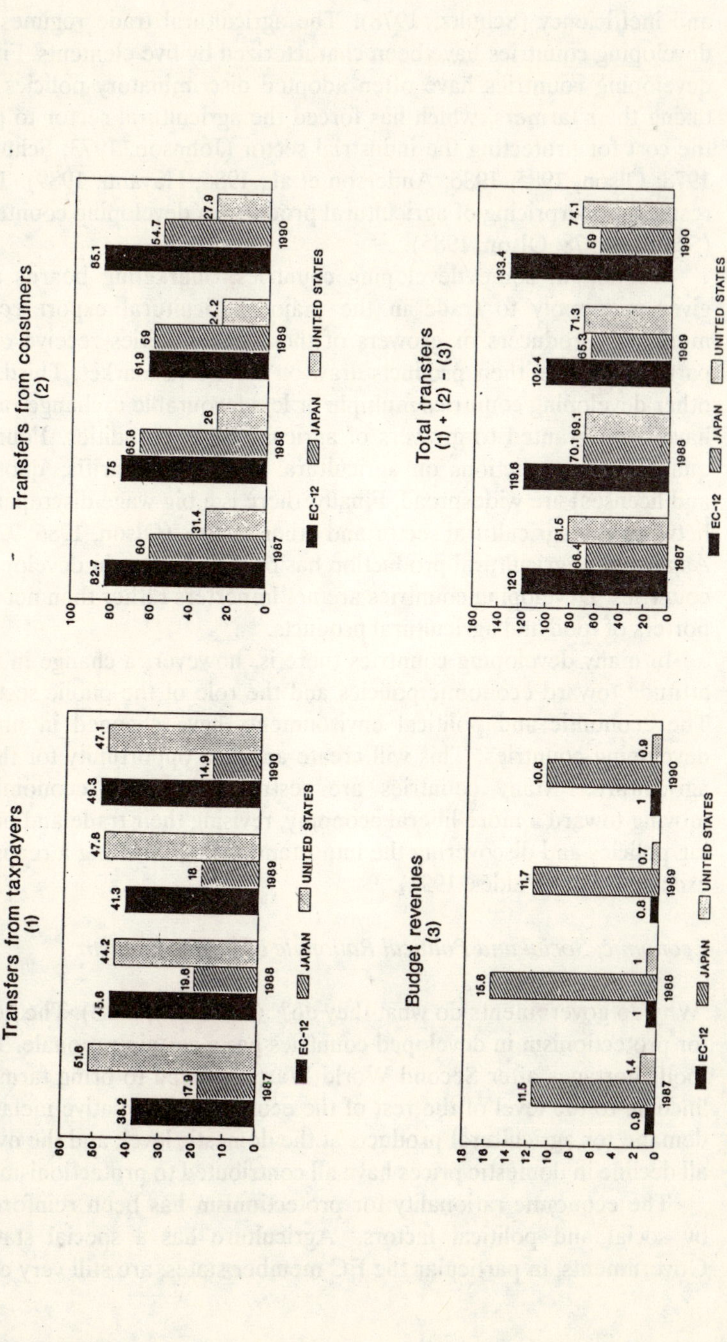

SOURCE: OECD, Monitoring Report, 1991

and inefficiency (Schultz, 1978). The agricultural trade regimes in developing countries have been characterized by five elements. First, developing countries have often adopted discriminatory policies by taxing their farmers, which has forced the agricultural sector to pay the cost for protecting the industrial sector (Johnson, 1973; Schultz, 1978; Olson, 1985, 1986; Anderson et al., 1986; Hayami, 1989). The result is underpricing of agricultural products in developing countries (Schultz, 1978; Olson, 1985).

Second, in some developing countries, marketing boards are given monopoly to trade in the major agricultural export commodities. Producers or growers of these commodities receive only part of the price their products draw on the world market. Third, in other developing countries multiple or less favourable exchange rates have been granted to growers of agricultural commodities. Fourth, quantitative restrictions on agricultural trade (e.g., tariffs, quotas, and licenses) are widespread. Finally, there is a big wage discrepancy between the agricultural sector and other sectors (Olson, 1986: 929). As a result, agricultural production has been very slow in developing countries. Developing countries are net importers rather than net exporters of food and agricultural products.

In many developing countries there is, however, a change in the attitude toward economic policies and the role of the public sector. The economic and political environments have changed in many developing countries. This will create an ideal opportunity for their agriculture. Many countries are restructuring their economies, moving toward a more liberal economy, revising their trade and pricing policies and discovering the importance of maintaining a realistic exchange rate (Valdés, 1991).

Economic, Social and Political Rationale of Interventionism

"Why do governments do what they do?" (de Janvry, 1983). The need for protectionism in developed countries has a certain rationale. The food shortages after Second World War; the need to bring farmers 'income to the level of the rest of the economy; the relative inelastic demand for agricultural products at the domestic level; and the overall decline in domestic prices have all contributed to protectionism.[7]

The economic rationality for protectionism has been reinforced by social and political factors. Agriculture has a special status. Governments, in particular the EC member states, are still very conscious of their own national interests and domestic agricultural policy in terms of political tradition and economic ideology (Senior Nello, 1984, 1989; Lueschen, 1990). There is also a strong emotional and historical bond between farmers and European societies. Farmers have always enjoyed public support and sympathy, in particular, in France, Germany and Japan. In the U.S., the rationale of preserving the traditional family farm, which characterized American agriculture in the past and continues to justify current policies, is no longer realistic for a highly specialized advanced agriculture (Tutwiler and Carr,1988:222).

The farm population, despite its reduced number, seems to be more successful than other groups in its rent-seeking politics. Many theories are advanced. Most prefer the power of interest groups and their ability to gain control of particular aspects of policy-making in defense of their own interests (Olson, 1965; Rausser, 1982; Senior Nello, 1984, 1989; Petit, 1985; Bonnen, 1987; Winters, 1987; Browne, 1988;). Agriculture's political power might be explained by the existence of powerful farmers' lobbies. In Germany and France the farmers' lobby is well organized and secures easy access to its national policy-makers. Farmers' unions such as the German Deutsche Bauernverband (DBV) and the French Fédération Nationale des Syndicats d'Exploitants Agricoles (FNSEA) are very powerful; they are firmly committed to protecting farmers' interests and are clearly in favour of the CAP as well as opposed to any cut in farm subsidies. In the U.S. commodity groups, which are strong in Congress and have significant influence within the executive branch (Moyer and Josling, 1990:133), still dominate the policy process.

At the EC level, agricultural ministers are policy-makers who have the power to formulate EC policies and to implement them. Agriculture ministers are also politicians, and therefore sensitive to their farmers' complaints that farm incomes have eroded. At the national level, domestic farm interests exert tremendous political power on the government.

The economic well-being of farmers has been reinforced by political coalitions between farmers and political parties.[8] Some theorists consider farmers marginal voters attractive to political parties (Hagedorn and Schmitt, 1985). For example, in Germany the farmers' power is based in the delicate ruling coalition between political parties. The Free Democratic Party (FDP) held the balance between the two main political parties, the Christian Democratic

Party (CDU) and the Social Democratic Party (SPD). The farm vote, which mainly accrues to the CDU, is crucial in maintaining the current political power of the CDU-FDP ruling coalition.

Japan reflects the case of high protectionism with her strong barriers for importing agricultural commodities. The increase in agricultural protection in Japan is due to the sharp decline in compar ative advantage due to rapid growth in industrial sectors. The decline in comparative advantage urged the rural population to pressure for protection. Such protection demand was organized in Japan by agricultural cooperative associations or NOKYO, a formidable political bloc (including 300,000 employees and 5 million members) and a "vote collector" (Hayami, 1989: 68-73).

The decline in comparative advantage is even stronger in Korea than in Japan. On one hand, international pressures are increasing for agricultural import liberalization, particularly from the United States. On the other hand, powerful domestic farm interests exert strong protectionist pressures on government (Lee et al., 1990).

Various explanations are advanced to explain government intervention in developed countries. Dependency theory – a theory of economic, social and political change – attempts to explain the lasting poverty and political instability of many poor countries in terms of their dominance by rich and powerful countries, in particular the dominance of Europe and the United States (Cardoso and Faletto, 1979). On the other hand, Marxian theory sees trade as "unequal exchange" between partners leading to the exploitation of one partner by the other. Economic and political power are essential to dominate and exploit others (Emmanuel, 1972; Amin, 1967).

Development theories are composed of conflicting propositions and questionable generalizations generated from particular processes observed in specific historical events and geographic locales. While attractive, these theories involve dangerous risks in conceiving notions of development and underdevelopment in the Third World developing countries. Most concepts of dependency try to classify very diverse and peculiar societies into one category (Boudon and Bourricaud, 1989). The main analysis within dependency theory most likely to last is the work of Cardoso and Faletto, who describe different forms of dependency over time and space, and include a detailed analysis of class structure in Latin America. "Class" theories of special interests using the state for their own benefit are more likely to survive (de Janvry, 1981; 1983). In the case of Latin America, more attention is given to agrarian class relations, working class power and the role of the state. Most Latin American countries did and some still have a significant number of landlords who managed to dominate and repress the working class. Agriculture, dominated by traditional latifundia/minifundia structures of land ownership, is unable to absorb the growing labour force (de Janvry, 1981; Mouzelis, 1986).[9]

However, Mouzelis (1988) argues that dependency theory is no longer adequate to explain the diversity of experiences in Africa, Asia and Latin America. For example, Latin American countries are "middle-level developing countries," where partial development and underdevelopment coexist (Evans and Stephens, 1988).

Distortions in Agricultural Policies

Protectionism has resulted in alarming distortions in agricultural policies, especially in cereals, milk and sugar (Commission of the European Communities, 1988). The situation is particularly serious for sugar worldwide. Japanese sugar producers receive 17 times the world price, and US and EC producers get nearly four times the world price. EC wheat price supports are twice the world price, while U.S. target wheat prices are about 50 per cent above the world price (Rausser and Wright, 1989:119). In the U.S., during the past decade, the grain, cotton, and dairy programs have been among the most expensive price support programs as measured by federal outlays (CRS Report for Congress, 1990).

Destructive Confrontation: Destabilization of World Agricultural Trade

World agricultural markets have been characterized today by a fierce confrontation between the European Community and the United States, the two giants of agricultural trade. The U.S. is the world' slargest exporter with a total value of $44.32 billion in 1990. The EC has become the world's second largest exporter behind the United States. EC agricultural exports almost quadrupled between 1975 and 1990, rising from $11.6 billion to $40.6 billion (Table 3.3).

TABLE 3.3: Value of Agricultural Exports, USA and EC, 1975-1990
(Data are for the EC-12 and exclude intra-EC trade unless specified.)

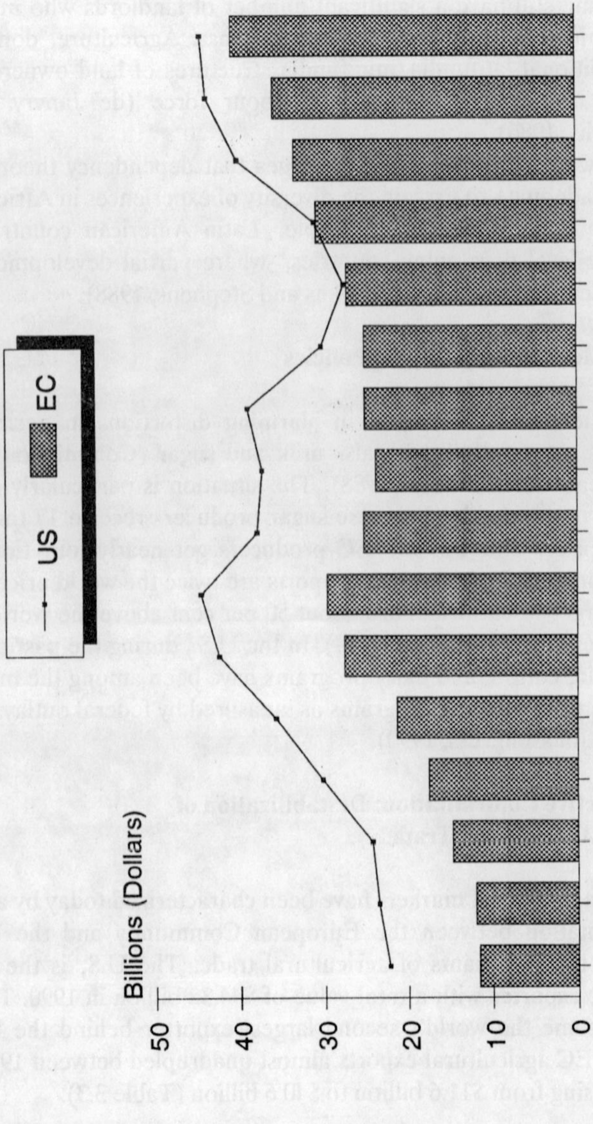

SOURCE: United Nations Trade Data, 1991.

Since the EC emerged as a major exporter of agricultural commodities in the 1970s, trade confrontation between the two giants has intensified into a full subsidy war. The EC is a fierce competitor for the U.S. in world commodity markets, particularly in grains (in contrast to the 1970's when the EC was a major market for U.S. grains). This results in fierce confrontations over third country markets, in particular in world wheat markets (Curry Foundation,1985; Petit, 1985; Petit, Rossmiller and Tutwiler, 1989). EC cereal exports increased by 150 per cent between 1973 and 1985 (Commission of the European Communities, 1989:56). This situation resulted in increasing tension between the major commodity exporters, poisoning relations between the EC and the United States (as well as with New Zealand, Canada and Australia). In addition, other large grain importer countries, such as China and India, became net exporters in the early 1980s.

This competition urged U.S. policy-makers to do something to reconquer the shrinking U.S. share of the world agricultural market. The result was the 1985 Food Security Act which introduced new provisions (making commodities more market sensitive), such as the Export Enhancement Programme (EEP) and the Target Export Programme (TEA), demonstrating the determination of the U.S. to be a competitive s upplier. The new 1990 Farm Bill continues the export oriented approach. The act contains a "GATT Trigger" in case of a non-agreement in the Uruguay Round. The trigger allows changes in prices and income supports, as well as export programmes, in case world agriculture is not liberated. The EC does not have such flexibility. But the EC is also determined to become more competitive in world agricultural markets through its policy of price intervention (Commission of the European Communities, 1991).

The confrontation has serious consequences for these two competing trading partners and for other countries as well. Big agricultural exporters benefiting from high incomes try to dump their surpluses in Third World markets. As a result, prices fall while market shares stay the same; however, budgets or costs of production increase. The losers are consumers and/or taxpayers in exporting cou ntries.

The distorted situation heavily influences North-South relations. Huge chronic surpluses from exporting countries compete on the international market and depress world commodity prices. Therefore, they have a negative effect on agricultural production in a number of developing and newly industrialized countries (with export prospects for certain products such as sugar, beef, and cereals). The International Monetary Fund (IMF) estimates that eliminating the industrial world's farm subsidies could boost Third World farm exports by $50 billion per year.

Toward Coordination of Agricultural Policies?

Coordination in GATT

The Uruguay Round is the eighth round of GATT negotiations and the most ambitious and complex round ever undertaken by GATT. It aims to set liberal new rules in 15 broad areas of trade, including a griculture, patents, financial services, telecommunications and textiles. Unlike other rounds, developing countries and smaller industrialized nations play an important role, and it is the first rou nd to directly confront the problem of agricultural protectionism.

In the Uruguay Round both the EC and the US have had to come with proposals to reduce farm subsidies. The initial U.S. "zero option" measures (the abolition of all domestic subsidies and broader measures with trade distortions within a decade) seemed an effort to dismantle CAP. Later, the United States, backed by the Cairns Group (which includes Australia, New Zealand, Canada, Argentina, Australia, Brazil, Canada, Chile, Colombia, Fiji, Hungary, Indonesia, Malaysia, New Zealand, the Philippines, Thailand, and Uruguay) proposed a cut of 90 per cent in export subsidies over ten years; a cut of 75 per cent in other farm supports, such as internal supports; and tariffication, or conversion of all non-tariff barriers into tariffs.

The European Community proposals included: a 30 per cent cut in overall farm supports over ten years starting in 1986; rebalancing or introduction of import quotas for feedstuffs and oilseeds (this implies increasing tariffs that are currently bound at zero or very low levels); reduction of import barriers in line with the dismantling of internal support; and unclear statements concerning export subsidies. The EC's proposed "less protection not free trade" is based on Aggregate Measures of Support (AMS), a device which seeks to capture all different forms of subsidies and benefits in a single measure to provide participants with the flexibility to choose their own methods of support and the balance of protection between commodities.

The negotiations were dominated by a bitter conflict between the EC on one side and the U.S., Canada, Argentina and other nations on the other side. The Community was reluctant to commit itself to a definite reduction of export subsidies. The Europeans, who were accused of paying the most generous farm subsidies, said that the opposing side was asking for cuts that were not politically feasible. In particular, France, with its many small farmers, resisted big reductions in farm subsidies and prevented the Commission from fixing the percentage of reduction. The Uruguay Round broke off on December 7, 1990, but resumed in February, 1991.

The EC position remains exactly the same. At the time of writing, progress was slow and difficult, with negotiations again deadlocked over the issue of agricultural subsidies, the most sensitive pa rt of trade because of strong farm lobbies in most countries. "There is something mystical about the farm industry. It is not a matter of surpluses or supports. Farmers are special," says GATT Director-General Arthur Dunkel (Time International, 1992:45). He presented a plan to unblock the stalled negotiations that would cut agricultural export subsidies 36 per cent over six years and domestic subsidies 20 per cent over the same period. EC trade and agricultural ministers rejected Dunkel's proposal because it would demand unfair concessions from European farmers. France and Ireland (one of the biggest beneficiaries of CAP payments) have led EC opposition. The French agricultural minister, Louis Mermaz, said that the Dunkel paper would be the "ruin of the European agriculture" (*The International Herald Tribune*, 1992a). President Mitterand called the compromise unacceptable. The German Minister of Agriculture, Ignaz Kiechle, and the powerful Deutscher Bauernverband were firmly committ ed to protecting farmers' income, while the German Minister of Economics, Jürgen Mölleman, sharply criticized CAP. "It would approach the borderline of insanity" if the EC does not make concessions at the GATT negotiations said Mölleman (*The Week in Germany*, 1992). Chancellor Kohl declared recently in Bonn that the future belongs to free trade not to protectionism. President Bush has refused to slash U.S. farm subsidies and to "disarm American farmers" without EC concessions (*Time International*, 1992). Japan, as culpable as any other actor with its substantially high levels of protection in some agricultural sectors such as rice, is also alarmed at an outbreak of protectionism. Negotiations are now under way involving country-by-country bargaining on specific commitments to make farm subsidy cuts as well as reduction in tariff and non-tariff barriers to imports of goods, including farm products (*The Economist*, 1992a).

Policy Reform

Both the United States and the European Community are particularly concerned with policy reform as they are burdened by enormous budgetary costs and huge surpluses of farm products. However, until now no significant change has occurred. The U.S. Congress passed the 1990 Farm Bill well before the current GATT negotiations will conclude. The new bill is a slightly modified version of the 1985 Food Security Act. The new bill requires, however, a reduction in agricultural spending, from $80 billion to $40 billion over 5 years.

This section focuses particularly on CAP reform.[10] The emergence of the EC as a major exporter has meant that the economic and external pressures (in particular from the U.S.) on the EC to reform CAP are tremendous. Reforming CAP is not an easy task because EC agricultural policy-makers have to deal with the different national interests of twelve member states with both their common and contr adictory characteristics (Petit, 1985; 1989; Petit, et al, 1987; Lueschen, 1990). At the same time, EC policy-making has shifted towards Brussels. Because of the primacy of agricultural policy within the EC, agricultural issues are discussed at the highest level. The summit meetings between political leaders are dominated by issues of milk, cereals, wine and other commodities.

The EC has already made some significant changes such as direct income support to farmers, budget discipline which imposes a ceiling on the increase in the agricultural budget, and other measures in cluding stabilizer mechanisms, milk quotas, set-aside of agricultural land, and a new oilseed support system.

Today the EC is faced more than ever with a new budget crisis as agricultural spending reached 32.5 billion ECU ($38 billion) in 1991, almost 5 billion ECU more than in 1990. More dramatic are the stockpiles of grains (30 million tonnes), beef (750 000 tonnes), and dairy products (one million tonnes). The budget crisis, added to external pressures, will be very important in forcing changes. In late January 1991, the EC Commission proposed a "Reflections Paper" to reform the CAP. The major advantages of the plan were to cut price supports, reduce production quotas, direct income aid to farmers, increase land set-aside, and protect the environment through extensification. New support mechanisms were introduced such as aid on a per hectare basis.

The Commission's proposal was criticized by the UK, the Netherlands and Denmark for discriminating against larger and more efficient farmers. However, the final decision depended, as expected, on the attitude of the German and French ministers of agriculture. Both faced a dilemma. Germany has always supported the small farmers because of their electoral power; and it was expected that the German minister would endorse the above-mentioned plan. But the influx of gigantic eastern farms, a result of unification, shifted attention from the small farmer. As a result, Germany opposed the plan, backed by the powerful farmers' organization, the DBV. France, as a big exporter of cereals, opposed the idea of aid on a per hectare basis. The French Minister of Agriculture sided with the UK in condemning the move toward discrimination against larger farmers. However, France also has a large number of small farmers who will benefit from the proposal. The Council of Agricultural Ministers met on February 4, 1991 to discuss the proposal but refused to endorse it. Instead, the Council asked the Commissioner to shift the focus to the annual price review.

Louis Mermaz, French minister of agriculture, announced that failure to reach agreement in GATT would push the EC to overhaul its agricultural policy. If there is no conclusion under GATT – which will happen if the Americans continue to be so "intransigent" – "we still have to set up this new Common Agricultural Policy," he said (*The International Herald Tribune*, 1992b).

As part of the 1991-92 price package, the EC has introduced a new set-aside programme in an effort to control production and expenditures, in particular in grains. In the new EC five-year budget prop osal, the farmers' share of the total budget would drop to around 47 percent (*The Economist*, 1992b).

Free-Trade Areas

Efforts to liberalize trade (including agriculture), and to "harmonize or unify economic policies" (OECD, 1991:107) are reflected through free-trade areas. The EC, one of the first, is expected to help Europe emerge with formidable power. The German unification has eliminated all customs and trade barriers between the former German Democratic Republic and the EC. The EC and EFTA signed a treaty creating a European Economic Area (EEA). Czechoslovakia, Hungary and Poland have been granted association status with the EC, but they are struggling for full membership. EFTA has also signed trade agreements with these countries. The aim is the creation of a free-trade area that will eliminate customs duties and quotas between the EC and the newly associated countries.

Other agricultural policy reforms are expected with the 1992 Single Market such as the elimination of internal trade barriers; free flow of goods, services and people between the twelve member state s; harmonization of food safety, plant, and animal regulations; and cooperation on labelling, packaging and additive legislation.

The EC operates a number of preferential trade agreements with developing countries. The Lomé Convention covers nearly seventy African, Caribbean and Pacific (ACP) countries in an effort to stren gthen North-South relations. Under the Lomé Convention many exports from ACP countries enter the Community free of customs duties and free of quantitative restrictions (while the ACP countries are not obliged to offer such concessions).

The EC has also negotiated various preferential trade agreements, with varying degrees of liberalism, with most of the Mediterranean countries. In some cases, these agreements have mentioned the possible creation of a customs union between the EC and appropriate countries.

The U.S., Canada and Mexico are forming a North American free trade area (NAFTA). One free-trade agreement between Brazil, Argentina, Uruguay and Paraguay has been signed. Mexico has signed a pact with Chile, and also plans a free-trade pact with Venezuela and Columbia (*The Economist*, 1991).

If the new trade-regions are really free-trade, they are not a bad accomplishment. But they may be used to exclude competitors; to create, for example, fortresses, in which trade would operate only within "walls." Eastern European countries would be very hard hit, as they desperately need EC markets in which to sell their low-cost steel, textiles and food that are very attractive to Western E uropean consumers.

Conclusion

As has been shown, the globalization of agricultural policies is a difficult task since many policies are designed and implemented by powerful countries and are useless to developing countries. Governments of developed countries are able to assemble an arsenal of policy mechanisms and direct controls to protect their economic interests. As result, these governments fail to control prices and trade policies in the best interest of both developed and developing countries. Current policies, especially those of the EC and the US, have introduced enormous distortions in the market, with consumers and taxpayers paying the burden of agricultural support.

This situation is the result of economic and political forces and, in particular, the relative power of farmers' organizations. The domestic determinants of agricultural policy-making are the most important elements of the CAP and its apparent irrationality (in economic terms). The continuity of the subsidization system attests to the importance of the national interests of the EC member states and the willingness of their governments to pay for it. The consequences of this is that any movement toward globalization of agricultural policies, for example toward free trade, is unlikely to happen considering that EC farmers have major political influence.

The success of the ongoing Uruguay Round depends heavily on a compromise or accommodation between the two giants in agricultural trade. It is important that the EC and the U.S. negotiate their compromise within the GATT multilateral arena. This is of course more difficult, but no country can afford to make a unilateral policy change in the direction of reducing protection. Given the political sensitivity of sharp reductions in farm income, policy reforms need a broader base of support. The political rationale for coordination is the general dislike of the present situation and the need for cooperation and coordination. The economic rationale for coordination lies in the effort of each country to reform its domestic agricultural policy.

Creating agricultural policy is an ongoing and changing process. The fact that agriculture is on the GATT agenda is an indication that countries are willing to discuss and change the current insane situation. Pressures on agricultural support are likely to continue as a result of significant changes in agricultural labour markets and rural economies in both Europe and North America. Perceptions of the role and function of rural areas and people in industrialized countries are also changing.

The focus on developed countries in this paper points out another problem of globalization in agriculture. Globalization implies the need to take into account the needs of developing countries.

The real success of the Uruguay Round shall be determined by the extent to which the industrialized countries will be able to adapt their agricultural production structures and markets to a new global trade situation in which developing countries will increase their agricultural production. The challenge for the Uruguay Round is to find alternatives that will achieve the goals of freer trade.

The new order will also have to take into account the current change and uncertainty of the centrally planned economies.

NOTES

1. Increased attention has been given by political scientists to the policy-making process in developed countries.
2. For the EC the variable levy is the main instrument of domestic price support policy. The U.S. considers it a trade barrier. For the U.S., target prices, loan rates and acreage set-aside are at the heart of domestic price and income supports. For the EC, these mechanisms are simply export subsidies. The U.S. system of payments is a government budget support with the burden on taxpayers; the EC farm payment is a price support with the burden on consumers. The U.S. system of protection sounds more economic; the American consumer buys his food cheaper than does the European consumer.
3. In particular, CAP's system of agricultural support has resulted in chronic surpluses (in cereals, sugar, dairy products, beef, poultry and wine), which, in turn, has required more support creating a vicious cycle and more disequilibrium. Since 1973, EC agricultural production has increased persistently above the level of self-sufficiency.
4. Various mechanisms have been used to compare the support levels. Josling has used the Producer Subsidy Equivalent (PSE) which is an extension and refinement of the Nominal Rate of Protection (NRP). The OECD has used the PSE and Consumer Subsidy Equivalent (CSE) concepts.
5. Total transfers include: subsidies specific to food processing and distribution; outlays related to rural transportation and communication and social payments (e.g., Food Stamp Programme in the U.S.); outlays for stockholding; and all budget outlays associated with PSE and CSE (OECD, 1991:137).
6. Forty-five per cent of the world's population is dependent on agriculture and is concentrated in the developing world, "with only one-fifth of the minimal prosperity levels in the lesser developed countries" (Harvey, 1991:312).
7. Ruttan (1980:20) argues that a rapid increase in imports accompanied by a rapid decline in employment in industry or commodity sectors always bring more protectionism. The instability in the glob al macro-economy further reinforces nationalistic tendencies in commodity trade (McCalla, 1989).
8. For a discussion of this theme for France and Germany see Averyt (1977), Duchene et al., (1985) Senior Nello (1984), and Coulomb et al.(1990). For a

discussion of the development of agricultural lobbies in the United States see Bonnen (1987). For a detailed discussion of the agri-business lobby see Browne (1988).

9. This is based on the assumption that dependent development was a particular inegalitarian form of capitalist development. The expansion of European capitalism has created economic development in the center and underdevelopment in the periphery.
10. CAP is blamed to a large extent for the global agricultural disequilibrium. It is considered a "dreadful" example of a highly protectionist agricultural policy. CAP's objectives are similar to those of other industrialized countries. CAP is, however, unique in that it combines a high level of internal price with a high production inducing the use of huge export subsidies (Tangermann, 198 5:90).

REFERENCES

Amin, Samir, (1967), Le Développement du capitalism en Cote-d'Ivoire. Paris: Editions de Minuit.

Anderson, Kym and Yujiro Hayami with Aurelia George... (et al), (1986), *The Political Economy of Agricultural Protection: East Asia in International Perspective*. Sydney: Allen and Unwin.

Averyt, William F., (1977), *Agropolitics in the European Community: Interest Groups and the Common Agricultural Policy*. New York: Praeger.

Bonnen, James T., (1987), "Institutions, instruments and driving forces behind U.S. national agricultural policies." Paper presented for the binational symposium on US-Canadian Agricultural Trade Challenges sponsored by the National Center for Food and Agricultural Policy, Resources for the Future, Washington DC, and the C.D. Howe Institute of Canada, Wayzeta, MN, July 22-24.

Boudon, Raymond and François Bourricaud, (1989), *A Critical Dictionary of Sociology*. Selected and translated by Peter Hamilton [First published in French in 1982 by Presses Universitaires de France]. Chicago: The University of Chicago Press.

Browne, William B., (1988), *Private Interests, Public Policy, and American Agriculture*. Lawrence: Kansas University Press.

Cardoso, Fernando H., and Enzo Faletto, (1979), *Dependency and Development in Latin America*. Berkeley: University of California Press.

Commission of the European Communities, (1988), Disharmonies in EC and US Agricultural Policy Measures. Luxembourg: Office for Official Publications of the European Communities.

—, (1989), A Common Agricultural Policy for the 1990s. Luxembourg: Office for Official Publications of the European Communities.

—, (1991), The Development and Future of the Common Agricultural Policy: Proposals of the Commission. Green Europe 2/91. Luxembourg: Office for Official Publications of the European Communities.

CRS Report for Congress, (1990), Provisions of the 1990 Farm Bill. Washington, D.C.: Congressional Research Service, the Library of Congress.

Coulomb, Pierre, Héléne Delorme, Bertrand Hervieu, Marcel Jollivet, and Philippe Lacombe, (1990), Les Agriculteurs et la Politique [Farmers and Politics]. Paris: Presse de la Foundation Nationale des Sciences Politiques.

Curry Foundation, (1985), *Confrontation or Negotiation: United States Policy and European Agriculture*. New York: Associated Faculty Press.

de Janvry, Alain, (1981), *The Agrarian Question and Reformism in Latin America*. Baltimore: The John Hopkins University Press.

——, (1983), "Why do governments do what they do? the case of food price policy." Pp. 185-212 in Gale D. Johnson and G. Edward Schuh, (eds.), *The Role of Markets in the World Food Economy*. Boulder: Westview Press.

Duchêne, François, Edward Szczepanik and Wilfrid Legg, (1985), *New Limits on European Agriculture: Politics and the Common Agricultural Policy*. London: Croom Helm.

Economist, The, (1991), "Latin America's economic reforms." October 19, pp.21-24.

——, (1992a), "GATT's trade talks final sprint-or-stumble." January 18, p. 69.

——, (1992b), "You thought five-year plans were dead?" February 8, p. 46.

Emmanuel, Arghiri, (1972), *Unequal Exchange: A Study of the Imperialism of Trade*. New York: Monthly Review Press.

Evans, Peter B. and John D. Stevens, (1988), "Development and the world economy." Pp. 739-773 in Neil Smelser, (ed.), *Handbook of Sociology*. Boulder: Sage Publications.

Hagedorn, Konrad and Gänther Schmitt, (1985), "Die politischen Gründe für eine wirtschaftspolitische Vorzugsbehandlung der Landwirtschaft." Pp. 279-300 in Jahrbuch fär Neue Politische Ökonomie, Bd.4. Tübingen: Mohr.

Harvey, David, (1991), "The production entitlement guarantee (PEG), option." Pp. 311-335 in Christopher Ritson and David Harvey, (eds.), *The Common Agricultural Policy and the World Economy*. Wallingford, UK: C.A.B. In ternational.

Hayami, Yujiro, (1989), "Agricultural policies in disarray." Pp. 56-88 in Harald von Witzke, C. Ford Runge and Brain Job (eds.), *Policy Coordination in World Agriculture*. Kiel, Germany: Wissenschaftsverlag Vauk.

International Herald Tribune, The, (1992a), "U.S. asks EC to 'relent' over GATT." January 13, p. 6.

——, (1992b), "France confident on EC stance in GATT." January 6, p. 11.

Johnson, D. Gale, (1973), *World Agriculture in Disarray*. London: McMillan.

Lee Yong S., Don F. Hadwinger and Chong-Bum Lee, (1990), "Agricultural policy making under international pressures: the case of South Korea, a newly industrialized country." *Food Policy*, 15:418-33.

Lueschen, Leila S., (1990), "The European Community Agricultural Policy-making Process: Interplay Among Actors and Conflicts of National Interests." Proceedings of the European Community Studies Association (ECSA), Inaugural Conference of the European Community in the 1990s. Washington, D.C.: Center for European Community Studies.

McCalla, Alex, (1989), "Improving policy coordination in agriculture." Pp. 212-245 in Harald von Witzke, C. Ford Runge and Brain Job (eds.), *Policy Coordination in World Agriculture*. Kiel, Germany: Wissenschaftsverl ag Kiel.

Moyer, Wayne H. and Timothy E. Josling, (1990), *Agricultural Policy Reform: Politics and Process in the EC and the USA*. Ames, Iowa: Iowa State University Press.

Mouzelis, Nicos, (1986), Politics in the Semi-Periphery: *Early Parliamentarism and Late Industrialization in the Balkans and Latin America*. London: Macmillan.

——, (1988), "Sociology of development: reflections on the present crisis." *Sociology*, 22.

OECD, (1991), Agricultural Policies, Markets and Trade: Monitoring and Outlook 1991. Organisation of for Economic Co-operation and Development: Paris.

Olson, Mancur, (1965), *The Logic of Collective Action:Public Goods and the Theory of Groups*. Cambridge, Mass.: Harvard University Press.

——, (1985), "Space, agriculture, and organization." *American Journal of Agricultural Economics*, 67:928-937.

——, (1986), "The exploitation and subsidization of agriculture in the developed and developing countries." Pp. 49-59 in Allen Maunder and Ulf Renborg, (eds.), *Agriculture in a Turbulent World*. Aldershot: Gower.

Petit, Michel, (1985), Determinants of Agricultural Policies in the United States and the European Community. Research Report #51. Washington, DC: International Food Policy Research Institute.

——, (1989), Pressures on Europe's Common Agricultural Policy. Washington, DC: International Food Policy Research Institute.

Petit, Michel, Michele de Benedictis, Denis Britton, Martijn de Groot, Wihlem Henrichsmeyer and Francesco Lechi (1987), Agricultural Policy Formation in the European Community: The Birth of Milk Quotas and CAP Reform. Amsterdam: Elsevier.

Petit, Michel, George E. Rossmiller, and M. Ann Tutwiler, (1989), International agricultural negotiations: the United States and the European Community square off. Pp.88-102 in M. Ann Tutwiler (ed.), *U.S. Agriculture in a Global Setting: an Agenda for the Future*. Washington, D.C.: Resources for the Future.

Rausser, Gordon C., (1982), "Political economic markets: PERTS and PESTs in food and agriculture." *American Journal of Agricultural Economics*, 64:821-833.

Rausser, Gordon C. and Brian D. Wright, (1989), "Alternative strategies for trade policy reform." Pp. 117-159 in Harald von Witzke, C. Ford Runge and Brain Job, (eds.), *Policy Coordination in World Agriculture*. Kiel, Germany: Wissenschaftsv erlag Vauk.

Ruttan, Vernon W., (1989), "Market integration in agriculture." Pp. 6-55 in Harald von Witzke, C. Ford Runge and Brain Job (eds.), *Policy Coordination in World Agriculture*. Kiel, Germany: Wissenschaftsverlag Vauk.

Schultz, T.W., (1978), "On economics and politics of agriculture." Pp. 3-22 in T.W, Schultz, (ed.), *Distortions of Agricultural Incentives*. Bloomington, Indiana: Indiana University Press.

Senior Nello, Susan, (1984), "An application of public choice theory to the question of CAP reform." *European Review of Agricultural Economics*, 11:261-283.

——, (1989), "European interest groups and the CAP." *Food Policy*, 14, (2):101-106.

Tangermann, Stefan, (1985), "Special features and ongoing reforms of the CAP." Pp. 84-106 in Confrontation or Negotiations. The Curry Foundation. New York: Associated Faculty Press.

The Week in Germany, (1992), "Green Week agricultural fair opens, accompanied by farmer protest." January 24, p. 4.

Time International, (1992), "Trade: stakes are high." January 27, pp. 44-45.

Tutwiler, M. Ann & A. Barry Carr, (1988), "An agenda for the future." Pp.221-232 in M. Ann Tutwiler, (ed.), U.S. Agriculture in a Global Setting: An Agenda for the Future. Washington, D.C.: Resources for the Future.

Valdés, Alberto, (1991), "Agricultural trade and pricing polices in developing countries: implications for policy reform." Pp. IS-IIIB-3 in Papers of the Plenary and Invited Paper Sessions, XXI International Conference of Agricultural Economists, August 22-29, 1991, Tokyo, Japan.

Von Witzke, Harold, C. Ford Runge and Brian Job, (1989), *Policy Coordination in World Agriculture*. Kiel: Wissenschaftsverlag Vauk.

Winters, L. Alan, (1987), "The political economy or of the agricultural policy of industrial countries." *European Review of Agricultural Economics* 14:285-304.

4

IMMIGRANT LABOUR IN THE INTERNATIONALIZATION OF MEAT-PROCESSING

LOURDES GOUVEIA

Introduction

The global character of the livestock complex, the essence of which was well captured in Sanderson's (1986) term "the world steer", has been documented by Friedmann (1990) and other authors. However, much of the discussion has concentrated on the "low end" of the production process while much remains to be known about the "upper" or processing end of the cycle. Meat processing has become inc reasingly global in recent years, spurred in part by technological changes such as the development of "boxed beef" and the growth of new food conglomerates which command control over the entire food chain and agro-industrial inputs. However, for some large firms, meatpacking remains an intrinsically domestic operation whose incursions into global capital circuits are restricted to exports and outsourcing of non-native labourers. This study considers the extent to which packers operating within the domestically constrained circuit of global capital (Bryan 1987; McMichael and Myhre, 1991), do in fact become dependent upon the mobilization of immigrant and minority workforces to remain competitive within the context of a global economy. Specifically, the paper examines the case of IBP, the world's largest beef processor and its operations in the U.S. Midwest.

Three large corporations slaughter and process around 80 per cent of the beef produced in the United States, up from 48 per cent ten years ago: Cargill, ConAgra, and IBP. IBP is currently the top producer. Despite this high level of market concentration, these meat-processing firms have seen their profit margins fluctuate widely in the last years brought about by a combination of factors: plant over-capacity due to reduced cattle inventories after the 1980s farm crisis, declining beef consumption in the home market, and competition with cheaper and leaner meats such as poultry and fish. This is also an industry with higher than average labour costs and relatively small profit margins per sale. These three firms have sought to recuperate and expand profit margins through a diversified set of restructuring strategies which today are well known to industry analysts and scholars alike (*Business Week*, 1983; Broadway, 1992). However, we have yet to understand the full-blown implications of these re structuring strategies within a new context of a globalized food and agricultural sector.

Starting in the late sixties, and following the lead of IBP, meat-processing firms undertook a series of cost-cutting strategies primarily concentrated on technological innovations and the re-organization of the production process. IBP opened its first plant in a rural community, Denison, Iowa, close to cattle on feed and away from high-cost unionized labour. It built the first of a new breed of large plants designed to take advantage of economics of scale and control a larger share of the market. It pioneered "boxed beef" (vacuum packed subprimal cuts of beef) which further reduced transportation costs and gave impetus to the standardization process of the commodity beef-enlarging its "distance and durability" which are critical in today's global food economy (Friedmann, 1990). It is also to IBP's tough stand against unions that industry analysts attribute the elimination of master contracts with meat-pacing unions and significant wage reductions – by the 1970s, for many beefpacking workers, these amounted to 40 per cent below pork workers with master agreements (*Business Week*, 1983). It further re-organized the labour process whereby more complex tasks where broken into simpler, repetitive ones, thus facilitating the incorporation of unskilled labour into the production process and increased labour productivity through the resultant acceleration of chain speeds.

By the late seventies, the pace of regional relocation accelerated and packers had fully re-organized their production process in line with IBP's (Broadway 1992). Expansions, mergers and acquisition s resulted in the current level of industrial consolidation. Finally, the composition of the meatpacking labour force began to change as the traditional pools from which meatpacking workers were recruited became either unavailable or unwilling to labour under new conditions. Women, part-time farmers, and most importantly new Hispanic and Asian immigrants constitute the core of the new meatpacking labour pools (Griffith, 1990). Once again, it is IBP which has been at the forefront of recruiting strategies aimed at mobilizing potential workers from depressed areas in the US-Mexico border.

While the essence of these cost-cutting strategies is well understood, the same cannot be said of the implications of the differential adoption of the same by each firm. As various authors have pointed out (Center for Rural Affairs, 1990; Broadway, 1992) IBP's expansion was accomplished through the building of new plants rather than new acquisitions and mergers. Its rise to dominance was also achieved largely through its philosophy of becoming "a master of fractions": to become (as it indeed was until recently) the lowest-cost producer by saving fractions of cost at every stage of the production process (Tintsman and Peterson, 1981). On the other hand, ConAgra and Cargill achieved their market dominance through the purchase and acquisition of two other packers, Monfort (1987) and Excel (1979) respectively. In a 1989 article Constance and Heffernan already noted the superior advantage enjoyed by Monfort and Excel through their association with a parent company with "deep pockets." What is even more significant than deep pockets in this new context of shrinking domestic markets and a globalized economy, is that they are transnational conglomerates, much better situated than IBP to scout the globe for workers, inputs and markets[1]. The question that inevitably emerges then is what survival strategies are now most crucial to IBP's survival.

A satisfactory answer to the question posed at the beginning of this paper would require an extensive look at the organization of production and corporate profiles of each of the three firms. Much of this paper is limited to the examination of IBP's specific practices, especially with regard to labour recruitment and workforce composition. Observations are also based quite substantially on IBP's operation in the small rural community of Lexington, Nebraska.

Methodological Note

Data for this study has been collected as part of an on-going field study in Lexington, NE and includes pilot interviews with local workers, community and company representatives, and social service providers. In addition, information has been obtained through company and government documents as well as newspaper and trade magazine articles. Lexington is a community of 6,600 located in the west-central part of Nebraska. According to the 1990 census, only 4.9 per cent of the population are Hispanic and 7.3 per cent are classified as minorities. IBP's Lexington plant began operating on November 8, 1990. Today, the plant employs over two thousand workers, over half of which are minorities and immigrants, and processes some 4,000 head of cattle a day.

Meat-processing in a Global Economy: Where IBP Stands

Despite IBP's impressive success in the past three decades, doubts have recently emerged as to whether it can continue to remain competitive and survive the latest struggle among the big three for a ddi-tional market shares. The company's earnings dropped from $48.3 million in 1990 to $ 1.4 million in 1991 – and a far cry from the $53.2 million ten years earlier (Rasmussen, 1992; Stuart, 1981). In its 1992 Board of Directors' meeting the company agreed to reduce dividends earned by shareholders – a move that has prompted some to wonder about the company's future. In contrast, though somewhat behind earnings of the previous year, ConAgra reported healthy (though not explicitly stated) 1991 earnings in its beef division, Monfort (ConAgra Inc, 1992). Earnings information on privately-owned Cargill is harder to obtain, but there has been no alarm sounded in the press as there has been with IBP.

ConAgra and Cargill are highly diversified and vertically integrated conglomerates whose commodities run the whole gamut of the food chain and livestock sector in particular. They are also the world's largest producers and traders of feed, fertilizer, and other key agricultural inputs. Both are keen examples of "global firms" strategically positioned to increase international sales and outsource labour and other inputs via their large number of direct and indirect investments in Europe, Japan, Australia, Asia, Canada, and Latin America. IBP, on the other hand, comes closer to the older type of multinational whose presence in the world market is confined to export sales (Gouveia, 1992). Global markets are recognized by all industry watchers as crucial for the survival of meatpacking companies (Kay, 1992). And while IBP may figure as the largest exporter of U.S. beef to Japan, ConAgra's and Cargill's direct investments in Asia and

Australia (where cattle will be raised for the Japanese market) override the relative significance of that fact. This is even more relevant when we look beyond beef and account for the inroads made by ConAgra and Cargill in U.S. and global production and marketing of poultry, pork, and fish. IBP competes with these two conglomerates for the pork market and has no investments in poultry and fish-beef's major competitors (Heffernan and Constance, 1992; Kay, 1992).

IBP's pioneering of modern production processes and technological innovations in the past also appears today to lag behind the other two major packers. For example, the move toward greater products tandardization that started with the introduction of boxed beef by IBP, is now being carried forward by the other two packers via, for example, case-ready and branded meats, as well as genetic and hot fat-trimming processes (Effertz, 1987).

IBP is still the world's largest meatpacking company (over eight million cattle a year) and alarms about its apparent loss of innovative capacity are dismissed by those who point to profit per head and similar indicators (Kay, 1988). But, today, competition from more globalized agro-industrial capital poses some undisputable dangers to IBP's earnings and future investment capacity. Some suggest IBP, in its traditional unique and independent way of doing business, is simply waiting in the wings for others to assume the risks associated with research and development to make its move into new products and processes. In fact, IBP's chief executive officer, Robert Peterson, has often spoken of the time when it will in fact be prudent to enter such terrains as case-ready beef and diversification within the core beef and pork business (Kay, 1990).

It is difficult if not impossible to forecast IBP's future success as capital accumulation strategies remain confined to a domestic field of investment. It is also impossible to predict whether IBP's current status as a national firm will change in the near future through, for example, new mergers or joint ventures – although entry into a global field of investment already dominated by global food conglomerates like ConAgra and Cargill, may prove as difficult as entry of new packers into domestic markets controlled by the Big Three. It is rather clear, however, that at present and in the near future IBP's capital accumulation depends heavily on a continuation of its old philosophy of saving fractions of cost at every stage of their domestic operations while attempting to expand export markets. It is in this context that access to pools of new labour force entrants such as newly legalized migrant farm workers, refugees, women, and in some cases, part-time farmers may be potentially significant. Also significant are subsidies of various sorts, training funds, and tax abatements from local states and municipalities. Utilization of immigrant and minority labour forces is not a new phenomena in the meatpacking industry (Stanley, 1988; Griffith, 1990). By the same token, extraction of concessions from municipalities and states is probably as prominent among the other two large packers. (See for example McNaughton, 1991; DED, 1991.) Nonetheless, current analyses have yet to determine the extent to which different circuits of globalized capital determine the centrality of such practices within profit maximization schemes.

IBP's Immigrant Labour Force in Nebraska and Other Midwest Communities: Contributions to a Domestic Firm

Evidence on an apparent trend within meat and poultry processing firms consisting in the replacement of native-born white minority workers by new immigrants and refugees has been accumulating for the past three or four years (See for example, Erickson and Stull, 1989; Griffith, 1990; Stanley, 1991; and various papers presented at the conference organized by Stull et al, 1992). However, information is still too dispersed and case studies not sufficiently standardized to produce conclusive evidence as to whether these are industry-wide trends or whether some fundamental distinctions must be drawn between regions, or firms of different sizes, organizational histories, and – in my view at least – degrees of internationalization. To complicate matters even further, the incorporation of new labour forces into meatpacking is a very dynamic process aided at the present time by, among other things, sophisticated state and private recruitment practices. Waves of different groups of immigrants, refugees and minorities can come and go in just a matter of months.

The case of IBP's presence in the Midwest, particularly its Lexington, Nebraska plant, is insufficient to answer the question as to whether its limited degree of internationalization constitutes yet one more factor shaping the increased hiring of new immigrants. Nonetheless, its examination generates some initial insights for this and closely related questions. Two specific issues seem to offer such insights: 1) Recruitment practices in IBP's recent history; 2) Examination of particular factors facilitating IBP's mobilization and recomposition of the meatpacking labour market.

Recruiting the New Meatpacking Workers

It must be said from the start that despite broad claims made by those who follow this issue closely (See for example PrairieFire Rural Action, 1991), I have yet to find clear evidence that ConAgra and Cargill employ a full-time labour recruiting team as does IBP. Instead, these companies seem to rely more heavily on network recruiting and conjunctural opportunities such as government and private agencies' efforts to situate refugees or migrant workers in permanent employment. Ironically, they also benefit from the migrant flows precipitated by IBP's more expensive recruitment methods.

IBP's recruiting teams are made up of well-trained full-time employees who travel constantly to low-employment areas with large minority or immigrant populations: Texas, California, Arizona, Colorado, and in some cases, the "rust-belt" area (Nuestro Mundo, 1990; *Omaha World Herald*, 1990). A Nebraska Department of Labour (DOL) official verifies this as well as the by now well-known role this organ ism and local job service offices play in meatpacking recruitment, the matching of job applicants with job offerings through a sophisticated nationwide computer network: From Nebraska, "on behalf of IBP we'll put in an order with the local job office in Texas, for example, for, say, 200 workers and specify what the pay and benefits will be . . . . we make sure those jobs are really there and they (the Texas job service office) are not going to be sending all these people without the jobs being truly available" (Gouveia personal communication with DOL official 4/5/1991).

Numerous press stories and other sources have documented the utilization of on-site recruitment (either through recruiters or local job offices) for several specific plants in both Nebraska and Iowa (See for example Nuestro Mundo 1991). As can be seen from Table 4.1, a moderate to large presence of New Hispanic or Asian immigrants can be observed in old and new, beef and pork plants alike. In general, smaller as well as older, unionized plants seem more likely to have smaller numbers of new immigrant workers. However, as suggested earlier, the incorporation of new immigrants into IBP's labour force is a very dynamic and relatively new process, gathering strength toward the end of the 1980s. IBP's flagship Dakota City plant, for example, has long been known for its lengthy and often

TABLE 4.1: Selected IBP Plants

Plant Location	Pork (P) or Beef (B)	Start-Up Date (1992)	No of Workers	Union	Estimated* Presence of New Immigrants workforce
Amarillo, TX	B	1975	2,800	Teamsters	M - H (LA)
Pasco, WA	B	1976	1,500	Teamsters	L - M (LA:increasing)
Dakota City, NE	B	1966	3,200	UFCW	H (LA)
Joslin, IL	B	1983	2,000	UFCW	L
Perry, IA	P	1989	775	UFCW	L - M (LA:increasing)
Waterloo, IA	P	1990	2,000	UFCW	H (LA)
Lexington, NE	B	1990	2,000	NO	H (LA)
Finney County, KS (Garden City)	B	1980	2,700	NO	H (A and LA-latter is plant's majority)
Storm Lake, IA	P	1982	1,200	NO	M - H (A)
Louis County, IA (Columbus Junction)	P	1986	3,200	NO	H (LA)
Madison, NE	P	1987	700	NO	L - M (LA: increasing)
Dennison, IA	B	1961	250	NO	L
West Point, NE	B	1968	325	NO	L

* Estimates are based on various research reports, articles, and personal communication with research informants and community representatives

Sources: Personal communication with IBP Public Relations Manager, IBP's 1990 10-K form, various research reports

A: Asians — M: Moderate
LA: Latinos — H: High
L: Low

violent union strikes. This old plant of 3,200 workers now hires a large and increasing number of new Latino immigrants, many of whom (at least initially) were recruited from states bordering Mexico (Petrowski, 1990). This is not entirely surprising as IBP has constantly fought to hire non-union workers and stem the power of the unionized workforce. According to IBP's Public Relations manager, new Latino workers are also arriving in increasing numbers in unionized plants in Washington state and Perry, Iowa, which he believes has hired 100 new Hispanic immigrants since 1989 (Gouveia: personal conversation 5/3/1992).

Similarly, some authors have noted that immigrants have tended to gravitate toward newer and larger plants (Griffith, 1990; Stanley, 1988). While this still holds true for the smallest plants, some medium-size plants like Madison, Iowa (700 workers), and the already-mentioned Perry plant, with a similar number of total employees, have been hiring increasing numbers of new Hispanic immigrants in the last two years – since IBP took over the operation of these plants and recruited heavily, for these plants specifically, in southern California and Louisiana (Broadway, 1992).

IBP's recruitment of new immigrants has also benefited from refugee assistance programmes for South East Asians, as was the case in the early phases of the Garden City, Kansas, and Storm Lake, Iowa plants' operations. While these programmes had a temporary status and much of this labour force has now dried up, the presence of Latino workers continues to intensify and even displace other minorities and immigrants throughout IBP's plants. IBP has offered bonuses, advertised periodically in areas of plant shut-downs and surrounding particular plants, and relied on network recruiting and word-ofmouth as important mechanisms of labour mobilization. Of lesser significance, but not entirely negligible has been the mobilization of women out of the household and low wage services and into these plants – from a 14 per cent average until the early eighties, to over 20 per cent by the early nineties.

New Hispanic and Asian immigrants have also moved into jobs provided by Excel and Monfort. Although exact figures are not available at this time, early indications suggest their presence there seem sat least uneven if not smaller – but most likely growing as well. Devoid of comprehensive recruiting strategies, these companies benefit either from their presence in communities like Greely, Colorado or Dodge City, Kansas, which have well-established

Hispanic migrant networks; or from the migrant streams generated by neighbouring IBP plants – as it has been the case in Grand Island, near Lexing ton, Nebraska.

As various authors have periodically pointed out, downgrading the labour process makes previously inaccessible pools of unskilled labour available to capital (Sassen, 1990). Low-skilled immigrants have historically served to lower production costs of production within the agro-industrial sector, and meat-packing in particular. From the point of view of IBP, the incorporation of great numbers of Latino and Asian immigrants since the mid – and late-eighties coincides with a series of related events. One crucial event was the farm crisis of the early eighties which led to an exodus of population from many rural counties where IBP operates (including Dawson County, where Lexington is located), shortening the supply of local labour. The crisis also reduced the number of cattle feeders which, in the context of plant over-capacity, has pushed up prices and accentuated the competition between packers. But the clear turning point for IBP came in 1987-1988 when its net earnings began a downward decline, experiencing its first quarter losses in 1989 when total earnings were almost half of 1987. What is significant about this particular period is that it marks the ascendancy of ConAgra as a major global food conglomerate and, through its 1987 purchase of Monfort and other packers, as IBP's major competitor (Constance and Heffernan, 1989). Although virtually impossible to document, it is logical to link IBP's profit squeeze, provoked by the emergence of meat-packing capital with wider doors to global markets, labour, and inputs, and its aggressive strategies for recruiting new immi grant and minority workers – one of IBP's only vehicles for reducing costs given its limited access to the expanding global economy.

There are other potentially significant contributions immigrant workers, particularly Hispanic immigrants, can make to meat-packing's profit margins. This has to do with the continuous seasonality of farm work which appears to have been efficiently incorporated into the meat-packing labour process, as well as calculations of workers' reproduction. In other words, fast line speeds associated with modern meat-packing lie at the bottom of this industry's higher than average turnover rates – in fact, the highest of any industry. Some suggest that this actually saves companies money as health and an other benefits don't kick in until after six months of continuing employment (PrairieFire Rural Action, 1991). At least some Mexican workers adjust to this demanding pace by quitting during the low-production period around Christmas Time – a time when hour reductions at these plants are common anyway, given seasonal drops in beef consumption – and resting from their potentially crippling jobs; a phenomena Griffith (personal communication 1992) calls cycles of "injury and therapy," which indirectly subsidize worker's health and subsistence costs in general. Likewise, there is some evidence from Lexington and in other assessments of the farm worker's current situation, that meat-packing is treated at times like another "crop"; workers leave meat-packing for the fields during various crops' peak cycles (Slesinger and Cautley, 1988). This mechanism for lowering workers' reproduction costs is not present among typical industrial workforces.

Other Factors Contributing to the Mobilization of New Hispanic Immigrants to Midwest Rural Communities: The Case of Lexington, Nebraska

The hypermobility of capital is not matched by similar rates of labour mobility. In fact, by most accounts, barriers to international migration have been increasing since the late seventies. When migration streams are present, they are hardly the result of simple "push-pull" factors as neo-classical economists have suggested. Rather, they occur within specific socio-economic contexts and are conditioned by a wide set of political and cultural factors as well.

First, potential migrants are constituted as part of a highly interconnected and unequal global economy which displaces workers within and across nations (Zolberg, 1991). For example, the advanced commercialization of Mexican agriculture in some areas, coupled with an export-oriented industrialization which produces low-wage jobs aimed at hiring of young, single women, has displaced large numbers of males (and increasingly females) from the local economy (Durand and Massey, 1992; Sklair, 1989). Based on pilot interviews and other field data, it can be safely said that the great majority of immigrants arriving in Lexington, Nebraska today are of rural origin. Often, they are migrant workers who have moved partially or totally into non-agricultural employment such as construction and, increasingly, meat-packing jobs in other parts of the country. Newspaper reports and case studies of other meat-packing communities in the Midwest suggest this is indeed a generalized phenomena (Griffith, 1990; Gouveia: personal communication with editor of the Perry Chief, 5/3/1992). Conversations with Mexican males coming from areas close to maquiladora (assembly for export) plants say that, in some cases, they have not even been allowed in the gates of the plant to obtain an application. Others point to the extremely low wages paid by these companies, which makes it impossible to support a family, except for households with multiple participants in the maquila labour force. Although in lesser numbers, other Central American immigrants have made their way into Lexington and the "meatpac king circuit" in particular. This is especially true in the case of Salvadorean refugees under the Temporary Protective Status which is due to expire in June of 1992.

Secondly, actual migration streams are conditioned by such factors as migration histories and the presence of viable economic niches and strong ethnic networks, or what Portes and Borocz (1990) call a "positive context of reception." Neither of these two conditions pre-existed IBP and were indeed quickly constituted through a series of actions and processes following its arrival. IBP-Lexington raised its base wage to $7.15 an hour, around $1 above that of any other plant, including unionized ones. Labour was particularly scarce in Dawson county which had seen its population decline by 11 per cent as a result of the latest farm crisis. Although underemployment is suspected to be high, unemployment in the county and the state as a whole was 2.8 per cent at the time of IBP's arrival. Most importantly, it soon became obvious that even this relatively high wage rate, was insufficient to spur the participation of "farm wives" and other under-employed workers into meat-packing employment and in the large numbers plant officials had hoped for. In fact, de-skilling of the labour process and reduction of wages and benefits constitutes a de facto strategy to by-pass much of the labour force and create an "economic niche" that has become once again identified with immigrant or "Mexican" labour. Interviews with cattle feeders revealed that their workers and relatives who, until the mid-eighties, had sought full or part-time employment in the now defunct Sperry New Holland plant (maker of agricultural implements), viewed meat-packing work with great destain: "nothing in life is worth that" remarked one (Gouveia interview 5/7/91). IBP officials sent mixed signals into the community, designed to placate fears of an invasion of Hispanics and other minorities, and yet suggest that their doors would be open to such groups. For example, through the local press and community forums, company officials repeatedly reassured the community that they expected most of its workers would come from the surrounding area. By the same token, they openly admitted to private groups and Spanish-speaking newspapers that large numbers of Hispanics were expected to be hired at the plant (Nuestro Mundo, 1990). Today, Latino immigrants make up around 50 per cent of the Lexington's plant workforce, and another 10 per cent are Asian immigrants and US minorities. Although no population census has been taken since the workers arrived, it is conceivable that Lexington's non-white population approaches 25 per cent.

As has been the case with numerous communities affected by the farm crisis, and eager to recruit new industries, IBP successfully recruited the town's leaders to spearhead efforts to culturally sens itize these predominantly white communities – or build a "positive context" of incorporation from scratch. Community forums, church teach-ins, multi-cultural workshops, the inauguration of services staffed with bilingual workers, such as a temporary shelter, and survival Spanish classes became a common occurrence during the weeks preceding and following the opening of the Lexington plant.

Finally, while US immigration laws have become more restrictive in recent years, they have also served as important mechanisms for channelling documented and undocumented workers into particular labour markets – an important one being meat-packing. The 1986 Immigration Control and Reform Act (IRCA), and especially the so-called agricultural or "SAW" (Special Agricultural Workers) amnesty provision, accelerated the move of seasonal agricultural workers toward non-agricultural employment which began in the sixties. In the context of declining manufacturing employment, meat-packing represents one of the few options available to these agricultural labourers. The majority of newly legalized workers contacted during the course of this project are SAW workers. IRCA's restrictions on cash assistance for legalized workers during a period of five years may also prevent turnover rates from getting too far out of balance. The Lexington plant, the first IBP beef plant to come on line after the enactment of IRCA, has experienced the lowest level of monthly turnover of any new plant. Finally, some suggest that IRCA's employer sanctions proviso has contributed to a deeper segmentation of labour according to legal status; further pushing undocumented workers into more dangerous and unregulated jobs. There is some indication of this from the Lexington case. IBP-

Lexington established an early reputation as a faithful complier of the new IRCA requirements. Although undocumented workers have been found to work at this plant, many understand that their best bet is with the cleaning company with which IBP subcontracts. Cleaning is the most dangerous job in meat-packing as it requires working with high pressure hoses and extremely toxic chemicals. Wages are lower and workers have complained of serious safety violations since it was last fined by OSHA in 1991.

Hiring a new immigrant labour force (especially when segmented along ethnic and gender lines) allows management to exercise a much greater degree of dominance over its labour force. During personal interviews workers repeatedly complained of unexpected line speeds, shortened breaks, and unpaid hours worked under various kinds of "informal" arrangements with line supervisors. Language barriers and fear of loosing their or their relatives' jobs precludes these workers from pursuing their complaints too far.

Small rural communities such as Lexington bear much of the cost associated with the opening of a meat-packing plant and reproduction of poor workers. Federal grants for community development have, for example, been transferred to IBP for construction of water treatment plants and other infrastructural projects. Additionally, IBP has secured a combination of federal and state funds to train its labour force arguing in its grant application that "it was not feasible to hire a skilled labour force" (DED, 1991) from the area. Ironically, in a newspaper interview originally given to the Houston Chronicle, an IBP spokesman states "'There is not an available workforce in either state (Iowa or Nebraska) to fill our needs. . . Keep in mind that we look primarily for unskilled labourers . . . the availability of those people just hasn't been there, it isn't there, and we don't see it in the future'" (Lincoln Star, 1990). Costs to these communities also come in the form of increased racial tensions as workers see themselves doing the dirty jobs for the benefit of a community that is not-uncommonly slow in opening up to them, and white residents see workers as threats to their cultural identity and safety.

Conclusions

The livestock complex, and its dominance by a small group of food transnationals has come to dominate the US agro-food system. The emergent context of globalization has given these companies new leverage for pressuring states, communities and subordinate classes for a whole host of concessions, political passivity, and give-backs. Nonetheless, the group made up by these three giant meat-packers is by no means homogenous with regard to their degree of participation within global capital circuits. As this study has demonstrated, IBP lags behind the other two in this sense, irrespective of its arguable status as the number one beef processor. Competition from ConAgra and Cargill is increasingly fierce. Survival strategies for IBP have depended heavily on cutting labour costs by instit uting aggressive mechanisms for the recruitment of non-native labour. Additionally, IBP has been busy securing help from state and local governments in places like Nebraska and Iowa, which the latest farm crisis nearly bankrupted.

But ConAgra, also based in Nebraska, has been even more effective than IBP in extracting concessions from the state – on whose coat tails IBP has indeed ridden – and forging the new capital-state relation that is characteristic of this post-Fordist era. The most telling example of ConAgra's influence was the passage of a historic 1987 tax-exemption bill, LB775 (Nebraska Investment and Employment Growth Act) which was literally drafted in ConAgra's CEO chairman's office (Limprecht, 1990). Threatening not to build its corporate headquarters and food labs in Omaha, as well as withdraw its support from agribusiness and biotechnology programmes in the state university system, ConAgra demanded, and got, passage of the bill with virtually no changes. Ironically, it is IBP that appears to have utilized these funds more frequently since the passage of the act.

IBP now finds itself in a position of again relying on the availability and loyalty of a labour force which not long ago was dismissed as a mere vehicle for fulfilling its philosophy of "fractions." Some suggest its stand on unions has softened (for the first time in history Dakota City settled its 1991 contract without a strike; and the new Waterloo plant was recently unionized), and often pays higher wages than the other two large packers (Constance and Heffernan, 1989). Lower turnover rates in Lexington have also been used as an indication of this seemingly emerging new capital-labour accord. It is too early to tell whether these are indeed signs of a new accord or of labour passivity in times of severe recession and unemployment. Yet, it is not unfeasible to witness new alliances among local classes and domestically constrained capitalists whose interests are equally threatened by the globe-trotting strategies of companies like ConAgra and Cargill.

NOTE

1. IBP had in fact experienced a merger situation when Occidental bought all of its stocks in 1981. By 1987 Occidental sold 49 per cent to the public and just last year it unloaded the rest at bargain prices. The total impact of this merger on IBP's financial security cannot be discussed here and is discussed in more depth in a forthcoming piece (Gouveia, forthcoming). Suffice it to say, however, that d espite early claims to the contrary made by former chairman Armand Hammer, the purchase of IBP can now be more clearly seen as designed to boost the financial stability of the oil company and not the other way around.

REFERENCES

Broadway, Michael, (1992), "Recent changes in the structure and location of the meat and fish-processing industry." Paper presented at the National Conference on New Factory Workers in Old Farming Communities: Costs and Consequences of Relocating Meat Industries. Wye Conference Center, Queenstown, Maryland. April 12-14.

Bryan, Richard, (1987), "The state and the internationalization of capital: an approach to analysis. *Journal of Contemporary Asia* 17 (3).

Business Week, (1983), "The slaughter of meatpacking wages." June 27:70-71.

Center for Rural Affairs, (1990), Competition and the Livestock Market. Report of a task force commissioned by The Center for Rural Affairs. Walthill, NE. April.

Conagra, Inc., (1992), Fiscal 1991 Annual Report. Omaha, NE: ConAgra.

Constance, Douglas H. and William D. Heffernan, (1989), "IBP's rise to dominance in the meatpacking industry: boxed beef and busted unions." Paper presented at the Agriculture, Food, and Human Values Society meeting. Little Rock, AR. November.

Durand, Jorge and Douglas S. Massey, (1992), "Mexican migration to the United States: a critical review." *Latin American Research Review* 27(2): 3-42.

Effertz, Nita, (1987), "What to expect from the 'big four (three)'." *Beef Today*. July.

Erickson, K. and D. Stull, (1989), "Bovine anthropology: pulling count in the packing house." Paper presented at the 1989 American Anthropological Association meetings, Washington, D.C.

Friedmann, Harriet, (1990), "Distance and durability: shaky foundations of the world food economy." Toronto. (unpublished paper)

Gouveia, Lourdes, (1992), "El estado, municipalidades, e immigrantes latinos en la internacionalizacion del circuito de la carne: un caso de Nebraska, Estados Unidos." Forthcoming in *International Journal of Sociology of Agriculture and Food*. Vol. 2.

Griffith, David, (1990), The Impact of the Immigration Reform and Control Act's (IRCA) Employer Sanctions on the U.S. Meat and Poultry Processing Industries.

Final Report submitted to the Institute for Multiculturalism and International Labor. State University of New York. Binghamton, NY.

Heffernan, William D. and Douglas Constance, (1992), "Restructuring of the U.S. meat, poultry, and fish-processing industries in the global economy." Paper presented at the National Conference on New Factory Workers in Old Farming Communities: Costs and Consequences of Relocating Meat Industries. Wye Conference Center, Queenstown, Maryland. April 12-14.

IBP, (1990), Annual Report. Dakota City, NE: IBP.

——, (1991), Annual Report. Dakota City, NE: IBP.

——, (1990), Form 10-K for the Securities and Exchange Commission. Dakota City: IBP.

Kay, Steve, (1992), "Globe-trotters. American meat companies increase their foreign presence as exports rise." *Beef Today*, February.

——, (1990), "You can't stand still." *Beef Today*, August, pp. 24-26.

——, (1988), "IBM sticks to its guns." *Beef Today*. May, pp. 22-24.

Limprecht, Jane E., (1989), ConAgra Who?: The Story of ConAgra's First 70 Years. Copyright ConAgra, Inc. ed. James Limprecht.

Lincoln Star, (1990), "Slaughter houses recruiting Texas' poor". September.

McMichael, Phillip and David Mhyre, (1991), "Global regulation versus the nation state: agro-food systems and the new politics of capital." *Capital and Class*, Vol.43:1-18.

McNaughton, Marie Thomas, (1991), "On the dark and bloody ground." *Meat and Poulty*. 18-26: September.

Nebraska Department of Economic Development (DED), (1991), "Summary of community development block grants by county 1982-1990." Lincoln, NE: Nebraska Department of Economic Development.

Nuestro Mundo, (1991), "Latinos search for hope in Norfolk, Nebraska." *Nuestro Mundo*. February: 5-6.

——, (1990), "IBP recruiting Latinos to Nebraska". *Nuestro Mundo*. July.

Omaha World Herald, (1990), "Hispanic influx becomes learning experience. *Sunday World Herald*: 20-21.

Petrowski, William, (1990), "Hispanics struggle in new life." *Des Moines Sunday Register*, 4-5A: January.

Portes, Alejandro and Jozsef Borocz, (1989), "Contemporary immigration: theoretical perspectives on its determinants and modes of incorporation." *International Migration Review* 23: 606-630.

Prairiefire Rural Action, (1991), Shattered Promises. The Plight of Non-English Speaking Workers in Iowa's Meat-packing Industry. *Des Moines*, IA: PrairieFire Rural Action.

Rasmussen, Jim, (1992), "Beef packers find profits elusive." *Sunday Omaha World Herald*. 19: 1 and 9: April.

Sassen, Saskia, (1990), *The Mobility of Labour and Capital*. New York: Cambridge University Press.

Sanderson, Steven, (1986), "The emergence of the 'world steer.' Internationalization and foreign domination in Latin American cattle production." Pp. 123-48 in F. Lamond Tullis and W. Ladd Hollist (eds.), *Food, the State, and International Political Economy*. Lincoln, Nebraska: University of Nebraska Press.

Sklair, Leslie, (1989), *Assembling for Development: The Maquila Industry in Mexico and the U.S.A.* Winchester, MA: Unwin Hyman, Inc.

Slesinger, Doris P. and Eleanor Cautley, (1988), Estimation of Migrant and Seasonal Agricultural Workers in Iowa, Kansas, Missouri and Nebraska. Submitted to National Migrant Referral Project, Inc., Austin, TX. October.

Stanley, Kathleen, (1991), "The role of immigrant and refugee labour in the restructuring of the midwestern meatpacking industry." Paper presented at the Midwest Sociological Meetings. April.

——, (1988), "Immigrant and refugee labour or the restrucuring of the midwest meatpacking industry." Proposal submitted to the Bureau of International Labor Affairs U.S. Department of Labour.

Stuart, Alexander, (1981), "Meat-packers in stampede." *Fortune*, 29: 67-71: June.

Stull, Donald D., Michael J. Broadway, Lourdes Gouveia, Mark A. Grey, and Robert Hackenberg (Co-organizers) (1992, National Conference on New Factory Workers in Old Farming Communities: Costs and Consequences of Relocating Meat Industries. Wye Conference Center, Queenstone MD. April 12-14.

Tintstman, Dale C. and Robert L. Peterson, (1981), Iowa Beef Processors, An Entire Industry Revolutionized. New York: The Newcomen Society in North America.

Zolberg, Aristide R., (1989), "The next waves: migration theory for a changing world." *International Migration Review* 23(3): 403-430.

PART TWO

GLOBALIZATION, BILATERALISM, REGIONALISM AND ETHICS

5

BILATERALISM, AGRICULTURE AND LDC'S: The Case of the North American Free Trade Agreement

AMY ANGEL AND C. PARR ROSSON, III

Introduction

The flourishing presence of free trade agreements in much of the world is evidence of the expansion of the agricultural trade sector and the push by governments and business to further this expansion. Free trade agreements have been a popular subject of study in recent years. The U.S.-Canada free trade agreement, for example, involves countries that, although differing in size, are at approximately the same stage of economic development. Much the same can be said of the European Community (EC), the Andean Pact nations, and the ASEAN countries of Southeast Asia, although admittedly some countries are more developed than others. The North American Free Trade Agreement (NAFTA) among Mexico, the United States, and Canada, however, presents an entirely different situation, which raises special issues which were not germane to the U.S.-Canada negotiations. Such issues may become relevant when any developing country is involved in trade negotiations with a more economically developed nation. This study will discuss some of these issues more relevant to agriculture, including agricultural structure, foreign investment restrictions, exchange rate policy, external debt, and infrastructural deficiencies in Mexico, as well as rural-to-urban migration. Because trade between Mexico and Canada is nominal, this analysis will concentrate on the relationship between the United States and Mexico.

The globalization of the agricultural and food sector has taken place from the seed planted in the ground to the food placed on the table. For example, advances in agricultural technology are spread worldwide wherever appropriate, and, unfortunately, sometimes where they are not. Overall, however, the increase in per hectare yields for most foodstuffs worldwide indicate this diffusion has been a success. Ownership of food production and distribution facilities by multinational corporations is tremendous. Media promotions allow many food products atypical of the standard cuisine of a country to become culturally acceptable and mainstream foods in much of the developing world.

Nowhere has agriculture and the food system become more internationalized than in the realm of trade. Due in large part to trade cooperation in the arena of the General Agreements on Tariffs and Trade (GATT), agricultural trade for many nations has expanded greatly. Countries which were previously self-sufficient now import foodstuffs, and many countries which previously relied on domestic sales now export large quantities of agricultural products. Other countries which were net food importers now are net exporters. Telecommunications have tremendously facilitated trade, where the respective parties may never meet face to face. The result has been a quadrupling in world food trade, which exceeded $200 billion in 1988. This expansion of trade is both a cause and effect of the "globalization" of agriculture; as trade grows and corporations establish their foothold in foreign markets, new technologies and food products are more easily introduced to countries, or, conversely, as demand for a new food product grows, the demand for imports of the product grows.

This expansion in global agricultural trade has come in spite of the existence of pervasive protective measures on the part of both importers and exporters in both developed and developing countries. Typically, developed countries protect their domestic agricultural producers against imports with tariffs, quotas, and other measures and subsidize exports, although sometimes implicitly in the form of input subsidies and direct producer compensation. Developing countries also protect their farmers against imports, although they often tax exports of agricultural products for much-needed government revenue. In the 1930's, the world experienced a trade war, brought about by the passage of the Smoot-Hawley Tariff Act in the United States. Countries progressively raised import tax levels until trade practically disappeared. In more recent decades, trade negotiations to reduce or eliminate these protective measures have taken place on a multilateral level, such as under the GATT, and increasingly on a bilateral or regional level. As regional trade agreements become more popular, the pattern of agricultural trade and the globalization of the agricultural and food sector will change, perhaps dramatically.

Bilateralism – A Substitute for Multilateralism?

Although Carla Hills, the U.S. Trade Representative, has called bilateral agreements complementary to and not substitutes for progress in multilateral negotiations ("Good Intentions," 1991), many analysts would disagree. Experts point to the shaky future of multilateralism, how long it took to even agree to negotiate in the current Uruguay round of the GATT, the many procedural opportunities to delay or block progress, the variety of reasons for key governments to drag their heels, and the growing numbers of bilateral or regional trade agreements (Diebold, 1988). Difficulties in agriculture include the steadfastness of European Community (EC) farm policy, the refusal of Japan to open its rice markets to imports, and the phasing out of the Multi-Fiber Arrangement in textiles.

The popularity of bilateral and regional trade agreements may stem from their simplicity. It is much easier to agree with one or two countries than with most of the world. Some of the significant advances in regionalism include those in the EC, Southeast Asia, South America, and U.S.-Canada. NAFTA appears to be the next step along this path toward regionalisation. Many analysts argue that a Western Hemisphere trading bloc could become a reality early in the next century.

Bilateral agreements are dealt with in the GATT under Article XXIV, where preferential arrangements are prohibited except for customs unions and free trade areas, which are allowed under certain conditions only, generally that the agreement must cover substantially all trade and must be achieved within a reasonable amount of time. Otherwise GATT required that whatever benefits are extended to the parties of bilateral agreements must be extended to all GATT members. The U.S.-Canada free trade agreement is allowed under the GATT framework, and NAFTA will likely bring no GATT opposition.

Toward a North American Free Trade Agreement

The United States began its pursuit of regional free trade with its 1988 agreement with Canada. In June of 1990, President Bush and Mexican President Carlos Salinas de Gortari agreed to begin negotiations on a comprehensive free trade agreement between their two countries. The agreement as envisioned by the presidents would involve "gradual and comprehensive elimination of trade barriers between the two countries, including: (1) the full, phased elimination of import tariffs; (2) the elimination or fullest possible reduction of non-tariff trade barriers, such as import quotas, licenses, and technical barriers to trade: (3) the establishment of clear, binding protection for intellectual property rights; (4) fair and expeditious dispute settlement procedures; and (5) means to improve and expand the flow of goods, services, and investment between the United States and Mexico" (The White House, undated). The agreement will most likely include the conversion of quotas to tariffs and the binding of those and other tariffs at some negotiated level, followed by a gradual reduction to near zero over time. Canada is also involved in the negotiations to secure their own position in the North American agreement. The combined GNP of the three nations would exceed $6.0 trillion, with over 360 million consumers and trade exceeding $1.0 trillion.

Levels of Economic Integration

The negotiations caused some confusion about the level of integration which can be expected among the participants in NAFTA. Official releases from both the Mexican and U.S. governments indicate that free trade area is the most appropriate term, where trade barriers are reduced or eliminated between the parties to the agreement, but the individual countries determine their own trade measures for the rest of the world. This level of economic cooperation is in contrast to a customs union, where a common external tariff is added to a free trade area, or a common market, which also allows the free flow of factors, such as labour, between member nations. The next level of economic integration is an economic union, which adds monetary coordination among member nations (Balassa, 1961).

Economic Relationship with the United States

Mexico and the United States have strong social, cultural, and even political linkages, but these relationships are certainly no more profound than that of these countries' two economies. The United States is Mexico's largest trading partner, receiving 71.6 per cent of Mexico's exports and sending 70.8 per cent of Mexico's imports in 1989. Agricultural trade between the two countries, shown in Figure 5.1, has also continued to increase. At $5.0 billion, agricultural trade accounts for about ten per cent of Mexican exports to the United States and nine per cent of U.S. exports to Mexico. The composition of this trade is shown in Figures 5.2 and 5.3. Finally, the United States contributed some $3.0 billion in aid to Mexico from 1970-1988.

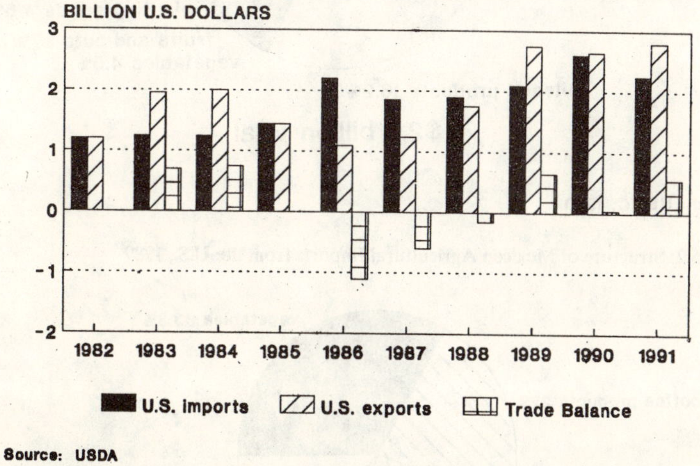

FIG. 5.1: U.S.-Mexico Agricultural Trade 1982-1991

The United States was the largest market for agricultural products from Mexico, and Mexico was the third largest market for U.S. agricultural exports in 1991, behind Japan and Canada. Over one-half of all U.S. agricultural exports to Mexico in 1989 were made under GSM-102 and GSM-103 Export Credit Guarantee Programmes of the U.S.D.A. Commodity Credit Corporation. General Sales Manager Export Credit Guarantees (GSM-102 and GSM-103) are available to developing countries facing foreign exchange constraints who might not otherwise purchase U.S. products. Export credit guarantees assure against default by the foreign importer's bank, and loans are made at commercial interest rates. Over two-thirds of the $1.25 billion export credit guarantees to Mexico in 1989 were used to import corn ($ 336 million), soybeans ($300 million), and grain sorghum ($190 million) (Rosson, et al, 1991:60).

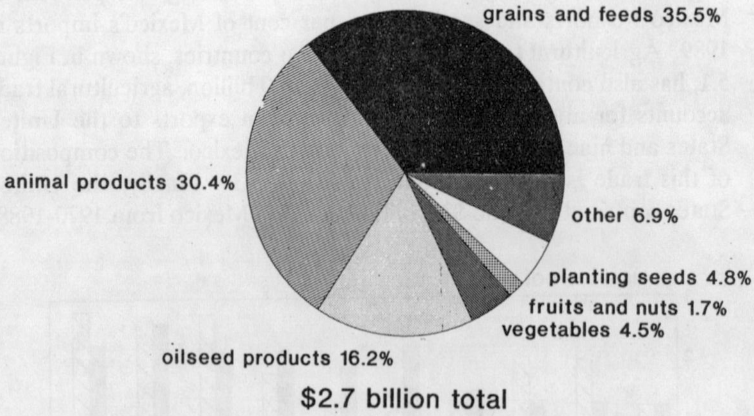

Source: USITC, 1990

FIG. 5.2: Structure of Mexican Agricultural Imports from the U.S., 1989

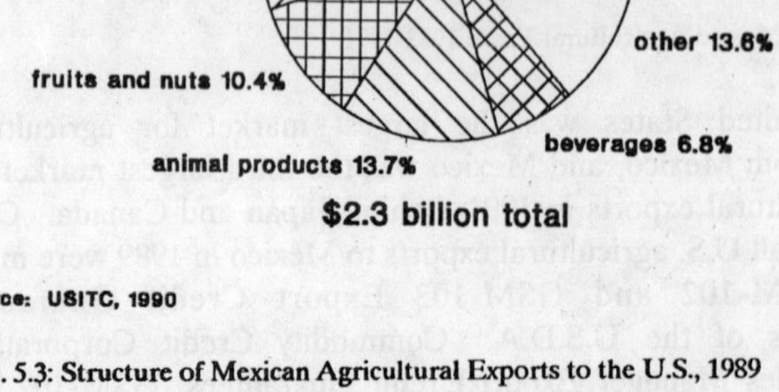

Source: USITC, 1990

FIG. 5.3: Structure of Mexican Agricultural Exports to the U.S., 1989

The Mexican Economy

Mexico has the fifteenth largest economy and eleventh largest population in the world, at ninety million people. Mexico, although technically a developing country, has an economy larger than many developed countries and most developing countries. Figure 5.4 indicates recent production figures in terms of gross national product (GNP). Mexico's GNP in 1990 was approximately $200 billion. Like most other Latin American countries, Mexico has struggled throughout the last decade. Gross national product actually declined after 1981, falling ten per cent in 1986. Per capita GNP declined even more rapidly due to Mexico's annual population growth rate exceeding 2.2 per cent. Mexico has one of the developing world's largest external debts, valued at $96 billion in 1990. Debt service requirements, coupled with declining oil prices and lower export revenues, led to the economic decline of Mexico in the early 1980's. Triple digit inflation and drastically lower real incomes characterized the Mexican economy from 1982-1987. Following a period of economic restructuring brought about by a moratorium on debt service, Mexico's economy began to recover in 1988. Income growth, and lower inflation, coupled with trade liberalization measures such as lower import tariffs, have resulted in an upsurge in food product imports from the United States.

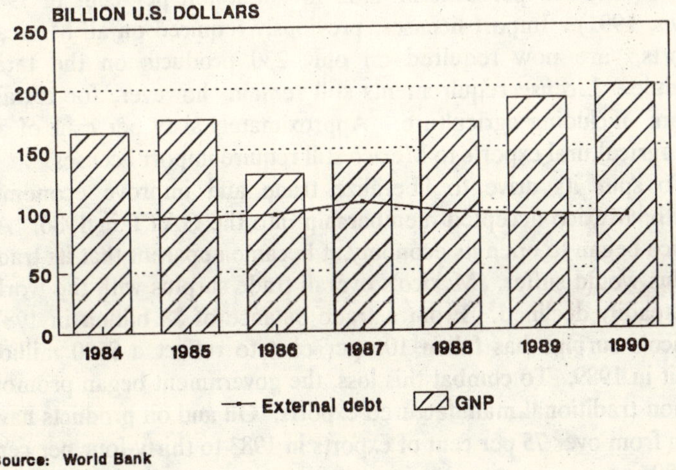

FIG. 5.4: Gross National Product (GNP) and External Debt for Mexico, 1984-1990

The contribution of various sectors of the economy to GNP in 1987 was nine per cent for agriculture, thirty-four per cent for manufacturing, and fifty-seven per cent for services (World Bank, 1990). Raw food products and value-added foods represent sixteen per cent of all imports and are a growing component of Mexico's overall imports. Exports of primary products contribute approximately seven per cent to Mexico's total exports.

Attitudes toward economic policy in Mexico are shaped by the economic and political history of the country. Nationalism remains strong, and foreign activity in the economy has traditionally been distrusted and discouraged. Mexico's economy could previously have been characterized as highly managed and protected by the government. Barriers to trade were plentiful, including export and import tariffs or taxes, import and export licenses, and quotas. The current administration of President Carlos Salinas de Gortari has instituted many broad-sweeping changes in economic policy, continuing and expanding the programme of his predecessor, President Miguel de la Madrid. Major, controversial changes in economic policy in Mexico have come in both the arenas of foreign trade and domestic agricultural policy. Before Mexico's entrance into the GATT in 1986, ad-valorem tariff rates were often over 100 per cent. Those rates are now less than 20 per cent. The trade-weighted average tariff fell from twenty-five per cent in 1985 to about ten per cent in 1989 (Davis, 1991). Import licenses, previously required on all Mexican imports, are now required on only 230 products on the tariff schedule. License requirements still remain, however, for certain sectors, including agriculture. Approximately sixty per cent of all U.S. agricultural exports to Mexico still require import licenses.

To spur its drive to liberalize trade and improve economic growth, Mexico accepted membership into the GATT in 1986. As Mexico began to open its economy, it became apparent that its trade surplus would suffer. Mexico's overall trade surplus with the world has steadily declined. From a trade balance of $8 billion in 1987, Mexico's surplus has fallen 106 per cent to reflect a $500 million deficit in 1989. To combat this loss, the government began promoting non-traditional manufactured exports. Oil and oil products have fallen from over 75 per cent of exports in 1983 to thirty-four per cent in 1989.

The Mexican Agricultural Sector

The importance of agriculture in the Mexican economy is, like most developing countries, greater than that of agriculture in more developed economies. Because of its significance, agriculture is an integral factor in NAFTA for Mexico. Nearly thirty per cent of the Mexican population is rural, and twenty-four per cent are employed in food and fiber related industries. Agricultural commodities rank second only to petroleum in terms of top earners of foreign exchange. Agriculture accounts for nine per cent of GNP and seven percent of merchandise exports (World Bank, 1990). Despite its overall growth, agricultural production has not kept pace with population growth, shown by declining per capita real agricultural production (Table 5.1).

TABLE 5.1: Total and *Per Capita* Agricultural Production and *Per Capita* GNP, 1984-1990

Year	Total Agriculture Index: 1980 = 100	Total Ag. per capita Index: 1980 = 100	GNP per capita (U.S. dollars)
1984	108.6	100.4	2151.52
1985	108.2	97.5	2205.14
1986	110.9	95.2	1681.82
1987	111.5	93.5	1729.13
1988	114.1	93.3	2023.62
1989	N/A	N/A	2153.04
1990	N/A	N/A	2276.09

Source: USDA/ERS, World Agricultural Trends and Indicators, 1989; World Bank, World Development Report, 1990.

Mexican agricultural production is ripe with contrasts. On the one hand are the large, commercial operations paralleling those of the United States. On the other hand are the collective farms and ejidos, on which the vast majority of farmers work. The ejido system was founded in 1914 and resulted in major land reform in 1940, when large portions of land were brought into production and agricultural output expanded. The second wave of land reform in the 1970's merely chopped up the already-existing parcels of land into smaller holdings.

Today, fifty-four per cent of all of the national territory belongs to ejidos and collective farms. Two-thirds of all arable land is now held in parcels of less than five hectares. Because of the subsistence nature of many ejidos, land is typically used to produce maize, rice, and beans, although some ejidatarios produce commodities for export, such as coffee. In general, however, the ejidos suffer from poor economies of scale because the land, much of which is only marginal, is in individual holdings which are overplanted and too small to warrant highly capitalized inputs or technologies. Agricultural policy in Mexico has relied heavily in the past on price supports and input subsidies. For several years, self-sufficiency in staple food production was the main policy goal, with fertilizer, seed, or irrigation given to farmers who would plant rice, maize, beans, or wheat, rather than more profitable export-oriented crops. This goal of self-sufficiency led to a skewed structure of agricultural production causing large plots of land to go unplanted and a loss of revenue necessary for further development. Food output per capita actually declined 3 per cent from 1979 to 1981. Subsequently, grain imports rose twenty-two per cent annually from 1970 to 1986.

The ejido system, however, will be altered or perhaps dismantled completely under the new land programme of President Salinas, in which the ejido lands will be converted to ordinary private property, which can later be sold, leased, or combined into larger, more efficient units. Many fear the end of the ejidos will lead to the further growth of large commercial farms and the continued displaceme nt of the rural poor. Others see it as a triumph for Mexican agriculture, allowing for greater returns to scale.

Despite the weakening performance of the ejidos and other subsistence farms, other regions of Mexico have a flourishing agricultural sector, particularly the Northern and Eastern coastal regions. These states produce primarily commodities for export to the United States, fruits and vegetables, cut flowers, and coffee.

Potential Free Trade Impacts

The final version of NAFTA will allow for more precise estimates of its impacts on Mexico and Mexican agriculture. For the purposes of this analysis, it is assumed that import licenses and quotas in Mexico are converted to tariffs, and that tariffs in all three countries are gradually reduced or eliminated. For domestic agricultural policies in Mexico, it is assumed that producer price guarantees will remain for only corn and beans, as preliminary reports indicate (U.S.D.A.,

1991). Some input subsidies may be eliminated, particularly in irrigation, and credit for input purchases may become less plentiful. While this analysis will make these assumptions, it is an important to note that the degree and speed of changes will have a great impact on the real effects of the agreement.

The potential gains from trade liberalization will depend on several factors. First, any progress made in the Uruguay Round of GATT will apply to NAFTA. Should countries negotiate and agree to low er levels of domestic support, reduced export subsidies, and greater market access, those provisions will be binding on any regional trade agreement which is negotiated. Second, current trade patterns will influence future outcomes in NAFTA. In the livestock and beef sectors, for instance, trade between the United States and Mexico is complementary, with the United States shipping processed goods and Mexico shipping live animals. This trade occurs with low tariffs and few import licensing procedures. Much of the gains from specializations have already been realized, indicating that "free trade" will have only minor impacts on these sectors. Relationships such as these necessitate analyzing agricultural sectors in great depth, leaving little room for broad generalization about effects of NAFTA on food and fiber trade. Third, to the extent that the United States already supplies a major share of Mexican consumption and imports, such as in grain sorghum, it seems unlikely that major gains in export expansion are to be expected without increases in consumption brought about from higher incomes. Finally, consumers and producers will adjust to changes in price and income. Their ability to adjust and the rate of adjustment make it especially difficult to measure exact impacts on trade.

Reducing trade barriers through NAFTA will have positive and negative impacts for both Mexico and the United States. For Mexican agriculture, exports of labour-intensive crops, particularly fruits a nd vegetables will likely increase. Cow-calf producers should also expect increased feeder calf exports. Increased imports from the United States would include animal breeding stock, beef, pork, poultry, variety meats and edible offals, dairy products, feed grains, especially corn and grain sorghum, and selected value-added fruits and vegetables.

The largest gains for Mexico are expected to come in manufacturing. Mexican workers should experience higher wages as increases in demand for some products place upward pressure on employment in some areas of Mexico. Also, consumers in Mexico should experience higher disposable incomes as tariff and non-tariff barriers to trade are lowered and goods are allowed to enter at reduced prices.

As incomes increase, diets are upgraded and consumers generally shift from more staple foods, such as beans and maize, to value-added and processed foods. The market for these value-added products is ripe for U.S. exports. Mexico's population, depicted in Figure 5.5, is relatively young, with fifty per cent under twenty years of age and sixty-one per cent under twenty-five. In other words, half of the Mexican population has yet to become adult consumers. The two requirements for effective demand, consumer want and ability to pay, would be satisfied by the expanding population and the expected increase in incomes. Increased imports from the United States means more jobs in the United States, or job shifts not job losses for U.S. workers.

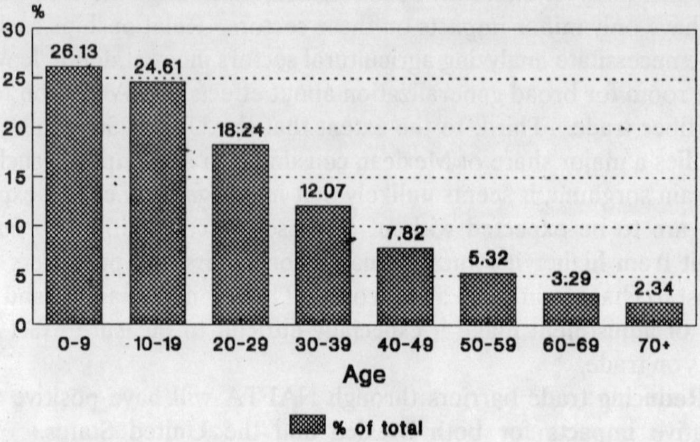

United Nations

FIG. 5.5: Mexico's Population by Age 1988

The important factor in this prediction is that incomes of the lower classes increase. Income distribution in Mexico is characterized as uneven, with forty per cent of the national income received by ten per cent of the population (World Bank, 1990). While per capita incomes may rise, the rural and urban poor may fail to fully experience these gains, leading to a lower demand for value-added foods. Still, agricultural exports particularly of fruits and vegetables would increase to a certain extent, and imports of staples and meats would also increase as explained previously.

Agricultural structure in Mexico will shift even more favourably to more highly capitalized, large producers of these commodities. The increases in most grain imports, pushing many small grain farmers out of the market, combined with the potential to sell land, will likely lead to increased concentration of ownership. Producers of agricultural inputs may experience difficulties both through increased imports from the United States and decreased demand for some inputs.

Perhaps the most important effect of a free trade agreement for the United States could be that of ensuring market access in the rapidly expanding market in Mexico, and vice versa. By negotiating and agreeing to specific levels of trade intervention, the two countries better ensure their access to the market and place an upper bound on tariffs and other trade measures should the next president of either nation be less in favour of an open economy. Other countries without free trade agreements, such as Japan and the EC, would not have that security.

Potential Constraints to Trade Expansion

External Debt

Many developing countries, like Mexico, are burdened by tremendous external debt. Mexico borrowed heavily in the late 1970's and early 1980's to subsidize inefficient industries and promote self-sufficiency in staple food production. In the early 1980's, external debt rose from around $50 billion in the early 1980's to a peak of $108 billion in 1988 and now has fallen to an estimated $94 billion for 1990 (Figure 5.4). In 1988, the per capita debt was $1202, or approximately half of per capita income. In fact, external debt represents approximately fifty per cent of GNP, one of the highest ratios in the Third World. Mexico became unable to pay even interest on external debt in 1982, depleting the government budget for many domestic programmes. Although presently under control, Mexico's external debt could become a crucial problem for prolonged economic development and overall growth of the Mexican economy. This problem will become particularly acute should U.S. interest rates in crease to relatively high levels.

Foreign Investment

An important incentive for developing countries to enter into free trade agreements is often the need for capital from foreign investors. Investment by foreigners in Mexico has a long history, but the preceding 50 years have seen severe limitations put on such investment. In 1973, the Law for the Promotion of Mexican Investment and Regulation of Foreign Investment limited foreign investment in most Mexican companies to a maximum of forty-nine per cent of capital stock and less equity in some strategic industries such as petroleum and communications. It also gave the federal government so le right to develop petroleum, electricity, and minerals (Rudolph, 1985).

Foreign investment was encouraged in the early 1980's, but is still restricted to less than a majority share. Despite all of the restrictions, foreign investment in the Mexican economy is strong. The United States is Mexico's largest foreign investor, holding sixty-three per cent, or $16.7 billion, of the total. Approximately ten per cent of all U.S. investment in other countries goes to Mexico. U.S. foreign investment in Mexican agriculture after a trade agreement is likely where commodities are exported to the U.S. and currently face relatively high tariffs, especially in labour intensive fresh foods, such as asparagus, cucumbers, onions, tomatoes, cantaloupes, and watermelons and in such processed products as broccoli, cauliflower, and tomato paste (Burfisher, 1991).

Questions also remain about the degree to which investment reform will be made a permanent part of Mexican law. Without such assurances, many foreign investors will be reluctant to undertake major long-term investment in Mexico.

Exchange Rate Policy

Currency stability is typically not an explicit consideration in trade negotiations, but in many cases when developing countries are parties to negotiations, it must become an implicit consideration. Exchange rates in Mexico were previously subject to a dual system, consisting of a controlled market, which was under a scheduled devaluation beginning in 1982 set by the Bank of Mexico, and a free parallel market, which is determined by market forces. The peso has been devalued over time from 143.9 pesos per U.S. dollar in 1983 to approximately 2950 pesos per dollar in 1990. The devaluation rate in 1990 was 80 centavos per day, and 40 centavos daily in 1991 until November 26, 1991, at which time the controlled rate was abolished. Exchange rates are now fully subject to free market fluctuations, which adds greater exchange rate risks to trading considerations. The recent low levels of inflation and expected economic growth would likely prevent any serious depreciations.

Transportation and Infrastructure

Many developing countries lack sufficient infrastructure to take advantage of increased trading opportunities that might present themselves through free trade agreements. The U.S. Government Accounting Office (GAO) reports that the Mexican land transportation system has been inadequate to handle the increase in trade Mexico has experienced in recent years. The rail system is outdated and lacks capacity to carry the increasing cargo from the United States. Storage capacity, especially refrigeration for perishables, is limited. Delays in loading, unloading, and movement within Mexico are frequently reported. Even with free trade, it is questionable how much additional cargo the Mexican infrastructure can accommodate without major investment and repair. The continued easing of foreign investment restraints, however, may make investment more feasible and more attractive, particularly as U.S. companies establish plants across the border in Mexico.

Rural-to-Urban Migration

In 1980, the rural population in Mexico was approximately 1.1 per harvested hectare, up from 0.7 persons per hectare in 1970, an increase of approximately fifty-seven per cent. The population as a whole in Mexico grew thirty-two per cent, reflecting some success in government efforts to keep rural residents on farmland parcels.

Because subsistence agriculture is an important component in Mexican agriculture, like most LDC's, a trade agreement would need to take special consideration of these farmers. A free trade agreement is likely to have large impacts on rural incomes, particularly for subsistence farmers, who may no longer be fully protected and heavily subsidized. In lieu of direct agricultural subsidies, the Mexican government has indicated it will substitute consumer subsidies and perhaps direct income subsidies. Whether these subsidies will be sufficient for the average farmer to remain on the land is unknown. If the displaced farmers do not have some local alternative for income, they will either head to the already overcrowded cities in Mexico or across the border to the United States. Despite the economic and employment growth expected in Mexican industrial cities, these areas are not prepared for a burdening influx of rural-to-urban migration, further taxing already insufficient city services and requiring housing which has yet to be built.

The problem of rural-to-urban migration and subsequent overcrowding is present in many developing countries. Economic growth through increased trade, if it is to occur, should be prepared for, with infrastructural and municipal improvements if the problems of so many third world cities are not to be exacerbated.

Conclusion – The Globalization of Agriculture?

With the trend toward bilateral and regional trade agreements overcoming the sluggishness of the GATT, one could question whether the globalization of agriculture is an appropriate term, at least in reference to trade. Although agricultural trade will continue to grow globally and agricultural economies will continue to become more interlinked through technology, communications, and consumerism, this globalization process may be limited somewhat by barriers to trade. Within regional trade agreements, this process will thrive. As this trend toward regionalisation continues, further questions will arise, such as what are appropriate measures to compensate injured industries or agricultural producers and should trade liberalization between developmentally different countries proceed in a different fashion than countries in similar stages of development. As trading blocs form, there appears to be an increasing likelihood that they will be used by governments to further the political agenda of major participant countries. Should this occur, what special role will food and agricultural policy play? All of these questions are being tested by the North American Free Trade Agreement.

REFERENCES

Balassa, Bela, (1961), *The Theory of Economic Integration*. London: Allen and Unwin.

Burfisher, Mary, (1991), "Prospects of U.S. Investment in Mexican Agriculture." Unpublished manuscript, U.S.D.A. Economic Research Service.

Davis, William L., (1991), "Breaking into the Mexican Market: Policy Shifts Offer New Opportunities," *AgExporter*, March 1991, pp. 4-8.

Diebold, William, Jr., ed., (1988), *Bilateralism, Multilateralism, and Canada in U.S. Trade Policy*. Cambridge, Mass.: Ballinger Publishing Co.

"Good Intentions", (1991), *The Economist*, March 2, (1991), p. 30.

Rosson, C. Parr, III, Ernest E. Davis, Eduardo Segarra, Amy L. Angel, Kris Schulthies, and DuBoise White, (1991), "The U.S.-Mexico Free Trade Agreement: Issues and Implications for the U.S. Livestock and Meat Sector." Pp. 3-96 in *North American Free Trade Agreement Effects on Agriculture*, Volume II: Li vestock and Dairy Issues. American Farm Bureau Research Foundation.

Rudolph, James D., ed., (1985), Mexico, a Country Study. Washington, D.C.: U.S. Secretary of the Army.

U.S. Department of Agriculture (USDA), (1991), Agriculture in a North American Free Trade Agreement, April 1991.

U.S. International Trade Commission (USITC), (1990), Review of Trade and Investment Liberalization Measures by Mexico and Prospects for Future United States-Mexico Relations, Phase II: Summary of Views on Prospects for Future United States-Mex ico Relations, USITC Publication 2326, Washington, D.C., October 1990.

White House, The, Office of the Press Secretary, "Joint Statement by the Presidents of Mexico and the United States on Negotiation of a Free Trade Agreement," no date.

World Bank, (1990), World Development Report. New York: Oxford Univ. Press.

Table 5.1. Total and Per Capita Agricultural Production and Per Capita GNP, 1984-1990

6

BENEFITS TO U.S. AGRICULTURE FROM TERMINATING EUROPEAN OILSEED SUBSIDIES

JAMES GLECKLER and LUTHER TWEETEN*

Globalization of world agriculture is partly a result of lower communication and transportation costs. In some cases, the trend toward globalization is reversed by trade barriers designed by govern ments to protect special interests in the domestic economy. As globalization continues, consumers and producers around the world are impacted by events far from home.

An interesting problem involves international trade in oilseeds. The U.S. has traditionally been the world's leading exporter of oilseeds, primarily soybeans. U.S. soybean producers usually produce a greater volume of other field crops. Soybeans play a minor role in corn and small grain rotations in the Midwest and Southeast, but there are few if any soybean-only producers. In parts of the Plains States and the West, on the other hand, soybeans are not commercially grown and many farms specialize in a grain crop such as wheat. This means that U.S. producers and farms in different regi ons may be impacted very differently when policies which affect these global-

---

* Respectively, Professor of Agriculture and Forestry, Northeastern Oklahoma A&M College, Miami and Anderson Professor of Agricultural Marketing, Policy, and Trade, Department of Agricultural Economics and Rural Sociology, The Ohio State University, Columbus. Comments of Norman Rask are much appreciated.

The financial and technical assistance of the Agricultural Trade Analysis Division of the ERS, U.S. Department of Agriculture in operationalizing the model used in this study is gratefully acknowledged. However, the authors are solely responsible for shortcomings and views presented herein.

ized markets are changed.

During the 1962 Dillon Round of multilateral trade negotiations, the European Community committed itself to no import restrictions on soybeans and soybean meal. But during the 1980s, subsidies paid to crushers for processing domestic oilseed rose dramatically. By 1986 the subsidy had increased European producer prices $216 per metric tonne. The oilseed subsidies alone were more than the world price of $208 per metric tonne and European producers responded by increasing their production over the period (Figure 6.1.)

In December, 1987 the American Soybean Association (ASA) filed a section 301 Unfair Trade Petition against the European Community (EC). The petition alleged that the EC oilseed subsidies constituted unfair discrimination against imports. The Dispute Settlement Panel of the General Agreement on Tariffs and Trade (GATT) ruled in December, 1989 that the European oilseed subsidies violate GATT trading rules and discriminate against oilseed imports. European Community officials agreed to abide by the ruling and will reportedly bring their programmes into compliance. The objective of this paper is to estimate the economic impacts on the United States and the European Community if the *EC* eliminates its oilseed subsidies. Conceptual Framework *A* conceptual model in Figure 6.2 depicts the effect of eliminating *EC* oilseed subsidy *Ps - P´w* where *Ps* is the *EC* supported price and *P´w* is the world price distorted by the *EC* subsidy. Without the oilseed subsidy, supply in the *EC* is *ss* and demand is *d*; supply in the rest of the world (ROW) is *S* and demand is *D*. Without subsidies, the world price of soybeans is P_w. *EC* supply quantity (production) is q_s and demand quantity is q_d. European imports of soybeans are $q_d - q_s = Q_e$ from *ROW*.

With the oilseed subsidy, the *EC* soybean supply function is *s´s*. European oilseed excess demand in world markets shifts from *ED* to *ED*', excess supply remains at *ES*, and world price falls to *P*. European oilseed imports fall from Q_e to a lower quantity $q_d - q_s = Q_s - Q_d = Q_e$.

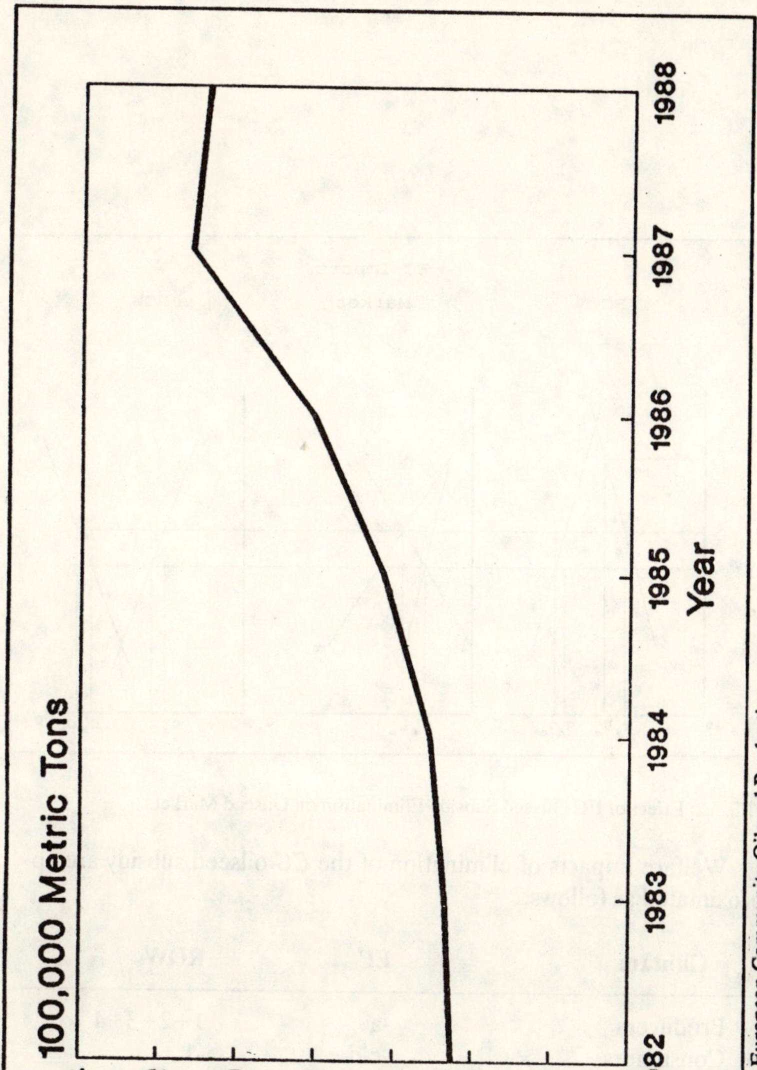

FIG. 6.1: European Community Oilseed Production
Source: ERS/USDA.

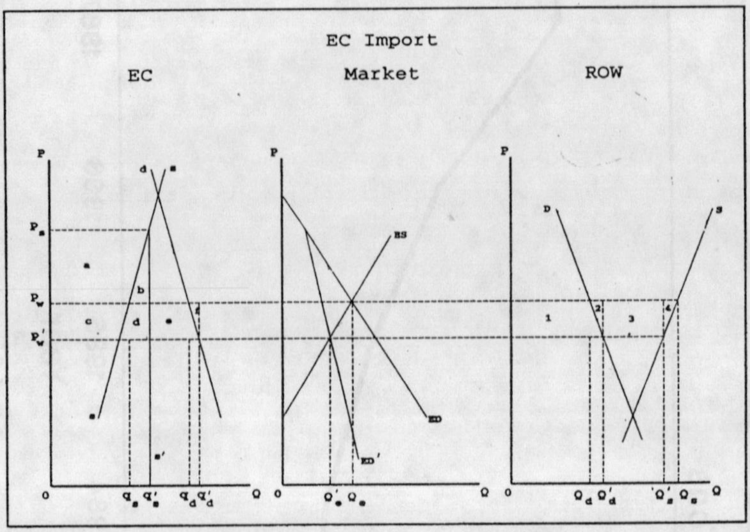

FIG. 6.2: Effect of EC Oilseed Subsidy Elimination on Oilseed Markets

Welfare impacts of elimination of the *EC* oilseed subsidy are approximated as follows:

Gain to:	EC	ROW
Producers	-a	1+2+3+4
Consumers	-c-d-e	-1
Taxpayers	a+b+c+d	—
Society	b-e	2+3+4
World (e+f=3)	b+f+2+4.	

With termination of the subsidy, European Community producers are worse off by area *a*. *EC* consumers lose area *c+d+e*. European taxpayers are better off by area *a+b+c+d*. Net gain to the *EC*, *b-e*, is positive if *b* exceeds *e*. *ROW* producers are better off by area 1+2+3+4 in the right panel. Consumers in *ROW* lose 1 so net gain to ROW is area 2+3+4. Net gain to the world is area *b+f*+2+4 from terminating the *EC* oilseed subsidy.

Area *b* in Figure 6.2 is gained because the *EC* no longer is producing oilseeds at costs above the border price (P_w), areas *f* and 2 are gained because consumers in the *EC* and *ROW* no longer are deriving less value than the border price from consuming oilseeds, and area 4 is gained because *ROW* no longer is foregoing production forthcoming at less than the border price. The border price, the equilibrium world price, is an opportunity return (cost) equal to the marginal value (cost) of oilseeds in production and consumption. The conceptual results for *ROW* apply to the U.S. because the U.S. also is an exporter of oilseeds.

The simplified partial equilibrium conceptual model does not account for individual country impacts or interactions among commodities. These are best analyzed with a mathematical international trade model. Impacts from oilseed subsidy elimination are quantified for the *EC* and the U.S. in the next section.

Empirical Analysis

Impacts of removing *EC* oilseed subsidies were quantified using a world trade simulation model developed at The Ohio State University. The model equations were written using the USDA SWOPSIM software. The model can be described as a static, non-spatial price equilibrium formulation incorporating the assumptions of neoclassical trade theory (see Roningen, et al., July 1986; Sullivan, et al., March 1989; Gleckler and Tweeten, 1990 for a further description of model). Data for 1989 were used to initialize the model. Results reflect changes from 1989 conditions and are in 1989 prices but the coefficients apply to an intermediate-run period of 4 to 5 years, other things equal. The model simultaneously estimates changes in markets for eight commodities: beef, pork, poultry meat, wheat, corn, coarse grains (excluding corn), oilseeds (principally soybeans, rapeseed, and sunflower seed), and oilmeal. Substitutability and complementarity among commodities are accounted for in behavioural equations.

Empirically estimated percentage changes in world prices following elimination of EC oilseed subsidies are presented in Table 6.1. Interestingly, proportional impacts on the price of wheat are as gre at as those on oilseeds. World coarse grain price is substantially lower as well. The origin of these price changes is production decisions by European farmers. Grains and oilseeds are substitutes in production. Oilseed subsidy elimination reduces oilseed acres and increases imports, resulting in higher world prices. Grains are substituted onto former oilseed acres. Increased EC grain expo rts and lower world prices result.

TABLE 6.1: **Change in World Prices from Eliminating the European Oilseed Subsidy**

Commodity	% Change
Beef	0.02
Pork	0.03
Poultry Meat	0.02
Wheat	−2.40
Corn	−0.26
Coarse Grain	−1.48
Oilseed	2.39
Oilmeal	1.15

Table 6.2 presents changes in EC production, consumption, and trade with the elimination of oilseed subsidies. The 33 per cent drop in production and one per cent rise in consumption combine for a 3,228,000 metric tonne increase in oilseed (mostly soybean) imports. In the past, subsidized production of oilseeds supplied low-cost feed ingredients for livestock producers. Elimination of the subsidies increases feed costs, drops beef, pork, and poultry production, and decreases European exports of these products an estimated 19,000 metric tons (3,000 + 10,000 + 6,000 metric tonnes).

TABLE 6.2: Impacts on European Community from Eliminating Oilseed Subsidy

Commodity	Production	Consumption	Trade (net exports)		
			1989 Quantity	Change	
	(% change)	(% change)	(1,000 MT)	(1,000 MT)	(%)
Beef	-0.04	0.00	269	-3	-1.01
Pork	-0.08	0.00	403	-10	-2.51
Poultry Meat	-0.09	0.00	314	-6	-1.75
Wheat	6.12	0.00	20,164	4,864	24.12
Corn	0.12	-0.02	-1,830	4	0.23
Coarse Grain	3.63	-0.02	5,728	2,019	35.24
Oilseed	-33.24	-1.10	-14,162	-3,228	-22.80
Oilmeal	-0.43	-0.50	-12,978	75	0.58

Because *EC* demand remains strong for oilseeds and is quite inelastic, and because world oilseed import supply is quite elastic, the reduction in *EC* subsidies shows up more in increased imports than in reduced consumption (Table 6.2). Wheat and coarse grain production, on the other hand, rise substantially in the European Community (Figure 6.3). Oil crops grow side-by-side with grain crops in Europe and at the same time of year. Lowering the effective EC producer price by 45 per cent (the 1989 subsidy amount) while continuing high grain price supports shifts production into grains. This is conceptualized by the shift from *s* to *s'* in Figure 6.3. Grain yields in metric tonnes per hectare are more than double oilseed yields and the shift brings substantial increases in grain exports. In Figure 6.3, *EC* grain exports increase from q_s-q_d to q_s-q_d when the support price is held at P_s.

Table 6.3 presents estimates of impacts on U.S. production and trade. Higher oilseed prices cause some soybean acreage expansion at the expense of corn and coarse grain acres. Lower world prices also contribute to grain production declines. Increased feeding costs cause a slight decrease in meat production. The U.S. trade position worsens in most commodities outside the oilseed sector. The 1,297,000 metric tonne increase in U.S. oilseed exports amounts to 40 per cent of the increase in *EC* imports (3,228,000 MT).

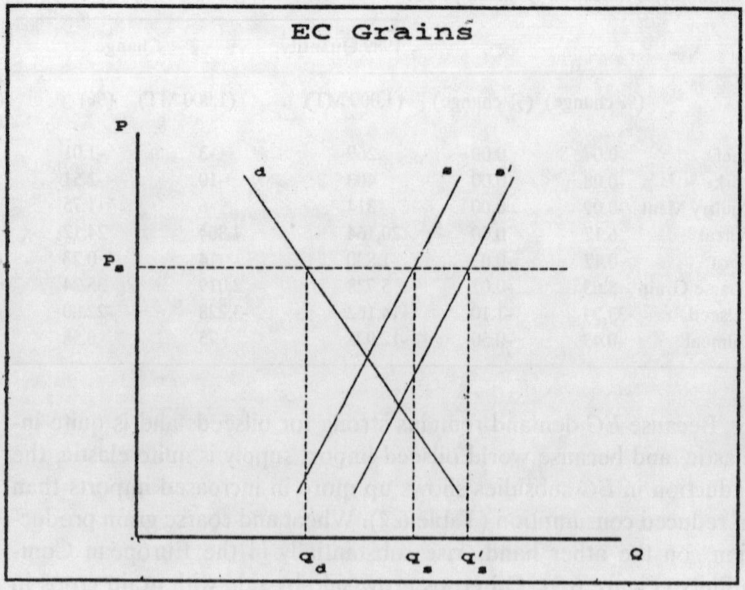

FIG. 6.3: Impact of Oilseed Subsidy Elimination on *EC* Grain Sector

TABLE 6.3: Impacts on U.S. Markets of Eliminating European Oilseed Subsidy

Commodity	Production	Consumption	Trade (net exports)		
			1989 Quantity	Change	
	(% change)	(% change)	(1,000 MT)	(1,000 MT)	(%)
Beef	-0.03	0.00	-579	-3	-0.52
Pork	-0.01	-0.01	-363	1	0.01
Poultry Meat	-0.07	0.00	426	-7	-1.67
Wheat	-0.81	0.51	34,128	-559	-1.64
Corn	-0.06	-0.03	54,537	-79	-0.14
Coarse Grain	-0.58	0.41	7,125	-274	-3.84
Oilseed	1.40	-1.06	15,897	1,297	8.16
Oilmeal	-0.43	-0.59	4,545	13	0.29

Welfare effects are presented in Table 6.4. As expected, *EC* producers lose substantial income from the elimination of oilseed processing payments. Some of this is recaptured in grain production. Oilseed consumers (processors) lose some from higher world price. Taxpayers in the Community gain $339 million more than producers and consumers lose. World price changes result in substantial U.S. producer losses especially in grains, but those losses are more than offset by U.S. producer gains in oilseeds. The producer impacts depend in part on the target prices and loan rates in effect when world prices change. All or part of producer losses might be transferred to taxpayers. Supply control and price enhancement mechanisms (as opposed to direct compensation) would shift cost to consum ers. U.S. consumers show a net loss primarily because of higher world oilseed prices. Grain producer and oilseed consumer losses combine to fully offset oilseed producer gains in the U.S.

Oilseed producers and wheat producers outside the U.S. and the EC (rest of world) especially benefit from terminating EC oilseed subsidies (Table 6.4). Deadweight welfare gains of $134 million more than offset any losses in the U.S. so that ROW welfare gains are positive as predicted by the conceptual model in Figure 6.2.

Conclusions

The GATT ruling on European Community oilseed programmes is a victory for the American Soybean Association. Estimates indicate the possibility for substantial income gains to U.S. soybean producers and European taxpayers if the EC eliminates oilseed subsidies. The biggest gainer from removing the market distortion is the EC which imposed it.

Almost 60 per cent of the gains to U.S. oilseed producers from eliminating EC oilseed subsidies is offset by losses to U.S. grain producers (Table 6.4). EC production shifts from oilseeds into grains which retain their high levels of support, significantly moderating potential benefits to U.S. farmers.

Globalization of agriculture means greater integration of producers and consumers around the world. Elimination of the European policy of subsidizing oilseed producers will impact U.S. farmers unevenly. As world agriculture continues to integrate, policy changes in Europe and other regions will increasingly impact U.S. producers and consumers. Because of the interrelated nature of agricultural commodity production, most of this impact will be uneven. Some farms and regions will benefit and some will be hurt. Current trends reversing trade liberalization may temporarily slow the globalization process and tend to insulate individual economies.

TABLE 6.4: Welfare Impacts of European Oilseed Subsidy Elimination

Commodity	Producers	Consumers	Taxpayers	Welfare
		($ million)		
European Community				
Beef	-5	0	1	
Pork	-8	0	4	
Poultry Meat	-4	0	2	
Wheat	534	0	-458	
Corn	3	0	1	
Coarse Grains	187	0	-75	
Oilseed	-1,662	-167	2,052	
Oilmeal	17	-83	0	
Total	-938	-250	1,527	339
United States				
Beef	-3	-3	0	
Pork	1	-4	0	
Poultry Meat	-4	-1	0	
Wheat	-110	44	0	
Corn	-26	20	0	
Coarse Grains	-27	22	0	
Oilseed	250	-178	0	
Oilmeal	29	-22	0	
Total	110	-122	0	-12
Rest of World				
Beef	15	-10	0	
Pork	20	-17	0	
Poultry Meat	10	-2	0	
Wheat	-986	1159	0	
Corn	-34	57	0	
Coarse Grains	-244	272	0	
Oilseed	633	-669	0	
Oilmeal	49	-119	0	
Total	-537	671	0	134

The GATT ruling comes at a time when the European Community is attempting to increase border protection and support of soybeans and oilseeds under the Common Agricultural Policy (CAP). Other crops in the EC (primarily cereal grains) are protected and supported to such an extent that "balancing" support to oilseeds is a central issue in current CAP policy formulation as well as in trade policy negotiations. ("Balancing" is a euphemism for moving toward equal levels of self-sufficiency or trade barriers among commodities through market intervention.) Although European welfare impacts are estimated to be positive with the elimination of subsidies, the ruling by the GATT is a serious setback to balancing producer support among oilseeds and other crops. This will probably increase the importance of soybeans in the ongoing trade negotiations. It may result in even more innovative methods of "balancing" the Common Agricultural Policy.

REFERENCES

Gleckler, James and Luther Tweeten, (1990), "The Economic Impact of a U.S.-Japan Free Trade Agreement." Pp. 87-104 in Luther Tweeten (ed.), *The Asian Market for Agricultural Products*. Columbus: Department of Agricultural Economics and R ural Sociology, The Ohio State University.

Roningen, Vernon, (1986), A static world policy simulation (SWOPSIM) modeling framework. Staff Report AGES860625. Washington, DC: ERS, U.S. Department of Agriculture. July.

Sullivan, John, John Wainio, and Vernon Roningen, (1989), A Database for Trade Liberalization Studies. AGES89-12. Washington, DC: ATAD, ERS, U.S. Department of Agriculture. March.

7

LIMITS TO AGRICULTURAL POLICY LIBERALIZATION IN BRAZIL: The Case of Collor's Government Agricultural Policy

PAULO ORTIZ ARAGAO and JOSÉ BOLIVAR ROCHA

Introduction

Like other civilian-elected governments in Latin America, such as Carlos Ménen in Argentina and Alberto Fujimori in Peru, Brazil's President Fernando Collor took power in March 1990 under the heavy burden of the so-called "lost decade" in the region. Brazil was badly hurt by a general economic and social crisis, aggravated by successive plans to fight inflation – beginning with the Cruzado Plan in 1986 – which brought the country to the brink of hyperinflation coupled with an enormous structural deficit. During the decade, the country experienced a sharp increase in absolute poverty. The continued migration from rural to urban areas helped to move the poor to the cities where in 1987 almost half of the population was below absolute poverty.[1] Under the assumption that the state was bankrupt, and it was necessary to restore its capacity to make economic policy and control over the market, the new government started with a bold and radical economic program, the so-called "New Brazil Plan" which included some features of the old stabilization plans such as a huge public tariffs increase, a currency devaluation, as well as something never tried before: a freeze of financial assets, bank accounts and savings of individuals and enterprises in the private and public sector.

Collor's government's first months in power were seemingly "insulated" from civil society; as if major social groups had no influence in the content and development of major government policies. These policies appeared as autonomous contributions of enlightened state officials, insulated from specific societal pressures, acting on behalf of the interests of society as a whole. This is particularly true in the case of the agricultural package that was delivered with the new plan. Those measures represented a radical attempt to redirect agriculture toward greater insertion in the world market.

For McMichael and Myhre (1991) the present regime of global capital accumulation has the effect of transforming the nation-state into a transnational state. They perceive the transformation of the nation-state and the state system as a response to the present crisis of the global economy. They believe that the transformation represents a new phase in the political development of capital. Capital is overcoming the barriers of national economic organization subordinating it to global commodities markets that cross national boundaries. The historical basis of the nation-state in the nationalization of capital are eroding. One consequence is the emergence of this transnational state.

Our paper focuses on a recent attempt of reorientation in state agricultural policy in Brazil, in the direction described by McMichael, emphasizing the particular relation between the state and social classes in agriculture. We concentrate on the obstacles in the way of a liberalization process and have made a deliberate choice of concentrating our discussion on two traditional and politically influential sectors that have an important presence in the political arena, namely sugar cane mill owners and wheat processors, which have resisted any attempt to change their partnership with the state, a move implied in the liberalization attempt. However, we ignored those dynamic sectors of Brazilian agro-food system that have been, since their creation, more export-oriented such as soybean, poultry, citric and fresh fruits. We argue, in this paper, that Collor's government's diagnostic and proposed reform of Brazil's agricultural policy was based upon an essentially "correct" perspective. By "correct" we mean that, for the first time, the government suggested policies to deal with particular interests of important fractions of the rural and agribusiness bourgeoisie such as the suga rcane mill owners (usineiros) and the wheat processing sector. Nonetheless, we argue that, given internal and external constraints, the chances of implementation and success of this new policy package are slim. We try to identify the forces that prevent state action.

Despite such apparent degrees of autonomy of state officials, the new policy proposal was not made in a vacuum. Therefore, we seek to explore why and how such policies were fashioned, and especially, to raise the question of whether, given internal and external constraints, can the new proposal be implemented. The paper calls attention both to the international environment, as well as to internal class dynamics, emphasizing the ability of the state to manage society's relation with capital. Also addressed is the problem of transition to democratization when the state attempts to recover the position of mediator between civil society and economic interests and faces new demands that are posed. Initially, we review the basic contours of the agricultural policy pursued during the period of authoritarian rule (1964-1984) to the first civilian government (Sarney's period 1984-90), taking into account the social-political context in which these policies were formulated. Then, we analyze Collor's agricultural package in order to compare both policies. We explore the volatile political situation, marked by an institutional breakdown which contributed to the appearance that the new government had a higher degree of autonomy vis-a-vis civil society. Part two focuses on the relationship of the state and social classes in agriculture. First, we examine closer the special relationship between the state and two sectors of the agrarian bourgeoisie in Brazil – the sugarcane mill owners and the wheat processing sector – as examples to demonstrate the kind of resistance the new government is likely to face when trying to create a new relationship with big agribusiness interests. Second, we examine the impact of the new agriculture policy on food production taken as a resp onse of the government to the growing demands of the popular sector to obtain improved food consumption. Finally, part three addresses the question of changes in the international economy and the external limits and possibilities for Brazilian agricultural production, especially the possibilities of profound changes in commodities market brought about by the recent GATT negotiations.

PART I

The 1964-90 Agricultural Policy

During the 1960s the military regime promoted a model of agricultural development that redefined the integration of agriculture and industry, the so called strategy of conservative modernization which was part of the regime's overall accumulation strategy. The heavy industrialization of the 1956-61 period had established the basis for industrialization of agriculture especially in the state of Sao Paulo. This redefinition was characterized by the passage from an extensive to an intensive agricultural model, requiring land and capital concentration into agro-industrial complexes benefiting the more advanced local and transnational enterprises and resulting in changes in the rural relations of production. As in the previous phase, the model of industrialized agriculture continued to emp hasize the production of commodities as a source of foreign exchange earnings.[2]

The military regime's model of agricultural development was meant to industrialize agriculture. The state agriculture policies were an attempt to articulate the expansion of agriculture with the ag ro-industrial complex, contributing to the internal supply of foods, with the accumulation of the capital goods and chemical industries – which were being promoted – and with export earnings vital to the model of industrial development being pursued.[3] The internationalization of the Brazilian economy had created the conditions for agriculture to become more capital-intensive through the utilization of modern industrial inputs such as fertilizers, and agricultural machinery. There was, therefore an increase in the sectorial interdependence between agriculture and industry: the pattern of agricultural development was subordinated to the pattern of industrial development under the leadership of transnational companies and financial capital.[4] State promotion in the agricultural and a gribusiness sectors, especially in the period 1970-75, created levels of subsidies unsurpassed in Brazil's history.[5]

Insertion of agriculture in the capitalist accumulation process implied the transfer of resources to the sector through the institutional credit system creating new opportunities of appropriation of agricultural surplus by industrial and financial capital (Goodman 1986).

The Political-Institutional Climate of the Economic Policies

This overall development strategy occurred in a period of military rule. The process of economic policy-making and the state administrative apparatus followed a technocratic orientation. The military and its technocratic allies envisioned the establishment of a higher level of rationality in the policy-making process; they wanted to establish a system that would assure rapid economic growth without overt political strife under the belief that the country could not achieve growth with an open political system. All political opposition was eliminated by the regime through a crackdown on poli tical parties, the legislature, trade union and other organizations. The elimination of the political opposition by urban labour and rural workers through repression permitted the regime to enjoy total freedom in policy-making. Without any effective opposition the regime monopolized the political process and was able to implement policies that mainly benefited the middle and upper classes.

The form of interest representation changed under the regime in allowing the well situated business community easy access to government agencies and increased influence upon government policies. As Abranches (1978: 68) puts it: "with society devoid of autonomous political organizations all political transactions are mediated by the state structure. Thus policy becomes circumscribed to the burea ucracy of the state". Agribusiness interests were able to take their case directly to government agencies. Cardoso (1979: 35-36) points out that the policy-making process helped to link the regime to civil society, although not in a corporative fashion. The regime discouraged the participation of class organizations in the decision-making process. However, the decision-makers encroached in the state apparatus selected individuals to participate in the decision-making process. Sector specific policies were utilized to obtain the support of the middle-class and the local capitalist classes b oth in agriculture and industry with economic growth becoming the road for the legitimation of the regime.

During this period, in the name of the need to better coordinate government action, economic policy-making was centralized, culminating in the creation of the Ministry of Planning and General Coord ination. However, as pointed out by Abranches (1978: 751), there was a segmentation of the state apparatus among different state agencies, resulting in disarticulation of state policies. Government agencies were unable to formulate "coherent, comprehensive and articulated policies", due to "the fragmentation of interests and the segmentation of the state apparatus. Comprehensive plans [had] alm ost no other function than providing the ideological ground for negotiation and for the legitimation of governmental actions. Most policies [were] effectively made by sectoral agencies, state banks and enterprises" (Abranches 1978: 440).

Under the state monopoly of power came the centralization of economic decision-making and it was under those conditions that the model of conservative modernization of agriculture was formulated. The present phase of the transition to democratization poses a host of new problems in terms of redefining the limits of state action and the creation of new mechanisms of policy formation.

From the mid-1980s the model of outward-oriented agricultural development in Brazil had began to show signs of exhaustion. One of the main determinants of this exhaustion has been the transformation in the world economy: the huge agricultural surplus of countries from the European Community (CEE) and the United States. This external constraint has been compounded by the fiscal collapse of the state resulting from large subsidies for agriculture and industry.

The "New Brazil" Plan: A Revolution from Above?

As it was stated before, as soon as it was inaugurated, the new government launched the most radical package of economic measures as ever seen in Brazil's recent economic history. We will focus brie fly on the main aspects related to agriculture in the new package.

According to the new government's perspective, the degree of state intervention in the sector after the 1950s made the agricultural sector in Brazil highly dependent on the state, almost a state-owned sector. It was argued that the growing state presence in the sector had placed agriculture under the custody of the state in that it completely imprisoned the sector into the mechanism of bureaucratic regulation implying a de facto state power of control over the agricultural production in the country.

Collor's agricultural policy was centered on two aspects: modernization of agriculture and the liberalization of the economy. In order to raise efficiency of the productive system, the government proposed to reduce import tariffs to expose the domestic economy to foreign competition. The argument was that, in the past, excessive protection had contributed to the creation of inefficiencies in the agricultural sector. The old policy of state custody, (i.e. the state as guardian of the sector), was rejected. Therefore, by decreasing subsidies for agriculture the aim was to lower the degree of state protection.

The main objective of the new policy was described as a "shift in the character of the process of production and income distribution, by expanding the productive chain of foods in order to meet the demand of the majority of the population, especially those located in the lowest stratum of income, and not the replacement of the state by the private sector" (Brasil 1990: 7). The document continues stating that the state function becomes one of manager of "public policies in order to guarantee, through instruments and rules clearly defined, the basic conditions, to obtain the increase of social safety, which is made possible, among other factors, by the guarantee of an adequate food supply" (Ibid: 7).

It was argued that Brazilian agriculture had the capacity to respond to market stimulus. The new role of agriculture, within the development model, being pursued was that the modernization of the ag ro-industry would create new demands to the agricultural sector allowing productivity increases in the sector. On the other hand, the expectation was that agriculture would create demands to the industrial sector, mainly the food industry and capital goods, providing stimuli for the increase of efficiency, competitiveness and industrial productivity of these sectors. The planners also envisioned the verticalization of production as "the basis to development" i.e. "the intersection among the different branches of the sector, and the industrial sector with agriculture" (Ibid: 7).[6] The incorporation of new land through the expansion of the agricultural frontier continues to be seen as strategic, as well as the reformulation of the instruments of government support to small and medium-size agricultural producers. The document also mention the ever present possibility of an agrarian reform (Ibid: 8).

In terms of credit for the sector, the new agriculture policy for the 1990/91 harvest differs from the prior years only on minor aspects. Staple crops such as beans, rice, corn and manioc would receive more financial support. Through financial mechanisms, the government would induce or redirect agricultural production toward potentially more productive geographical regions. One of the main points of the new government policy was the use of the minimum price policy as an instrument to redirect the productive potentiality. Minimum prices would be equalized nationally thus increasing the mar gin of profit of more efficient producers and forcing those less inefficient to shift to crops better suited for each region. The idea was that producers would react to a decrease on its profit and shift to more profitable crops.

The discussion about the new agricultural policy took place during the first months of the new government when the annual harvest was already in progress. As a result, not many changes were observed, but the discussion created a great deal of uncertainty among rural producers. This political climate, coupled with drought in some regions, resulted in a decline of 9.8 per cent in the 1990s harvest as compared to the 1989 harvest (Conjuntura Econômica 1991: 93).[7] As a result, the 1991 harvest was expected to be the lowest of the last twelve years, requiring the import of basic foods for internal consumption.

PART II

State and Social Classes in Agriculture

The question of the degree of autonomy of the state vis-a-vis the classes is central in the debate about the nature of the capitalist state. It is generally argued that the state depends on sectors of the bourgeoisie to implement economic policies. Therefore, can the state position itself above the classes and implement independent policies or is the state always constrained in its action? For O'Donnell (1973) the state has a certain degree of autonomy vis-a-vis the ruling classes, however, it essentially embodies the existing class structure and therefore is structurally incapable of devising or implementing policies contrary to the interests of the dominant classes.

The state autonomy discussion in Brazil varies from a position of considering a great degree of state autonomy in policy-making to the position of considering the state as constrained by the classes despite the authoritarian nature of the regime which prevailed in Brazil since 1964. Cardoso (1979) sees the local classes as lacking a "vocation for hegemony" perceiving themselves as politically subordinate to a state apparatus they do not control. In the same line Evans (1982), following Abranches (1978), sees the bourgeoisie as controlled by the state and having little to say about state policies, even though the state has to advance the interests of the bourgeoisie. He sees the state role as mediator between global capital, the national bourgeoisie and the working class (Evans, 1979).

Regarding the rural elites, Nunberg (1986) argues that despite the authoritarian nature of the Brazilian state, they maintained a great deal of influence over policy-making. She casts doubts about the view of attributing supremacy in the policy-making process to the authoritarian state and argues that the agrarian elites maintained a great deal of autonomy from the state. Even during the military rule, agricultural elites have maintained a great deal of power and influence on policy-making because their political support was crucial for the regime's legitimacy and stability.

Agricultural modernization policies in Brazil during the 1970s were formulated in an authoritarian and exclusive context whereby the interests of a few groups and classes in agriculture and industry were privileged.[8] Policies that benefited groups and class fractions linked to agro-industrial complexes were implemented while small producers were excluded.

The Collor's government was elected by a coalition involving conservative rural interests, the middle class, fractions of the industrial bourgeoisie that saw in his opponent a threat to the capitalist order, and mainly by the descamisados (literally those without shirt) attracted by the candidate's reformist discourse. The descamisados were those left out of the development process of the last re gimes: the process of conservative modernization followed by the military regime and continued during the transition government of the New Republic (1985-90). As a candidate, Collor's ticket did not receive open support from the most important fraction of the national bourgeoisie, Sao Paulo's industrial bourgeoisie. As a consequence, at the beginning of his term in government, he was able to assume a defiant and uncompromising position, a position of absolute autonomy. In fact, during Collor's first months in power, he was essentially "insulated" from civil society. It was as if major social groups had no influence in the content and development of major governmental policies. His policy was presented as an autonomous contribution of state officials insulated from specific societal pressures, with the governmental system showing strong tendencies toward autonomous state action; state officials claiming to know and represent "general" or "national" interests presented themselves as especially capable of formulating holistic and long-term strategies transcending partial, short-sighted demands from profit-seeking capitalists or narrowly self-interested social groups.[9] The liberalizing discourse envisioned to deprivatize the state decreasing subsidies and rationalizing the process of credit concession in agriculture. Two cases will be briefly reviewed to show the limits of market liberalization.

Wheat processing

Wheat processing is a case which illustrates the constraints the government has had to face in dealing with some powerful fractions of the bourgeoisie in its attempt to globalize the economy and decrease the fiscal burden of the state. Wheat processing is an activity that has been heavily controlled by the state. In 1967, during the first military government, Roberto Campos, the liberal minister of planning, devised a unique system to organize the industry that ended up on heavy state subsidies for the sector, whereby access to the market was guaranteed only for a few privileged members of the cartel. The system worked in such a way that only those few who had access to subsidized wheat bought from the government (the only supplier) for processing, and the product was – and still is – delivered by the government at plant site. Ever since, the system has become even more concentrated with a reduction in the number of processing plants from more than 500 in 1967 to 1979 presently. Today only twenty privileged groups control 80 per cent of the market.[10] Less powerful wheat producers, on the other hand, did not receive from the government the same generous treatment. In September 1990, the Collor government attempted to deregulate the industry by withdrawing the state from the role of sole buyer and distributor of the product. However, Congress opposed the new policy and blocked the liberalization attempt proposing instead a transitional period in order to industry to adjust to the new situation. During this period, only the few members of the cartel would be allowed to import wheat. It remains to be seen whether the new government will be able to substantially alter the terms of the wheat cartel.

Usineiros

The case of *usineiros* is also illustrative of the internal limits and difficulties of liberalization. President Collor comes from a Northeastern state – the state of Alagoas – where *usineiros* interests are the dominant ones. During his tenure in Congress as state representative, he staunchly defended renegotiation programmes for the chronic debts of the sector, a policy opposed by Brazil's Central Bank and the state-owned Banco do Brasil. As president, despite his neoliberal discourse and promises to rationalize the state, Collor has not been able to come up with a coherent and uniform policy for agriculture. To face the sector's virtual bankruptcy, the government has come out with a bail out plan for renegotiation of an estimated 1.7 billion dollars debt of the *usineiros*.

In addition, in Collor's government, sugar has received special status as the only product directly managed by the presidency.[11]

In sum, *usineiros* and wheat processor are class fractions, politically important, that have skillfully used the legislative to receive government concessions and advance their interests. Sugarcane is an economically important activity in the country and the usineiros, as they have done in the past, have used the threat of social unrest in the populous sugarcane region if the demands of the sector are ignored.

Democratization poses the problem for the government of having to share with civil society and other spheres of power the formulation of economic policies, resulting in a difficult adjustment process and a non-synchronization among the different sphere of power (executive, legislative and judiciary).

Agricultural Policy and Food Production

The agricultural policy of the 1960s was designed mainly with the objective of internationalization of the economy, but it also pursued self-sufficiency policies as part of an ideology of national security. Subsidized credit, technological research and rural extension were established and geared toward export and energy crops. This explains why food production in Brazil – in a short period – has declined ever since, while energy and export crops have boomed, placing Brazil as a major exporter for the world market. The agricultural frontier, in the government's perspective, would simulta neously make possible the production of export, energy and food crops. However as Ryff (1982) pointed out, in the main agricultural producing states, there was no frontier area. Therefore, any increa se in a kind of crop would mean competition with the others.

Collor's agricultural policy departs from the old policies, dropping the objectives of self-sufficiency, to specialize in crops in which the country has comparative advantages in the world market. In the case of food for domestic consumption, the country would rely more on imports, for instance buying more wheat from Argentina. Several studies provide evidence about the difficulties of reconciling the two objectives, production for the world market and food for domestic consumption. There seems to be a contradiction between the two policy goals (Barkin et al. 1990: 18).

The new agricultural policy follows a neo-liberal discourse. It holds the belief that the market gives answers for the economic problems, and that farmers would respond immediately to market opportunities. However, as many authors have pointed out, during the period of military rule, agricultural credit policy was concentrated in agricultural production for export and fuel crops. In the case of food for internal consumption the positive response from producers to market stimulus did not occur due to factors such as concentration of subsidized credit on energy-exports crops, non-availability of seeds, inefficient distribution systems and government price control for basic foods. In part as a result of generous subsidies for agriculture, a situation of fiscal crisis has been created in Brazil (Wilkinson, 1989). The new government has come under pressure from multilateral agencies such as the IMF and the World Bank to begin a process of "deprivatization" of the state.[12]

In order to deal with this fiscal crisis, one of the responses of the new government has been to search for greater rationality of the agrarian sector. To compound the financial problem, there was a bad business climate in Brazil, marked by instability, contradictory policies and a high level of uncertainty about the future. The economic policies of the present government have only worsened the problem. Recent data about capital flows in Brazil shows that the country has become net exporter of capital with an estimated US$ 2 billion exported in 1990 (Brasil, 1991b). The impasse on the renegotiation talks of Brazil's huge external debt has also cut off the country from its important and traditional sources of external finance. The Collor government's commitment to neo-liberal policies has been impaired by difficulties in solving the enormous debt of backward but articulated sectors of the rural bourgeoisie such as the usineiros.[13] The process of making agricultural production more efficient and less dependent on the state seems endangered. Whether the state can be deprivatized or whether agricultural interests prevail and continue to dictate state policies for the sector remains to be seen.[14]

PART III

Limits and Opportunities for Brazilian Agricultural Commodities Exports

In this section we will discuss the external limits of the domestic policy of liberalization launched during the new government's first months in power. Globalization implies that competition and price formation is international and the level of international efficiency has to be internalized. Capital and technology has to adapt to the new demands of the world market. Since the international commodities market is volatile and heavily dependent on the state for credit, subsidies, research and development of new technologies and on signaling what to cultivate, the state in Brazil, as elsewhere in the world, has had also to play a central role in the stabilization and regulation of the market through mechanisms of price fixation, credit concession, subsidies, research, and intervention in the supply and distribution of foods, and so on.[15]

The new government has attempted to face the agricultural, as well as the overall economic problem mentioned above through market liberalization. In the agricultural sector, one of the main tenets of the policy was to make agriculture more efficient and internationally competitive, by cutting subsidies and inducing farmers to abandon inefficient crops. This policy was grounded in two main assumptions: (1) that the countries of CEE in the Uruguay Round of talks would make concessions toward agricultural liberalization and (2) a deepening in the integration with South Cone countries that would supply Brazil with commodities it cannot produce efficiently, such as wheat. Brazil's strategy was that by following a liberalization policy in the industrial area (computers, pharmaceuticals, intellectual property, and so on) as well as implementing more liberal rules for foreign investments and services, it would be rewarded by a significant reduction of agricultural subsidies and other commercial barriers to the flow of agricultural commodities. This expectation did not materialize. On the contrary, the last Uruguay Round of negotiations has shown that concessions from CEE countries will not easily follow, providing evidence of the shortcomings of the liberalization policy.[16]

The government's initial expectation was that the present round of GATT negotiations, initiated in 1986 in Punta del Este, Uruguay, would lower European countries agricultural subsidies and other barriers to agricultural products, thus contributing to the opening up of new opportunities for Brazilian agricultural exports. The GATT negotiations involve a complicated system of bargaining between developed and developing countries. The Uruguay Round has focused on areas traditionally left out of GATT negotiations and is a first attempt to create multilateral rules in what has been called the "new themes:" liberalization in the areas of services, including financial services, intellectual property and international investment and commerce, reevaluation of textile protection and reduction of agricultural subsidies in developed countries. In the Brazilian case, the sensitive issues have been the introduction of more liberal legislation in areas like patents, intellectual property and norms for foreign investments and services. In the case of the developed countries like CEE and Japan, they were expected to make concessions reducing agricultural subsidies. The talks have come to a deadlock exactly in the area that constitutes an old unresolved theme, the agricultural question.[17] The organized agricultural interests of Europe succeeded in obstructing an agriculture reform and a broader reform proposal from the CEE countries thus causing the round of talks to collapse.[18] The lesson from the CEE countries position is that agricultural policies in those countries, as else where, are heavily determined by the organizations of agricultural producers with the state having to consider seriously their interests.[19]

Due to the agricultural question, the December 1990 meeting in Brussels finished at an impasse and despite the pressures from the U.S. and the coalition of 14 developed and developing countries, including Brazil, known as the Cairns group (an Australian city), to bring reforms to the Common Agriculture Policy of the CEE, a compromise has not been reached. The main issue was the magnitude of reductions in subsidies and other measures of internal support to agriculture defended, on the one side, by the U.S. and, on the other, by the CEE proposal. The American proposal was of a 90 per cent reduction in subsidies for agricultural exports and a 75 per cent reduction in measures of internal support for agriculture and commercial barriers in a 10 year period starting by 1991. The CEE proposal represents a reduction of subsidies in 30 per cent based on 1986 values.[20] A final collapse of the talks would have important consequences for the agricultural sector of countries like Brazil, a major player in the commodities market, and certainly would constitute a major problem for agriculture liberalization policies in Brazil.

Conclusions and Discussion

We will pinpoint now the main obstacles to what we see as a significant change in agricultural policy in Brazil. We also try to outline the implications of Brazil's case to theory concerning the limits of state autonomy.

To start with, the government has come up with a proposal that is sharply different from its original discourse. Actually, from a strategic point of view, there was little change in the official policy for agriculture and significant changes were left on paper. On the external side, a gradual liberalization of agriculture through the elimination of instruments of bureaucratic regulation and tariff reductions requires the liberalization on a global scale. The present difficulties at the Uruguay Round of GATT talks have highlighted the obstacles of globalization. Therefore, it is naive to suppose that Brazil can liberalize unilaterally. Developed countries' policies of supporting their farmers involves the purchase of their agricultural surplus at subsidized prices. These surpluses have to find their way to the global market, at any price, since they obviously cannot be sold in the internal market of the developed countries, thus jeopardizing their policy of price stabilization. Therefore, globalization in Brazil poses the question of whether the government can afford the political cost of liberalization by failing to "deliver the goods" for its supporters.

The regional integration of South Cone countries represents another difficulty. This point can be nicely illustrated by recent attempt by the U.S. to undersell Argentina in Brazil wheat imports, thr eatening the yet incipient common market of the South Cone countries (MERCOSUL).

We believe that the case of Collor's agricultural policy is useful in highlighting the narrow limits of state autonomy when the state faces difficulties in both the domestic and international environment. In this case, even for a powerful and ever present state as the Brazilian one, with a strong historical tendency toward autonomy, intervention in the economy and with a strong and professional bureaucracy, the possibilities of maneuvers are quite reduced. To a large extent, the external environment sets up the structural possibilities for state autonomy. In a good external climate, it wou ld be much easier for the government to overcome the internal crisis. If the economic policy of the last thirty years deeply changed the Brazilian class structure, creating the conditions for the emergence of a government that could position itself above the classes would be easier. However, this is not possible due to the combination of external constraints with the internal crisis. Special in terests and the commitments to its support base have had to be addressed. During the period of authoritarian rule, which took place in an expansionary world economy – the "miracle" years – the possibility of autonomous state action was much higher. The present period of a transition to democracy in a recessionary scenario makes it much more difficult to sustain autonomy from the dominant class, reminding us that state autonomy, as the state role itself, is not a static category but an historically determined one.

Our paper indicates that the way toward globalization is not one that is easily obtained but one full of obstacles. The process results in winners and looser. Some sectors of the national agro-food system are already greatly integrated into the international circuits of capital and are less dependent on state custody and support. However, other sectors such as sugar/alcohol and wheat processing are historically dominated by local capital and have maintained a special relationship with the state, resisting liberalization policy and globalization attempts. The reaction of rural producers to the directives of the Collor's government agricultural policy is illustrative. With the government reduction of financing for crops, the government was forced to spend 2 billion dollars in the 1991 fiscal year on the import of foods for internal consumption.

Globalization discussions of the agro-food system picture the process as an inexorable one with the state becoming a facilitator (McMichael and Myhre, 1991). Even though the state tries to overcome the 'constraints of national economic organization' in order to subordinate the economy to global markets as pointed out by McMichael and Myhre (1991:107), this process can generate resistances from internal social and political forces. The higher the intersectorial disparities of the agro-food system in terms of degrees of modernization and globalization, the greater would be the difficulties in the establishment of a liberalization and globalization policy. As recognized by the authors, although there is an universality in the process of globalization of national economies, the process is not a linear or inevitable one.

NOTES

1. The deteriorating standard of living is evidenced by the growing cost of the basket of basic goods for the low income urban and rural population, with the minimum wage becoming increasingly insufficient to cover the living costs. Data available from the Brazilian national sample survey (PNAD) shows that between 1980-87 poverty increased in all but one Brazilian region. The overall rate of those living below the level of absolute poverty rose from 17.7 to 23.3

per cent (HÇlio Jaguaribe, 1991, quoted in Folha de Sao Paulo, April 23, 1991). The data shows a sharp increase in poverty on those living in urban areas (from 36.6 to 46.4 per cent), while in the countryside a significant decrease in absolute poverty levels was observed (from 63.3 to 53.6 per cent) in the same period. Each year 1.5 million person moved from rural to urban areas indicating a massive transfer of the poor from rural to urban areas.

2. For discussions of the post-1964 development model see, among many others: Sorj (1980), Wanderley et al. (1979), Graziano da Silva (1981), Ryff (1982), Mueller (1982), Szmrecsnyi (1983).
3. For a discussion of state promotion of the capital goods and chemical industry in the Geisel government period, see Evans (1982).
4. See Muller (1982).
5. In the mid-1970s the state was already providing generous incentives for purchases of agricultural equipments in order to push demand for the capital goods industry that had been established in the country and was also being promoted. A new stage of import-substitution industrialization was initiated with the installation in the country of subsidiaries of transnational corporations.
6. In a departure from the old policies of expanding the agriculture frontier regardless of the cost and level of subsidies involved, the new policy orientation is intended to be more cost oriented avoiding high levels of subsidies. In 1991 Embrapa, the state agricultural research company presented an agro-ecologic map of Brazil. This map pinpoints the areas better suited for each crop, indicatin g which areas should be maintained as preservation and which areas should be used for cattle raising. The government intends to use this information in order to guide its policy of minimum prices and rural credit directing production to areas that result in the highest possible yield. (José Ramos, *Jornal do Brasil*, August 12, 1990)
7. This represents an estimate for 1990.
8. Among those especially benefitted from those policies were the *usineiros* through the huge state-sponsored programme for fuel-alcohol production, the PROALCOOL Programme.
9. Skocpol (1985: 7) discusses how . . . "a fundamental rethinking of the role of states in relation to economies and societies" is taking place, inspired by the writings of Max Weber.
10. According to Lawrence Pih, owner of Moinho Pacífico, Folha de Sao Paulo March 19, 1991.
11. The special treatment received by the usineiros during the present government are: (i) the continuation of subsidies for northeastern and Rio de Janeiro state usineiros; (ii) after the freeze of fina ncial assets the usineiros had their bank accounts transformed in cruzeiros (the new currency) rather than waiting eighteen months to do so as for everybody else; (iii) the sector continues protected fr om open competition. This means that in order to install a new sugar mill or distillery, there must be government authorization; (iv) it was the only sector in the Collor II Plan (February 1991) to rec eive a price increase (46.7%) among the overall increase in government's tariffs.
12. More on the discussion about the role of multilateral agencies in McMichael and Myhre (1991).

13. The government has proposed a bail out package for the usineiros with the renegotiation of their debt with the state in 15 years at interest rates oscillating between 5 and 15 per cent.
14. In order to decrease the role of the state in financing the agricultural sector, the new agricultural package brought some changes in the financial system such as the creation of "price insurance", the term used by the banks to call the government authorization to finance operations with agricultural commodities in the future market; the obligation of the banks to direct 10 per cent of the resources from the savings accounts to finance agriculture and the creation of titles of rural captation. The price insurance reveals also the government interest to modernize the process of price guarantee fo r producers through market mechanisms. In the old policy of minimum prices the government would guarantee the price in the case of unfavourable market conditions during the harvest period. In the new policy the price is guaranteed by the buyer from the moment the operation is closed in the future market, and the bank can finance the harvest already sold. (Maristela Mafei, Folha de Sao Paulo, August 19, 1991).
15. Even such staunch defenders of free trade, like Japan, CEE countries and US has maintained state protection for their agricultural sector — which shows that in no country in the world can the agr icultural sector survive without state intervention and support.
16. João Mauro Boschero, president of state company in charge of food policy (CNA), has declared that there were two proposals for liberalization during the period immediately before the inauguration.

    A radical one defending a complete market liberalization and a moderate one, which won, defending the continuation of the state action as coadjutor of the market. According to Boschero "liberalism does not exist, nobody in this government is liberal." For him the government action is directed to open tne economy in order to rationalize the internal production (Folha de Sao Paulo, June 19, 1990).
17. See Carlos Alberto Primo Braga, Folha de São Paulo, April 15, 1991 and Dornbusch (1991).
18. The main protagonists of the European resistance to reform are the COPA (Committee of Professional Agricultural Organizations of the European Community) and Cocega (General Committee of Agricultur al Cooperation of the European Economic Committee) the two most powerful of 57 European organizations of agricultural interests representation. COPA, created in 1958, congregates 23 national organiza tions of agricultural producers and 5.4 million producers and Cocega, created in 1959, congregates 10 national organizations, 40,000 cooperatives of processing and distribution and 10 million produce rs. Cocega is the political organization of the cooperative movement in Europe. Since the beginning, these organizations have resisted any liberalization trying to maintain the basic principles of the Common Agriculture Policy and rejecting any concession in the GATT that would risk the internal policies of CEE countries. The food companies of the CEE, although interested in a general reduction of tariffs which would contribute to reduction in the costs of inputs, did not want to antagonize those powerful organized interests. Some segments of the food industry with more close contact with a gricultural producers did

not support the agricultural reforms (Mauro de Resende Lopes, Folha de Sao Paulo January 18, 1991).

19. In a recent conference for Brazilian entrepreneurs, the neo-liberal former prime-minister of France Mr. Raymond Barre gave an illustrative example of the difficulties of developed countries in adopting neo-liberal policies. About the GATT round, he said that "the agriculture is made of human beings and the withdrawal of subsidies can not be made abruptly" (quoted in Rabêlo, José Maria 1991: 44). The difficulties are not just from the countries of CEE, Japan also has made clear its position about the import of rice: "we would never abandon our initial idea, that the production of rice is a question of national security" said Michiru Okuma director of the Division of International Economic Affairs of the Japanese Ministry of Agriculture (Ibid:44).
20. Carlos Alberto Primo Braga, Folha de Sao Paulo, April 15, 1991.

REFERENCES

Abranches, Sérgio H. Hudson de., (1978), "The Divided Leviathan: State and Economic Policy Formation in Authoritarian Brazil." Ph.D dissertation, Cornell University. Ann Arbor: University Microfilms.

Barkin, David; Rosemary Bart; and Billie DeWalt, (1990), *Food Crop vs. Feed Crop: The Global Substitution of Grains in Production*. Boulder: Lynne Reinner.

Brasil. Ministério da Economia, Fazenda e Planejamento, (1990), Brasil 90 - Diretrizes do Governo para Modernizar a Agricultura. Brasilia.

Brasil. Banco Central do Brasil, (1991b), Relatório Anual. Brasilia.

Brown, Lester R., (1990), "Food or Fuel: New Competition for the World Cropland." Worldwatch paper 35. Washington, DC.

Cardoso, Fernando Henrique, (1979), "On the Characterization of Authoritarian Regimes in Latin America." In David Collier (ed.), *The New Authoritarianism in Latin America*. Princenton: University Press.

Conjuntura Econômica. "*Retrospectiva da Agro-pecuária*," 1991, Vol. 44 (2):93-111. Rio de Janeiro: FGV, 1991.

Dornbusch, Rudiger, (1991), "O Gatt e o Comércio Mundial — A Rodada Uruguai." *Conjuntura Econômica*, Vol. 44 (2):53-55.

Evans, Peter, (1982), "Reinventing the bourgeoisie: State Entrepreneurship and Class Formation in Dependent Capitalist Development." Pp. 210-247 in Michael Burawoy and Theda Skocpol (eds.), *Marxist Inquiries*. Chicago: The University of Chicago Press.

Figueiredo, Vilma, (1984), "O Trabalhador Rural e a Modernização da Agricultura." *Revista Brasileira de Tecnologia*, Vol. 15 (4):12-18.

Goodman, David, (1986), "Economia e Sociedade Rurais a Partir de 1945." In Edmar Bacha and Herbert Klein (eds.), *A Transição Incompleta. Rio de Janeiro*: Paz e Terra.

Graziano da Silva, José, (1981), Progresso Técnico e Relaçhes de Trabalho na Agricultura. Sao Paulo: Hucitec.

McMichael, Philip and David Myhre, (1991), Global Regulation vs. the Nation-State: The Agro-Food Systems and the New Politics of Capital. Capital and Class, 43 (2):233-252.

Mueller, Charles C., (1982), "Formulações de Políticas Agrícolas." *Revista de Economia Política*, Vol. 2 (5):89-122.

Muller, Geraldo, (1982), "Estado e Classes Sociais na Agricultura." *Estudos Econômicos*, Vol. 12 (2):81-94, 1982.

Nunberg, Barbara, (1986), "Structural Change and State Policy: The Politics of Sugar in Brazil since 1964". *Latin American Research Review*, Vol. 21:53-92.

O'Donnell, Guillermo A., (1973), *Modernization and Bureaucratic-authoritarianism: Studies in South American Politics*. Berkeley: Institute of International Studies. University of California.

Rabêlo, José Maria, (1991), "Ricos Nacionalistas Querem Pobres Neoliberais." *Cadernos do Terceiro Mundo*, Vol. 138:44-47.

Ryff, Tito, (1983), "A Cornucôpia Agrôcola: Mitoe Realidade." In Maria da Conceópao Tavares e Mauricio D. David (eds.), Rio de Janeiro: Vozes.

Skocpol, Theda, (1985), "Bringing the State Back In: Strategies of Analysis in Current Research." Pp. 3-37 in Peter Evans, Dietrich Rueschemeyer and Theda Skocpol (eds.), *Bringing the State Back* In. New York: Cambridge University Press.

Sorj, Bernardo, (1980), *Estado e Classes Sociais na Agicultura Brasileira*. Rio de Janeiro: Zahar Editores.

Szmrecsanyi, Tamás, (1983), "Anlise Crítica das Políticas para o Setor Agropecuário." In Luiz G. Belluzzo and Renata Coutinho (eds.), *Desenvolvimento Capitalista no Brasil*. São Paulo.

Wanderley, Maria; Nazareth Baudel; Vilma Figueiredo; Lúcia, (1979), Alice Guedes Pinto e Abdias Vilar de Carvalho. *Reflexoes Sobre a Agricultura Brasileira*. Rio de Janeiro: Paze Terra.

Wilkinson, John, (1989), *O Futuro do Sistema Alimentar*. Sao Paulo: Hucitec.

8

CONSUMERS, LAND AND FOOD:
In Search of Food Ethics

GLENN EDWARDS MCGEE

With the coming into prominence of a "global" agricultural community in which interdependences are recognized and intertwinings of practice occur, it is hard to miss the magnitude of the North American role in energy and food consumption. This role, pronounced at the statistical, political, economic, agricultural, and cultural level, represents a certain (at times ironic) leadership position for American food practice, in which American agriculture tends to set the tone for the second and third worlds (Swaminathan, 1988).

American consumption of food represents an astonishingly global endeavour, which reshapes the polity and culture of the world both by example and through direct intervention (Schusky, 1989:103-120). This consumption belies, I will argue, its "noble roots in technological advancement," giving voice instead to an interesting but dangerous understanding of food; a kind of technological food ethics.

By exploring the roots and manifestations of these ethics in American agriculture and food, we can better come to diagnose one dangerous overtone to the globalization of agricultural and food practices.

Once a week, most Americans take a twenty-minute walk through a clean, well lighted place. North American grocery store shelves are a modern cornucopia, a celebration of plenty and a symbol of conta ct with every corner of the world. They are also a symbol of a new relationship with food. Though Americans take the smorgasbord for granted, the modern grocery store is the culmination of years of a gricultural, industrial, and technological growth. Today, mass-American eating is different economically, aesthetically, and ethically from the past. A different, new kind of "consumer" connection with food bears little resemblance to other animal food chains or the self-sufficient farming communities of humanity's yesteryear. The consumer role has new implications for society and the earth, and poses a challenge to those interested in sustainability and responsible living. After all, our relationship with food is also our relationship with the land. The three sections of this paper deal with the emerging rift in the developed world's apprehension of the reality of food, some of the political and historical factors involved in that rift, and suggest a provocative, localized solution that begins with recapturing the reality of food and ends in a reduction of energy consumption and human alienation.

Food, Advertising, and the Human Condition

Suffice it to say that people love food. Only slightly less interesting than sex, eating is the most natural thing humans do. Before any questions of aesthetics, ethics, or politics take the stage, it seems fitting to suggest that people feel their finest when they are fully fed. Most of the behaviours we observe in animals before they eat, after they eat, and when they are deprived of the pleasure of eating are mirrored in human behaviours. These same behaviours have taken on vast mythical significances throughout time in rituals celebrating the entanglements we have with food (Lévi-Strauss, 1969).

Modern technology has created a new ritual for the American (and increasingly, European) consumer: shopping. Shopping in the modern grocery store is a seductive experience. Every possible avenue for advertising is exploited to teach us not to think about food, but instead to develop "gut feelings" about various food products and brands. Pictures of "serving suggestions" on glossy packaging sell a brand name, a taste, and feelings of safety and fullness and virility and success. The grocery story is a sensory odyssey for the hungry of body and spirit alike, who enjoy being sold food as much if not more than eating that food. Wendell Berry suggests that modern consumers "think of food as an agricultural product perhaps, but . . . do not think of [our]selves as participants in agriculture. [We] think of [our]selves as 'consumers'" (Berry, 1991). Berry continues:

> Most urban shoppers would tell you that food is produced on farms. But most of them do not know on what farms, or what kind of farms, or where the farms are, or what knowledge and skills

> are involved in farming. For them, then, food is pretty much an abstract idea – something they do not know or imagine – until it appears on the grocery shelf or on the table.

Many shoppers, it seems, would prefer to just "have" food; that is, to purchase the preparation, cooking, farming, and political implications at the check-out stand. The wealthy have always been able to afford a pathos of distance from the preparation of food, but until 50 years ago the North American middle class was actively involved in preparing the daily meat and vegetable from the garden. Distance from food and food is a conditioned and abstract idea: our minds sew the seeds of techno-industrial food.

Food was not historically clean, but instead something that needed to be boiled or roasted by the cook to "kill critters," and incorporated into a plentiful American meal. Disease and parasites were a real concern for the housewife of yesterday. Learning to cook meant learning to keep your family safe and healthy. The luxury of modern convenience ameliorates safety concerns, and thus the immediate need to know a great deal about the chemistry and biology of food. Today's food has been sanitized by technology and advertising. As Berry remarks,

> The passive American consumer, sitting down to a meal of preprepared or fast food, confronts a platter covered with inert, autonomous substances that have been processed, dyed, breaded, sauced, gravied, ground, pulped, strained, blended, prettified, and sanitized beyond resemblance to any part of any creature that ever lived (Berry, 1990).

Anyone can cook boxed, bagged food. In fact, anyone could eat bagged food "raw." Increasingly, raw means only "not microwaved yet." Wearing various emblems, seals, and certifications, even frozen pizza today is "Zestfully" clean. Cooked and marketed to death, processed food bears no onus of consequences. Fast food is an obvious instance in which the power of advertising helps to clean up the food process. A fast-food hamburger might spend hours under a heat lamp, yet fast-food environmental commercials bombard the airwaves with the picture of "good" food fresh from a "good earth" and brought to fruition by a franchise restaurant.

Clean, safe, modern food will appear on North American tables if the consumer pushes seven telephone buttons. It will be here within 30 minutes, and will require no consumer preparation. Twenty years ago Americans marveled at the variety of canned foods they could buy and heat. Ten years ago the miracles of colour and flavour and preservation carried these possibilities even further. Three years ago, some frozen dinners no longer required freezing – they were just dried and treated. Today, at the apex of modern convenience, cooking is increasingly more an "art" for the affluent few-and less a way of life. It would seem that in America, if you can make food easier, or faster, or cleaner, or more magical, there is money in your mailbox.

Doubtless, tomorrow's shoppers, raised on boxed macaroni and powder dinners, will carry the technological torch still further. On the horizon is food with no fat, no calories, just synthesized flavour. We will add our nutrition packets to this malleable "flavour stuff." "Indeed," says Berry, "this sort of consumption may be said to be one of the chief goals of industrial production."

The new food isolates us from our actions, our beliefs, and our world. When Gabriel Marcel wrote in his Men Against Humanity of the effects of technology "on the average [hu]man," he counseled of a "pessimism" that is not "so much thought out as worked forth" (Marcel, 1952:42-44). Max Scheler invokes this same dull sound and fury (signifying nothing) as a "mixed up state" that occurs in the wake of disillusionment with one's natural origins-when humans become able to see themselves as wholly other to nature and natural process, they come to feel and be depressed, alienated, and pessimistic (Scheler, 1961:4-6). Industrial food provides a different and shocking alternative to home-cooked, home-grown agriculture: a new, industrial food "product." This product's impact on our lives is important:

> The products of nature and agriculture have been made, to all appearances, the products of industry. Both eater and eaten are thus in exile from biological reality. And the result is a kind of solitude unprecedented in human experience, in which the eater may think of eating as, first, a purely commercial transaction between him and a supplier, and then as a purely appetitive transaction between him and the food (Berry, 1990:127).

The nightmare is driven by alienation of human beings from their labour, nature, and the value of their actions: every purchase of a microwave burrito tends to drive local competition out, increase monocultural growth, destroy traditional cooking methods, decrease emphasis on learning how to cook burritos, increase incidence of cancer caused by additives, microwave use, and bad diet. Where did the burrito come from? Most Americans would answer, "the store." Modernity's memory and understanding of food's impact on ecosystemic diversity and geopolitical stability typically ends there: the store. In a nation and milieu in which even bananas have brand names and food has acquired new powers through advertising, it is difficult to be an accountable consumer. The senses in which we relate to food are so invested with the labour of advertising that accountability might itself take on a "lite" character, divested of the quasi-religious relationship of the American ancestors to their land (Campbell, 1990:38).

Politics, Economics and Food

As food and agriculture increasingly become a global enterprise, emerging patterns of consumption cast an alarming pall over the character of American eating-especially given the tendency of other first and second-world nations to imitate American cultural and economic trends. If the consumption practices of the American middle-class are disruptive in ethical terms, they are even more dangerous politically and economically, as the nation that consumes the most food and energy sets the trend for a new century. Indeed, American consumption singularly lays to waste entire Latin American societies with the creation of singular agricultural markets, tailor-made to provide cheap coffee or bananas to the first world. The economics of globalism portend an ethics of food which is equally threatening.

Thirty-five per cent or more of every food dollar pays for advertising (Moore Lappé, 1982:145). Add to that more than 9 per cent for packaging, and it becomes apparent that a sizable portion of every North American food dollar subsidizes aggressive marketing of food products. Big budget advertising allows quick accumulation of market share by the big food corporations (MacDougall, 1979:1). Thus, a group of corporations, typified by those once subsumed under the name Beatrice, has gradually swallowed up regional food producers by employing a political and economic psychology that plays to the human desire for mannah from heaven, or at least from the microwave (Zwerdling, 1980).

Food power is not solely economic. As we noted above, modern global agricultural practices often diminish the sustainability of third-world agriculture in order to provide cheap food for North America. Such transactions are facilitated by the polity, which draws its legitimation from the people. From Moses to Reagan to Gorbachev, politicians have had to learn the hard way that food is primary in politics. Cheap food means happy constituents, and industrial agriculture promises cheap food. American food industry organizes to request the indulgence of polity, and the lobby of technological food takes on a momentum of its own (Giddens, 1984).

In the modern human community described by Royce, the provider of food is, then, the leader of humans. If one applies Josiah Royce's community understanding of values to the history of food in the United States, a number of guiding commitments emerge, each of which has worked toward our present state. Paul Thompson traces the loss of agrarianism in technological America in terms of the shifts in power that accompanied both globalization and the modernist and pragmatist schools of thought (Thompson, 1990:6-7).

Though industry advertises in order to grow and make money, several externalities of such food advertising are able to emerge in themes, not the least of which is a concealment of the real relations hip between industrial food and industrial farming. Is it a conspiracy to deprive us of the knowledge we want? Not at all. Americans come to want the luxury of a pathos of distance from food, and often simply have no desire to know about the effect that massive industrial farming has on the environment. Trusting that if some nutrition or health or dolphin crisis arises they will be notified by a warning label or the nightly news, the public placidly enjoys the fruits of energy-intensive, geopolitically destabilizing agriculture. The food industry benefits from this complacency, and remains loyal to the belief that the less people have to think about a food X, the more they will purchase of that food X. As I argue above, the goal is to transfer the meaning of food from food qua foodstuff to food cum feelings. Thus, "hamburger helper helps your hamburger help you make a great meal." Public awareness of industrial reliance on monoculture, pesticides, inhumane veal production, in short on "energy intensive farming," would change the perception that industrial agriculture is fashi oned of cleanliness and efficiency and homespun, provincial practice. For example, the "good food from the good earth" notion stands in stark contrast to the reality of fast food and its effects. Public funding is not about to change public attitudes. The federal allocation for nutritional education was less than 1/100th of one fast-food chain's advertising budget in 1989 (McCarthy, 1990).

We have discussed some of the constellation of reasons for governmental apathy toward agricultural and nutritional education, but the extent of the apathy is astounding, as John Block, Secretary of A griculture under President Reagan often demonstrated. When asked about nutrition education, Block wields the governmental attitude that has come to be typical:

> I know that they are not the same, but hogs are just like people. You can provide protein and grain to a hog, and he will balance his ration. He will eat the right amount of protein to go along with the grain. People are surely as smart as hogs. Really, I think people deserve that prerogative. I am not so sure that government needs to get so deeply into telling people what they should or should not eat (McCarthy, 1990).

Finding Responsible Food Attitudes

Stop reading the moment that this paper suggests that Americans ought to forgo a measure of convenience. One of the most developed psychological notions, which provides economics with part of its impetus, is that human beings will forgo a substantial amount to prevent a certain dissonance that accompanies the erosion of *status quo* reality. Food, as a modern idea, is a part of modern reality. Most Americans have the ability to purchase this reality, and will give it up only if forced to by some much more pressing, vital, personal concern. Until the environment becomes more than a best-selling trend, food in its modern, convenient form will outrank all ecological concerns. If our wants are not malleable, though, perhaps our mindset is.

Obesity is caused in large part by the reallocation of the food role in the emotional process. Food can replace friends and assuage sadness only when it acquires a mental dimension. We can replace the idea that food is a weapon, or a friend, or a band-aid with a more authentic and less anthropomorphic mentality. "I begin with the proposition that eating is an agricultural act. Eating ends the annual drama of the food economy that begins with planting and birth (Berry, 1991:36)."

We must find accountability and knowledge to make informed change. This means coming to know industrial practices, and teaching children that choosing pre-prepared food means choosing these practices. It is a grapple with a societal immovability. Once we know this, though, we can make decisions about whether we want packaged lasagna or a balanced world; clean-well lighted places or healthy farm lands (Simon, 1982).

The most alien environment, obviously, is the urban environment. There the need for change and awareness is greatest, so it is there that little things can be most vital in terms of instruction. A window box, as Berry suggests, can be a teaching labouratory for young and old alike to recycle kitchen scraps for fertilizer, and see the "energy cycle that revolves from soil to seed to flower to fruit to food to offal to decay, and around again" (Berry, 1991:37). Cooking, housekeeping, and understanding can be coextensive, if only the ethos of consumption can be disabused of some pervasive notions about cleanliness and goodness and pleasure as they relate to the consumption of time, energy and resources. Of course, knowledge is "intensive" in this recognition.

Every time we prepare our own meals, we take a measure of control over our bodies, actions, and selves back into our own hands. The choices we make about what we eat, and where it comes from, and how it was raised are likewise critical to personal responsibility. Buying from a local farmer sends a message about preference directly to the source, and has impact on the food market by helping to eliminate the entire group of transporters and wholesalers and such who thrive on irresponsible land use. Learning about what is in season tells us a great deal about when it is responsible to buy things. Learning about regions that produce crops in strange, expensive times of the year is also useful.

In sum, the critical measure of food awareness is this: how accountable is the consumer for food choices. Advertising that has altered the fundamental reality of our relationship to the world, and economic theory that subsumes people under the "selfish agent" category has made it absolutely dangerous to participate passively. Accountability, then, depends on understanding and adroit responsiveness to the demands of a sick planet. One vital way to increase public awareness begins with government spending more on food education (McCarthy, 1990:1). Another is the simple education of restraint in living (Campbell, 1990:49). Education, experimentation, creative and holistic living are often difficult and even costly enterprises. Words like "sustainable" and "ecologically sound" can themselves become trappings of advertising for everything from motor oil to tampon shields. The staggering implications of personal choices about food are interesting, though, and demand more than cursory examination.

Food plays an enormous economic role in culture and polity. With the globalization of food, I have argued, also comes a set of choices that have ethical dimensions. Consumer roles in agriculture can become obscured, even obfuscated, by advertising, technology, and the fundamental reordering of consumer priorities in energy-intensive society. Technological food comes to be seen as "clean" and wh olesome, even as that same technology works against environmental and agricultural diversity and stability. Likewise, the low-cost "convenience" of first-world food works to the disadvantage ("disconvenience") of those in the third world. Consumers in the United States and other first-world nations must come to recognize the impact of food choices, rather than passively subjectifying the environment and the third world in the name of frozen pizza and cheap coffee. Wendell Berry and others have taken an important first step to educating us about the possibilities for an authentic food ethics: first, we must learn to intuit that there are limits-and that in the "new world order," our cheap coffee is another person's poverty. As the global community in agriculture brings with it sweeping and at times abstract notions like "interdependence," we must take care in our theory and our praxis to remember that personal choices set the tone for North America, which in turn holds substantial purchase on agroeconomic trends in the globalizing world of the future.

REFERENCES

Berry, Wendell, (1991), "Know That What You Eat You Are." *Harper's*, Vol. 283 (1688):36-40.

——, (1990), "The Pleasures of Eating." Pp. 125-131 in R.Clark (ed.), *Our Sustainable Table*. Berkeley: North Point Press.

Campbell, James, (1990), "Personhood and the Land." *Agriculture and Human Values*, Vol. 7 (1):39-43.

Giddens, Anthony, (1984), *The Constitution of Society: Introduction to Theory of Structuration*. Berkeley, University of California Press.

Lévi-Strauss, Claude, (1969), *The Raw and the Cooked*. New York: Harper and Rowe.

MacDougall, A. Kent, (1979), "Market-Shelf Proliferation-Public Pays." *Los Angeles*

Times, May 27.

Marcel, Gabriel, (1952), *Men Against Humanity*. London: Harvill Press.

McCarthy, Colman, (1990), "A Thin and Pasty Gruel." *The Washington Post*, November 10.

Moore Lappé, Frances, (1982), *Diet for a Small Planet*. New York: Ballentine.

Scheler, Max, (1961), *Man's Place in Nature*. New York: Noonday Press.

Schusky, Ernest L., (1989), *Culture and Agriculture*. New York: Bergin and Garvey.

Simon, Julian, (1982), "The Farmer and the Mall: Are American Farmlands Disappearing?" *The American Spectator*, Vol. 15 (8):18-40.

Swaminathan, M.S., (1988), "Our Common Agricultural Future." Pp. 120-130 in B.W.J. LeMay (ed.), *Science, Ethics and Food*. Washington, Smithsonian Institution Press.

Thompson, Paul, (1990), "Agrarianism and the American Philosophical Tradition." *Agriculture and Human Values*, Vol. 7 (1):6-7.

Zwerdling, Daniel, (1980), "The Food Monsters: How They Gobble Up Each Other – and Us." *The Progressive*, Vol. 44 (3):16-27.

PART THREE

GLOBALIZATION AND THE ROLE OF AGRICULTURAL RESEARCH, EXTENSION AND EDUCATION

9

GLOBALIZATION, DEPENDENCE AND UNDERDEVELOPMENT: Towards Understanding the Context of Agricultural Research Institutions in India and the U.S.

SHRIPAD D. DEO and ROSALIND P. HARRIS

Followers of a faith may be expected to spread their particular gospel to less fortunate people who have not yet seen the light....It makes little difference whether a new religion is needed or wanted, there being only one true religion, everyone should have it whether [s]he wants it or not.

—*F. T. de Vyver (1964: 216-7)*

Whatever we do, we always look to the West and see what they are doing.

—*An Indian scientist quoted in Shiva and Bandyopadhyay (1980: 577)*

Introduction

For the post-colonial societies of Africa, Asia, and Latin America, the period after the Second World War was characterized by dramatic and far-reaching changes in virtually all facets of economic, socio-cultural, and political life. In many respects, these changes represented a continuation of the colonial policies of European nations, but with new rulers, regimes and "clergy." It was during this period that post-colonial societies were advised, cajoled and more often than not, coerced to modernize through the process that we have come to call development. This requires a very specific way of shaping how we think about the relationship between the lives and circumstances faced by people in post-colonial and Western societies. We call this way of naturalizing a very specific kind of relationship between post-colonial and western societies the development discourse.

In the 1950s and 1960s, the development discourse established the dichotomy, pre-modern and modern, to designate historically conditioned geopolitical realities, the modern West and pre-modern non-West. The societies that were encouraged to follow the path of development were at once encouraged to accept a particular interpretation of the history of Western societies wherein achievements of science and technology (S&T) were presented as a dominant factor in their accomplishment of apparently endless material well-being. A concomitant argument posited that the development of S&T and their use in industry, agriculture or virtually any field of human endeavor, was a sign of modernity. As such, the absence and/or underdevelopment of institutions of science and science-based industries were assessed to be clear indicators of backwardness. Scientific preeminence involvement of state in scientific/industrial research, and direct or indirect promotion of industry and other economic activities were viewed as being necessary for supporting "national" interest.

A strategy encoded within the concept of development and designed to assist post-colonial societies with the modernization process was the "development of educational institutions, particularly universities, in those areas that foreign policy architects determined to be of strategic economic and geopolitical importance to the U.S." (Berman, 1983: 66). U.S. philanthropic foundations, influenced by the Rostovian vision of world 'development' where nations were seen as airplanes lined up on the path to development, poised for take-off to self-sustained growth, focused on establishing western type institutions and elite/leaders in those countries that were most likely to accommodate the western ideas that would lead to the transformation of rural agrarian societies. The process of establishing institutions and selecting and grooming leaders sympathetic to development was facilitated by the fellowship programmes of U.S. foundations which provided educational opportunities at selected American and European universities.

American universities played a key role in the transfer of educational and research institutions by providing the model upon which first generation "university development centers" within the post-colonial societies would be developed. Essentially, the post-war foreign policy architects of the U.S. envisioned the elaboration of a network of vanguard institutions, developed through the efforts of technical experts from U.S. universities, that in turn would reiterate the process of transmitting the knowledge that had originated within a uniquely American context. Nowhere is this more dramatically played out than in the growth and proliferation of agricultural institutions within the post-colonial societies.

Though the land-grant model was shaped by the unique constellation of economic, political and social forces driving the transition to an urban-industrial based economy in the mid-19th century within the U.S., it was transferred wholly unchanged to respond to very different circumstances within many post-colonial societies in the mid-20th century. As a result, institutional practices and expert knowledge was often geared to displacing agrarian food systems long characterized by their small scale, diverse and ecologically particular responses to food production and food security needs in favour of monocropping operations dependent on the importation of U.S. agricultural chemicals and technologies. Moreover, agrarian rationalities long key to the dynamism of traditional food production systems were often de-legitimated in tandem with the legitimation of agricultural science rationalities from the West. These institutional practices and expert knowledge contexts have had the effect of spawning crises of consequence within many post-colonial societies. Such crises have been characterized by the creation or intensification of poverty, hunger and malnutrition, the alienation of longstanding agrarian populations from the land and the obliteration of traditional or indigenous agricultural knowledge.

In this paper we examine the establishment and development of Indian Agricultural Universities (IAUs) and Black Land Grant (BLG) institutions, as examples of institutions profoundly influenced by the U.S. land grant model. The first agricultural institutions in India were established by the British colonial rulers in the early 1900s to study tropical agriculture for the benefit of British commercial and industrial interests and plantations. The establishment of IAUs in the 1960s with the help of USAID and their expansion thereafter has been a subject of critical evaluation by domestic and international organizations with respect to their "mission" and impact on Indian agriculture.

In contrast, BLG institutions were created within an internal colonial context. They were created through the 1890 Morrill Act, a provision enacted to accommodate the separate, but equal sentiment that reflected the spiralling national sentiment against genuine black social, political and economic empowerment during that period. The involvement of BLG institutions in post-colonial food systems has been coordinated primarily by USAID through the Title XII Programme. The exploration of the role played by BLG institutions in post-colonial food systems is an area open for considerable critical inquiry (cf Harris 1990).

This comparative framework provides us with the opportunity to examine how colonial, internal colonial and post-colonial forces have shaped the role of institutions that are currently working within post-colonial food systems. We pay particular attention to the ways in which western agricultural knowledge has been reproduced within these institutions and globalized as an extension of the white land grant (WLG) institutions. To assist with this examination, we will first explore theoretical work that will help to illuminate key issues before turning to our case studies.

Theoretical Discussion

In recent years, social scientists have focused their attention on understanding and explaining the phenomenon that has come to be called globalization. This phenomenon is viewed as a multidimensional, transnational and trans-societal process which takes on a variety of forms, but nevertheless is conceived to accomplish the westernization or homogenization of cultures throughout the world. The political and economic leveraging of Nation-states facilitates the "flow of goods, people, information, knowledge, and images" (Featherstone, 1990: 1) from the West to the rest of the world. Our perception of globalization builds on this understanding and views it as the next phase in the process of modernization and the quest for modernity. As Giddens puts it, "We have not moved beyond modernity but are living precisely through a phase of its radicalization" (Giddens, 1990:51).

In many respects, the radicalization of modernity is realized more through the conjunctures of knowledge and power and the subtlety of persuasion than through insistence and force. For example, know ledge contexts that were once imposed upon colonial subjects in an effort to maintain political and economic hegemony are now woven into the very fabric of individual intellectual and institutional forms.

As Goontilake argues, such knowledge contexts become a normalized and naturalized part of the knowledge frameworks of 'dependent intellectuals', "the structure of knowledge that is transmitted to a social system and absorbed by its population. . . . acts as a form of social control"(Goonatilake, 1982:189).

We pay particular attention to this dynamic in examining the role played by universities in the international distribution of knowledge. Spitzberg argues that universities play a key role in the production and transmission of knowledge in a "complex international network of interdependency." He argues, moreover, given that "{t}he power of the First over all other worlds has now become one based upon the domination of knowledge production and dissemination. . . ." we need to "understand the relationship both between universities and their societies and among universities and societies. . . ."(Spitzberg, 1980:x).

Since we are interested in understanding the role that second generation land grant institutions play in globalizing a particular kind of agricultural knowledge, it seems reasonable to pay attention to theories that problematize the power dynamics among universities within the international knowledge system. Altbach (1980) argues that we must understand how the knowledge frames that particular universities employ are conditioned by their positions within the international knowledge system, that the positions that these universities occupy within the international knowledge system largely parallel the positions of their countries within the global economy. Therefore, centers and peripheries exist within the international knowledge system. Also, in light of the uneven social, regional, political and economic development within countries, they occur within national knowledge systems as well.

Continuing the analogy, Altbach argues that peripheral institutions, by and large, reproduce "dependent" knowledge contexts, that is, knowledge that is not generated in response to local i. e., national imperatives and needs, but is generated instead by agendas set in the center which more often than not correspond with its needs for capital expansion. This is why, for example, we find an emphasis placed on employing and disseminating techniques associated with the valorization of large scale commodity operatives rather than techniques associated with small scale farming operations in the programs of many Third World universities.

If we accept, as Altbach (1980) suggests, that the directions taken by the peripheral institutions of today have largely been conditioned by the colonial imperatives of the past which placed the needs of the colonial power before that of the colony, we must concern ourselves with identifying processes that either interrupt or reinforce these imperatives. In this regard, Altbach argues that "relatively few (peripheral) institutions present alternative models or go in radically different directions" (Altbach, 1980:43) from center institutions because neocolonial processes have succeeded in narrowing epistemological and practical choices. They have done so by effectively privileging and legitimizing Western academic knowledge contexts and devaluing and de-legitimizing the organic knowledg e tied to indigenous contexts and realities. As a result, peripheral institutions, largely staffed by expert/intellectuals trained in the West rely on center institutions to "give direction, provide models, produce research, and, in general, function as the pinnacles of the academic system" (Altbach, 1980:43).

Land grant institutions are indeed part of the international knowledge system. Moreover, they are an integral part of an emerging global agricultural research system. Altbach's "University as Center and Periphery" framework helps us identify and examine the ways in which the land grant frame has been "globalized" through the work of IAUs and BLG institutions.

Indian Agricultural Universities

In India, the initial decade after independence was dominated by debates over the nature of the development to be instituted. Nehru, India's first prime minister and the chosen political heir of Gandhi, asserted that rapid industrialization was the logic of universal history, because that is what happened in Europe, the U.S. and the Soviet Union. He further emphasized that there was a "need to catch up, as far as we can, with the Industrial Revolution that occurred long ago in Western countries. . ." (Nehru, 1954: 83).

The origin of IAUs can be traced to the work of the University Education Commission (UEC) which advocated that educational facilities be established for rural populations, that intensive agriculture and community development programs be developed through the efforts of the Rockefeller and Ford foundations and that the U.S. provide assistance to India on the basis of President Truman's Point Four Programme. The Point Four programme explicitly problematized the status of Third World countries in terms of their economic deficiencies, that is, what they lacked materially and technically. As such, it called upon those agencies within the U.S. that were most equipped to transfer to the third world the expertise and technologies responsible for the modernization of the U.S. economy. Having targeted the eradication of hunger and malnutrition through increased food production as a major objective, President Truman was able to inspire the commitment of U.S. land-grant institutions.

When the UEC put forth the idea of a "rural university", the dominant thought among the policy-makers was to increase agricultural production through institutional reforms. The emphasis was on "rural" rather than "agricultural" development. It was still believed that agriculture was only one, albeit a major one, of the rural activities and hence, there was unwillingness to concentrate on agriculture alone. The development of IAUs began against the background of general food shortages, failure of monsoons resulting in drought conditions in many regions of India, the slow pace of earlier programmes for improvement of agriculture and rural communities, substantial food imports and widespread rural discontent. This scenario made it imperative to define India's agrarian problem in terms of increasing food production and productivity. It is at this point the UEC conceptualization of "rural university" as an appropriate mode for educating larger numbers of people in rural areas in a practical and vocationally oriented manner was interpreted as synonymous with the concept of "agricultural university" advocated by the U.S. universities and the USAID with emphasis on modernizing agriculture in India and increasing agricultural production. India was quickly moving away from the milder end of the advice-aid scale and the donor advice and interpretation prevailed.

Dean Harold Hannah of the University of Illinois prepared a Blueprint for a Rural University in India (1956) outlining the role of IAUs and developed a model act for setting up universities in various states. The emphasis in the Blueprint was not on 'rural' development as envisioned by the UEC but on 'agricultural' development. There was no doubt that there had been pressure from donors to change the focus of rural universities from extensive rural social uplift to a narrow focus on agricultural modernization and an increase in agricultural productivity. The Blueprint by Hannah outlined the administrative structure of an American land-grant university, using Illinois as a model, and suggested guiding principles for a rural university in India. The criteria for setting up agricultural universities were laid down and enforced through the Agricultural Universities Committee. It has been argued that these criteria were used as control mechanisms to direct efforts in a particular direction and to reject alternatives as a waste of efforts (Abrol 1983).

In general, the support for the "agricultural university" concept came from those Indians who had studied at one of the U.S. land-grant universities. They were the severest critics of the tradition al Indian agricultural colleges and the strongest supporters of the U.S. land-grant concept. The cultural and intellectual orientations of these western-educated scientists transported back to India provided the necessary foothold for the cultural-structural invasion implicit in the transfer of technology and institutions to post-colonial societies (Goonatilake, 1984; Reddy, 1976; Busch, 1984). The emissaries were influenced by the land-grant model but were not influenced by the reality of the Indian agrarian situation. The reaction of the emissaries was predictable: they wanted an exact model of the system they had seen in the U.S.

In a recent report it is observed that institution-building was developed in the U.S. in the 1960s as a form of social engineering. Its expressed goal was to bring about rapid social change in post-colonial societies by working with elites in a top-down fashion (Busch, 1988:24). IAUs were part of that institution-building strategy. It is not surprising that there were supporters of this idea among graduates of U.S. land-grant universities, bureaucrats cornered by grim food situations, and political leaders who saw an opportunity to influence agricultural policy at the state level through these institutions. Even as early as 1967, a participant observed that in "the U.S., universities may have assumed too much from the start that they knew what was needed and they knew how to do it. The 'land-grant' banner was carried high and too literally; it was not recognized that the task was more than a simple 'transplant' job" (Kiehl, 1967:9). Institutions were xeroxed without consideration to Indian traditions, values and institutions.

The first IAU was founded in Uttar Pradesh in 1960 with the collaboration of the University of Illinois. By 1972, when the U.S. program was disbanded, there were eight IAUs and a post-graduate agricultural research institute. When the program of setting up agricultural institutes was disbanded, the U.S. land-grant system was also being criticized from within and outside. It was faulted for its research orientation with large farmers in mind while neglecting the needs of small farmers in the U.S. It was criticized for its linkages with agribusiness, specifically the suppliers of agricultural inputs (Hightower, 1973). It was also argued that the land-grant schools had not paid enough attention to the negative consequences of agrichemicals on the environment and users (Carson, 1962). An important criticism was that the colleges of agriculture had neglected basic research (NRC, 1972). It is interesting to note that when IAUs were being set up, it was argued that research emphasis of new institutions should be "on adaptive, protective and applied research. . . with basic fundamental studies postponed until later (Moseman, 1971: 101). Today, there are 26 IAUs (with several states having more than one), and two national research institutes. This agricultural research and education system is the second largest in the world (Busch, 1988; Deo, 1987).

By most standards, the institutional transfer to India was inappropriate. The idealized and optimistic version of land-grant system, devoid of its socio-economic and political context in the U.S., could not have replicated the results of the same magnitude in India. Yet these institutions in the Indian context have brought about basic changes in Indian agriculture through increased penetration of capitalist modes of production. It has long been recognized by those observing the transfer of technology and institutions to post-colonial societies that agricultural research has changed and continues to change the social structure of these societies in a fundamental and irreversible way (Levins and Lewontin, 1985; Busch, 1984).

Today, the researchers in these institutions conduct their research in isolation from each other and from the farmers who were to be helped. In his study of the first IAU at Pantnagar in Uttar Prad esh, Paul Brass has examined the question of institutional transfer of technology at length. He argues that:

> The form of technology transfer undertaken at Pantnagar had foreseeable undesirable consequences, some of which are associated with the general process of large-scale commercialization of agriculture, others of which arise out of specific north Indian conditions; that these consequences were not foreseen and the transformations taking place before their eyes were not analyzed by the research community at Pantnagar; and that there were alternative forms of organizing and extending the kind of

technology generated at or processed through Pantnagar that could avoid these consequences.

(Brass, 1982: 104)

Busch has rightly observed that research in these institutions is mostly a one-way activity. Researchers zealously sticking to the western model of agricultural research, in a large measure, have failed to appreciate vast stores of practical knowledge that farmers have accumulated over years. Unfortunately, "as a result of the lack of farmer input to agricultural research, all too often techno logy has been developed that is of high quality but inappropriate for circumstances of farmers. Needless to say, these technologies have not been widely adopted by Indian farmers" (Busch, 1988: 61).

The National Commission on Agriculture (NCA) in India observed that "What often passes as fundamental research in agriculture is but a variation of a similar study done elsewhere having little or no relevance to our conditions. Sometimes, research workers. . . work in sheer oblivion of the actual problem" (1972: 93). The report comments that "most often the researcher gets at the problem by reading scientific literature in his own discipline, either Indian or foreign. Rarely does he go out into the field and pick up his problem from his own direct observation or those of his colleagues enga ged in field work" (NCA 1972: 95).

Busch has diagnosed a part of the problem facing the IAUs correctly. He argues that initial emphasis on production agriculture by the IAUs was perhaps "a necessary and appropriate response to food shortages in the early days", but that narrow focus has become an impediment (Busch, 1988:49-50). It may be recalled that the IAUs were set up during the period when the green revolution technology w as being introduced globally. Also the network of IARCs concentrating on specific commodities and regions was growing. The international division of labour that was envisaged entailed concentration of fundamental research in agriculture at these centers while national agricultural systems were to focus on adaptive, protective and applied research (Moseman, 1970:101; Abrol, 1983). It is, therefore, not too difficult to understand why the focus has remained narrow in the work done by the IAUs. Gajbhiye and Hadwiger indicate that "the international agricultural research system. . . has served as a very important link between U.S. agricultural research and small farmers of the third world" (Gajbhiye and Hadwiger, 1986:241-54). It is noteworthy that in their study of agricultural scientists at IARCs, Gajbhiye and Hadwiger conclude with this thought: "Aspects of the U.S. system [the land-grant system] have served as models for the international research centers. Both the U.S. and the international centers played important roles in the development of the national research institutions within the developing countries" (Gajbhiye and Hadwiger, 1986:252). U.S. institutions have trained half or more of agricultural scientists at IARCs, just as they have trained agricultural scientists in other post-colonial societies, including India. It then becomes clear that the process of mobilizing and incorporating various elements of agricultural research has facilitated the process of globalizing knowledge production.

Black Land Grant Institutions

BLG institutions have also played an important role in globalizing the scientific agricultural knowledge of the West. Though the strategies and mechanisms involved in this process have not been explored to the extent that they have been in the Indian case, what emerges from this brief discussion on the history of their development and the nature of their investiture within the international agricultural research system is instructive. The 1890s in the United States were marked by "the regression of black civil rights and economic opportunities" (Schor, 1983:1). The vigorous efforts seeking equality in all walks of life, came to an end in 1901 when the last African-American individual in the Congress retired. The new African-American "leader", Booker T. Washington, who emerged on the scene renounced "social equality, [and] accepted at least temporarily a subordinate role [for African-Americans] in politics" (Schor, 1983:2). Washington chose the path of educating African-Americans in industrial and agricultural arts which would enable them to get jobs provided by southern friends (Logan, 1967: 195-6; Schor, 1983:2). Black people were effectively denied equal status in southern society, but were allowed to learn/acquire skills which would make them available to the industrial/agricultural sectors in need of trained labour. Not all southerners were bent on African-American disfranchisement but they were atypical and less influential.

The Morrill-McComas Act of 1890 was passed during this period of African-American disfranchisement primarily to respond to pressure by agricultural scientists and businesses. They were demanding more appropriations to cover the cost of residential instruction for "the more complete endowment and maintenance" of WLG institutions (Marbury, 1979). Only indirectly did the 1890 legislation provide for the creation of separate land-grant institutions for African-American people. State agricultural experiment stations established through the Hatch-George Act (1887) were located in WLG institutions and generated much needed revenues for them and helping them in establish themselves as legitimate research institutions. Research funding allocated under the Hatch Act remained unequal from the beginning until the late 1960s. Only one of the 17 BLGs received Hatch funds prior to 1971. As a result even though the 1890 Morrill Act, though vague about higher education of African-Americans and delayed by 28 years after the original legislation, provided for residential instruction but not for agricultural research or materials and equipment needed for the development of physical infrastructures. This was consistent with the dominant ideology of African-American education at that time, which placed emphasis on preparing teachers and on the practical training of a marginalized and dependent work force. This had the effect of reproducing the class structure of modern agriculture.

The institutional resource constraints combined with socio-political and economic discrimination had led BLG institutions to develop an agricultural knowledge base quite distinct from that developed within WLG institutions. This knowledge base reflected the agrarian wisdom of small farmers and the ingenuity and resourcefulness developed through the reliance on home grown methods and technologies used by BLG agricultural faculty. Concerns about agriculture were also, always addressed in tandem with the broader community concerns, from which they could not be disconnected. Though the differences in approach that distinguished BLG institutions from WLG institutions were conditioned more by circumstance than conscious choice, they nevertheless indicate the existence of a knowledge context not wholly shaped by the imperatives of scientific agriculture as developed within the WLG system. This is important to bear in mind as we consider the changes brought about within BLG institutions by desegregation and by their incorporation within the international agriculture research system through U.S. foreign assistance mandates.

The desegregation mandate of 1954, inspired according to Emerson and Kilson (1966) by America's need to appear racially tolerant within the context of its post-war efforts to establish economic ties with the Third World resulted in dramatic changes for the operations of BLG institutions. In the name of integration, many BLG programmes were either eliminated or absorbed uncomfortably into WLG programmes (Schor, 1983). Moreover, African-Americans were increasingly afforded the opportunity to train as agricultural scientists within WLG institutions, returning to BLG institutions as teachers and researchers eager to pursue interests inspired during their years of training within WLG institutions. Many were thwarted in their attempts, however, by the lack of research infrastructures and financial support needed to carry out such activities. Nevertheless, BLG institutions were in the process of being fundamentally altered by their incorporation within the land grant mainstream. Between 1967 and 1981 the U.S. Congress enacted legislation designed to compensate BLG institutions for historical deficiencies in research funding by providing money for the development and proliferation of research activities and facilities. A condition of the legislation required that BLG and WLG institutions coordinate planning and decision-making activities in setting the agricultural and rural development research agendas for their respective states. In many instances this resulted in organizational restructuring that meant that respective BLG institutions, in whole or in part were ultimately accountable to the WLG institutions in their states for the decisions they made regarding their research and extension programmes.

A similar provision for institutional collaboration between BLG and WLG institutions was mandated for agricultural work within the Third World by the U.S. Agency for International Development (USAID.) The major impetus for USAID's attention to increasing the involvement of BLG institutions in Third World activities was the concern that such efforts "contribute to the implementation of the U.S. Government's Affirmative Action programme by increasing minority representation in foreign assistance teams" (AID document "Guidelines for the Preparation and Submission of Proposals for Minority Institutions", August 1984:1). Increasing the representation of minorities on foreign assistance teams was of considerable concern apparently "because of the great diplomatic liabilities of the "all white " teams usually provided by the other universities" (AID memorandum to BIFAD regarding Strengthening Grants to Minority Institutions, February 20, 1981:2).

As a result special provisions were made for involving BLG institutions in AID's Title XII Programme. Title XII amended the 1961 Foreign Assistance Act in 1975 to reflect a formalization of relations between the Agency for International Development (AID) and American universities. It committed the federal government to using the resources and expertise of land grant institutions, in particular, to relieving hunger and famine within the Third World. Title XII itself was enacted in the wake of legislation passed in 1973 to redirect AID's foreign assistance efforts toward the needs of the rural poor in post-colonial societies.

Title XII specified that university resources should be employed to assist small scale or limited resource farmers in the Third World with their food production concerns. However, it was recognized that the land grant system "had been aimed with certain exceptions at increasing the productivity of farmers with access to resources, not the marginal farmers. . . . {Thus} a reorientation of U.S. unive rsities would be needed if they were to truly meet the needs of the poorest of the poor – or even limited resource farmers" (Flora and Flora, 1989:27). This recognition stimulated the development of legislative and programmatic mechanisms to help universities prepare themselves to address the needs of the limited resource farmer. These mechanisms included institutional Strengthening Grants and Project Support Grants. The latter are provided for by memorandums of understanding (MOUs) and joint memorandums of understanding (JMOUs) between universities and AID which call for the elaboration of long-term relations between the two universities in carrying out agricultural activities within the Third World. The JMOU arrangement, in particular, pairs a BLG institution with a WLG institution in a long term relationship with AID. This has been the primary mechanism for involving BLG institutions in AID projects.

By structuring the terms of the JMOU programme so that BLG institutions work in subordinate positions to WLG institutions it has virtually placed BLG institutions under tutelage to WLG institutions. D ifference, that is a different agricultural knowledge base, within this context is held to be undesirable, something in need of change so that it conforms to the standard so that the BLG difference is held to be something in need of upgrading – of change. The circumstances under which people from BLG institutions work within AID and within the Title XII Programme specifically do not appear to be co nducive to allowing possibilities to emerge. First and foremost Title

XII is a programme within a bureaucracy that values the science-based agricultural knowledge WLG institutions have produced for decades and exported post-colonial societies. It is also a programme that values familiarity with the rules and regulations that govern project contracting.

Essentially, the structure of the JMOU programme provides little incentive for BLG institutions to use their traditional knowledge bases and approaches, approaches that could potentially provide much needed sources of support to limited resource farmers and disadvantaged groups in their involvements in post-colonial societies and for informing the insights and practices of their WLG collaborators as well. Reconsidering the basic objectives of Title XII to address the food and nutritional needs of marginalized groups within post-colonial societies and the concerns of small farmers, in particular, it seems ironic that the capabilities of BLG institutions were never considered within AID to be conducive to addressing these goals. Moreover, if we refer to the argument advanced by Flora and Fauna, that WLG capabilities were in need of a reorientation to the needs of small scale farmers in order to balance their capabilities for responding to the needs of large scale farmers, it also seems ironic that Title XII mechanisms were put into place to provide tutelage to BLG institutions having such capabilities. These ironies can only be understood if we seriously consider AID's commitment to continuing patterns of agricultural practice within post-colonial societies that place the knowledge and capabilities historically developed within WLG institutions at the forefront of development activity.

Through their work in the Title XII programme, universities are mobilized to become part of the global agricultural research system comprised of national research centers within the tropical and semi-tropical regions of post-colonial societies and are supported by a system of 13 International Agricultural Research Centers (IARCs). The conceptualization and operationalization of a network of the IARCs, according to the Consultative Group on International Agricultural Research (CGIAR), is based on the ever increasing need to apply science to agriculture to increase production.

For WLG institutions whose agricultural research infrastructures are strong, participation in this scientific "indigenization" process has proceeded accordingly. And although the IARC focus, including farming systems research, has been heavily criticized for its lack of attention to the genuine needs of small scale farmers in post-colonial societies (Richards, 1985) WLG institutions continue to be heavily subsidized for their research activities in post-colonial societies. For the majority of BLG institutions with weak or fledgling research capabilities, participation in the Title XII programme has been looked upon as an opportunity to learn by example from WLG institutions.

Summary

In this chapter we explored the concept of globalization as a cultural phenomenon. In particular we examined how Indian Agricultural Universities and Black Land Grant institutions have been conditioned to reproduce the agendas of historically white U.S. land grant institutions within post colonial societies. Our discussion was undergirded by a critique of globalization that identifies it as an outcome of culturally specific strategies that assume a view of human progress which we have come to call development, a view that continues to assume that human progress can only be measured in economic terms and that the material wealth of the advanced industrial societies was possible largely because of the role played by scientific and technological knowledge. In essence, this view holds that by expanding the domains of these knowledge contexts it would be possible for "underdeveloped" societies to become like "developed" societies; that by following a unilinear process of advance, it then becomes possible to valorize the universalism of science. Given this definition of the problem, the task then becomes one of institutionalizing the solution. That is, to establish scientific institutions within post-colonial societies capable of disseminating the appropriate knowledge.

By comparing the historical contexts of development for IAUs and BLG institutions, a number of common themes emerge from seemingly very dissimilar situations. First, each set of institutions developed within milieus where more tradition bound approaches to agriculture and rural community development were important to the people they were to serve. In the Indian case this consisted of indigenous knowledge and approaches to community welfare that embedded concerns regarding agricultural development rather than subordinating it to agricultural development. In the black case this consisted of local wisdom and practices regarding food production that were largely unmediated by the lessons being disseminated on agricultural practices within white communities. In the black case, such wisdom was realized and explored with an awareness of the fuller constraints to community power posed by the political economy of the South. Second, in each case, popular leaders accommodated to the overarching trends that would help to shape the respective sets of institutions, conditioning them, in many respects, for the roles they currently play within the international knowledge system. Nehru, in contradistinction to Gandhi, enthusiastically endorsed the idea of rapid industrialization and the roles that would be played by Western science and technology. As a result, IAUs were primed to accept their roles in compliance with national imperatives. Even in the face of considerable criticism over the last two and a half decades, IAUs continue to function within a fairly traditional land grant frame. On the other hand Booker T. Washington accommodated the socio-educational ideology that prevailed during the early 1890s, that sought to exclude blacks from any educational experience deemed "white." As a result, he helped to shape a tradition of self-sufficiency and self-reliance basically in defense of black survival and in recognition of the fact that BLG institutions might never be fully linked with the land grant mainstream. Since the knowledge BLG institutions did develop came to be considered inferior knowledge because it did not have as its basis the same tradition of scientific research as that developed within WLG institutions, BLG institutions have largely been viewed as novices with respect to generating legitimate scientific agricultural knowledge. As a result they have been treated as such within the international agricultural research system.

Third, U.S. foreign policy played a key role in framing how IAUs and BLG institutions would be developed for work in the food systems of Post-colonial societies. In both instances the mechanisms that were implemented to "train" the institutions were tied directly to USAID programmes that were focused on modernizing agriculture. In the case of the IAUs, policy provided for model institutions such as the University of Illinois to direct the development of agricultural institutions. In the case of BLG institutions, policy provided for the development of JMOUs that would place WLG institutions in mentor position vis-a-vis BLG institutions.

Finally, IAUs and BLG institutions have been organized within the emerging international agricultural research system to carry out work within the food systems of Post-colonial societies. To date, they would appear to be conforming to Altbach's notion of peripheral institutions. And if we are to give ultimate credence to Altbach's argument, there would appear to be little room for peripheral in stitutions to maneuver within a system dominated by the imperatives of central institutions.

We would like to consider in closing, however, that despite an undeniable degree of homogenization, there are differences for these institutions to draw upon in creating space for maneuver. For instance, both sets of institutions have alternative, albeit subjugated knowledge contexts to draw upon, intellectual traditions critical of mainstream interventions and the vital group specific, culture specific everyday experiences and counterdiscourses of subordinated peoples to mediate the often finely veiled tyranny of globalization.

REFERENCES

Abrol, D., (1983), "American Involvement in Indian Agricultural Research," *Social Scientist*, 11(10):8-26.

Altbach, P.G, (1980), "The University as Center and Periphery" in Universities and the International Distribution of Knowledge. Edited by Irving J. Spitzberg, Jr., New York, Praeger.

Berman, E. H., (1983), The Influence of the Carnegie, Ford and Rockefeller Foundations on American Foreign Policy: The Ideology of Philanthropy. Albany, NY: SUNY Press.

Brass, P., (1982), "Institutional Transfer of Technology: The Land-grant Model and the Agricultural University at Pantnagar" in *Science, Politics, and the Agricultural Revolution in Asia*. Edited by R. S. Anderson, P. Brass, E. Levy, and B. M. Morrison. Boulder, CO: Westview.

Busch, L. M., (1984), "Can Agronomy Feed the World? Agricultural Research Policy and World Hunger". A Paper presented at the Right to Food: An International Conference on Freedom from Hunger, Montreal, Canada. May.

——, (1988), Universities for Development: Report of the Joint Indo-U.S. Impact Evaluation of the Indian Agricultural Universities. Washington D.C.:United States Agency for International Development.

Carson, R., (1962), *Silent Spring*. Boston: Houghton Mifflin.

de Vyver, F.T, (1964), "The Transplantation of Trade Unionism to British Africa" in *The Transfer of Institutions*. Edited by W.B. Hamiliton. Durham, NC: Duke University Commonwealth Studies Center.

Deo, S. D., (1987), "Indian Agricultural Universities: Review of the Literature". Unpublished manuscript.

Emerson R. and M. Kilson, (1966), "The American Dilemma in a Changing World: The Rise of Africa and the American Negro" in *The American Negro*. Edited by T. Parsons and K. B. Clark. Cambridge: Riverside Press.

Featherstone, M., (1990), "Global Culture: An Introduction" in *Global Culture: Nationalism*, Globalization and Modernity. Edited by M. Featherstone. London: Sage. 1-14.

Flora, C.B. and J. Flora, (1989), "An Historical Perspective on Institutional Transfer" in *The Transformation of International Agricultural Research and Development*. Edited by J. Lin Compton. Boulder, CO: Lynne Rienner Publishers.

Gajbhiye, J. and D. Hadwiger, (1986), "U.S. Agricultural Research and International Aricultural Research Centers: An Institutional Comparison" in *The Agricultural Scientific Enterprise: A System in Transition*. Edited by L. Busch and W. Lacy. Boulder: Westview.

Giddens, A., (1990), *The Consequences of Modernity*. Stanford, CA: Stanford University Press.

Goonatilake, S., (1982), *Crippled Minds: An Exploration into Colonial Culture*. New Delhi: Vikas Publishing.

——, (1984), *Aborted Discovery: Science and Creativity in the Third World*. London: Zed Books.

Hannah, H. W., (1956), Blueprint for a Rural University in India. New Delhi: Indian Council for Agricultural Research.

Harris, R.P., (1990), Black Land Grant Institutions and Third World Agriculture Within the Title XII Program: Is There Room for Maneuver? Unpublished Dissertation, University Park, The Pennsylvania State University.

Hightower, J., (1973), *Hard Tomatoes, Hard Times*. Cambridge, MA: Schenkman.

Kiehl, E., (1967), "The Objectives of the Indian Agricultural Universities" in Proceedings of the 11th Campus Coordinators' Conference: Agricultural Universities Development in India. Urbana, IL: University of Illinois.

Levins, R. and R. Lewontin, (1985), *The Dialectical Biologist*. Cambridge, MA: Harvard University Press.

Logan, R. W., (1967), The Betrayal of the Negro, from Rutherford B. Hayes to Woodrow Wilson. New York: Collier Books.

Marburry, C. H., (1979), "The Decline in Black-owned Rural Land: Challenge to the Historically Black Institutions of Higher Education" in *The Black Rural Landowner-Endangered Species*. Edited by L. McGee and R. Boone. Westport, CT: Greenwood Press.

Moseman, A., (1971), Building Agricultural Research Systems in Developing Nations. New York: Agricultural Development Council.

National Commission on Agriculture, (1976), Report of the National Commission on Agriculture, 1976. Part XI: Research, Education and Extension. New Delhi. Governemnt of India, Ministry of Agriculture and Irrigation.

National Research Council, (1972), Report of the Committee on Research Advisory to the U.S. Department of Agriculture. Glenn Pound (ed.). Washington, D.C.: National Technical Information Services for the National Academy of Sciences.

Nehru, J., (1954), *Jawaharlal Nehru's Speeches 1949-53*. New Delhi: Publications Division, Ministry of Information and Broadcasting, Government of India.

Reddy, A., (1976), "Trojan Horse'. *Ceres*, (March-April): 40-43.

Richards, P., (1985), *Indigenous Agricultural Revolution: Ecology and Food Production in West Africa*. Boulder, CO: Westview Press.

Schor, (1983), "The Black Presence in the U.S. Cooperative Extension Service to 1983: A Profile". Typescript. Revised Edition.

Shiva, V. and J. Bandyopadhyay, (1980), "The Large and Fragile Community of Scientists in India". *Minerva*, 18 (4): 575-94.

Spitzberg, I.J., (1980), "Introduction" in *Universities and the International Distribution of Knowledge*. Edited by Irving J. Spitzberg, Jr., New York, Praeger.

UEC Report, (1962), The Report of the University Education Commission (December 1948-August 1949). Vol. I. Publication No. 606. Reprint of 1950 edition. New Delhi: Ministry of Education, Government of India.

10

BILATERAL CURRICULUM DEVELOPMENT FOR ASSISTANCE IN FOOD SECURITY FOR LUSO-PHONE AFRICA

TIMOTHY L. KOEHNEN, JOSÉ PORTELA and ARTUR CRISTÕVÃO

Introduction

Prior to the development of the major globalization theme of this paper, the authors would like to address briefly the role of extension by extension agents in the improvement and transformation of low and medium resource family farms in developing nations to enhance quality of life. Although the issue of training extension agents will be discussed in some detail, a brief overview of an individual extension agent strategy and philosophy will follow. These ideas have developed from individual study and contacts with international and professional associations. They play a leading role in stimulating dialogue between and within developing nations in order to improve extension education in the context for decreasing the disadvantages from the haves and have nots.

The field level agent is an educator, not a regulatory agent, who also needs adequate communication skills to discuss general agriculture problems or events with his/her constituency. The traditional ideas encountered in these groups and community gatherings require that the agent understand, identify, verify and appropriate catalogues for the further study of endogenous knowledge prior to accepting or rejecting the technologies. The process of informing other potential users of endogenous knowledge or farm activities that are successful or failures only occurs through cultivated linkages with all actors in the agricultural system, including a multidisciplinary subject matter specialist team. The problems and needs not resolvable by the farming community and field level extension agent require that agents communicate with a subject matter specialist team for a holistic appraisal; and who in turn can be backstopped by regional agricultural research institutions to effectively work in the transformation of the low resource farming community.

The field level extension agents or educators also require skills for assisting the low resource farmers in improving their leadership and organizational skills and thereby empowering farm families in the democratic development process which can improve food security. The low resource farm family communities participate in decision-making to assist policy-makers in visualizing the reality of the situation of these families in the formulation of policy that balances national, regional and local interests.

One other component, outside of the farm community and family (utilize), and yet a part of the agricultural knowledge system, encompasses the preparation of extension educators and other human power resources to work effectively in the development process. The paper will now describe a specific research study within an active participatory curriculum development project in northern Portugal. The project involved the teaching-learning process in the formal educational system, which enhanced the professional knowledge and skills of mid-career extensionist and educators.

The success within the interactive curriculum development process can form a proposed skeletal design for similar types of Luso-American initiatives encapsulating a future vision to design and implement agricultural and rural educational and development programmes for luso-phone Africa. For example, a future bilateral working group (University staff from United States and Portugal) can involve themselves with the host government in a cooperative effort to transform and implement educational programmes that are relevant for the luso-phone African conditions. Specifically, the prudent initiatives can assist to improve the food security for the continent.

How does a curriculum development project in northern Portugal relate to the improvement of food security in Africa? We have recently read of the influential cooperative effort by the Luso-American peace effort in Angola. These diplomatic successes are communicated to a world-wide audience overnight. However, the authors believe the less spectacular cooperative efforts within integrated rural development activities open the door for pressing, African educational and rural development projects for Portuguese speaking nations: Angola, Mocambique, Guiné-Bissau, São Tomé e Principe and Cabo Verde. The Universidade de Trçs-os-Montese Alto Douro(UTAD)/Fundaĩio Luso-Americana para o Desenvolvimento (FLAD) educational project initiates a possible continuous Luso-American partnership dedicated to the improvement of the African global food situation.

The vision of the authors is to diversify and extend the Luso-American development effort into Africa. The FLAD, a bilateral foundation, or a similarly structured organization with the assistance of the Portuguese and United States of America agricultural universities can negotiate and implement assistance programmes and projects with the particular African nation government as the partner. A tri-partnership process in the organization of activities can assist the African nations to identify their future development goals and the resources available to them to carry out the development process. The specific types of development programmes to be highlighted by the above proposed institutions fall within the agricultural knowledge system. One example of cooperation can encompass the study of extension's and agricultural research's role in the development process. Early projects must link to educational programmes for the training of the necessary human resources which can expand the knowledge system in luso-phone Africa. This involves the training and development of administrators, technicians, and front-line workers to assist rural populations to increase their food production and consumption. The understanding of the knowledge system for the training of these key development workers precludes indigenous participation in the formulation of a relevant agricultural educational system. The system eventually matches the needs of the nation through human resource development and thereby establishes compatible preparation for the world of work. The process should involve a complex appraisal of the present situation in these countries in order to understand their specific needs. It also requires donor nations which can interact effectively and integrate their experiences in order to begin the many initiatives and actions for the recuperation and development of these countries. The on-going and past cooperative efforts and actions by donor partners can serve as a catalyst to promote additional development in the African luso-phone agricultural knowledge system.

With the above situation in mind, the bilateral experience in northern Portugal points the way for further multilateral projects outside the region. The bilateral effort of UTAD and FLAD in educati onal and rural development within the less developed region of Trçs-os-Montes establishes precedents for cooperation with the countries of Africa lacking food security. The precedent of the interactive initiative suggests a possible form of curriculum development for Africa. The spin-off from the curriculum development project to be discussed and other rural development projects in Portugal can stress a people-oriented process for an innovative multi-lateral development effort for Africa.

Let's take a look at the specific case in which funding from a bilateral foundation has institutionalized an educational programme. The programme will be described briefly in the background context for an interactive curriculum development process for the understanding of the African agricultural knowledge systems.

The UTAD with FLAD consultative and financial assistance has initiated the first Master's Degree in Rural Development and Extension Education in Portugal. The design and implementation of the Master's degree has taken place within a university which had been described until quite recently as a Polytechnical Agricultural Institute with many faculty working toward a doctorate. The recent institutional building involved various established institutions and foreign government donors. After the preliminary institutional building, the University still had no graduate programme with a design involving coursework and thesis. In addition to the lack of an on-going graduate programme within the concept of a European or North American Graduate College, the university had inadequate library materials and computer facilities for graduate research which parallels the disparity of the region in which the university has developed.

The design and implementation of a new degree programme within a relatively new University required additional time and financial resources to get the programme established and fine tuned than is the case, for example, when the curriculum falls within an institutionalized graduate college with adequate library and computer facilities, etc. In this type of implementation process, one cannot piggyback or be backstopped on non-existing infrastructure. Therefore, additional financial resources were required for educational infrastructure such as the purchase of instructional and library materials, capital expenditure for equipment (computers, copier, office equipment) and transport as well as the hiring of a long and short term staff including expatriates. It was also necessary that a line item for the training of faculty members to a Master and Ph.D. level be considered for educational programme continuity in the future i.e. replacement of expatriate teaching staff. These factors were considered within a proposal developed and approved through a joint-venture between a funding agency, FLAD and the UTAD. This type of joint-venture should be proposed for assistance programmes in luso-phone Africa.

The grant from FLAD provided partial funding to reduce the constraints in implementing a degree programme in a newly functioning university. The FLAD, a newly created institution in Portugal, assisted to defray some of these costs for the implementation of a degree programme at UTAD. The FLAD has some innovative characteristics, the major financial source for the foundation are part of a donor as sistance package to Portugal. The foundation funds are invested in both money-making activities (to ensure the survival and longevity of the foundation) and development related projects such as the Master's Degree in Rural Development and Extension Education at UTAD. A similar foundation might be appropriate for the African Portuguese speaking countries.

This type of foundation can be a prototype or model for future development programmes in luso-phone Africa. The foundation model allows for a more active participation of the host country in the development process. Also, the host country professionals can be a part of a supervised experienced career entry programme by working with and alongside experienced donor staff placed in the foundation in the early stages of operations. We would suggest that donor and host government (i.e. the foundation) need to collabourate in a partnership mode to layout relevant development policy and strategy. After donor financial and consultative assistance ends, the foundation survivability is strengthened with a continuous agenda for other development projects through the auspices of country personnel. The foundation personnel should have representative perceptions and viewpoints for the development of the agricultural knowledge system.

One specific type of project that is crucial and relevant involves curriculum development for the conditions in Africa. The cooperative effort between Portugal, United States and the African country is more complex, but establishes one important element in the process for the improvement in the agricultural knowledge system in the former colonies of Portugal. The common language between the luso-phcne African countries and Portugal with U.S. consultative and financial assistance establishes a relevant tri-partite developmental action. Every partner has to make sacrifices, investments and contributions in the process, to improve the global food security.

Curriculum Development Study

In the particular research study, the authors explored the perceptions of a population of directors of extension at the local level of the Portuguese rural extension system. In order to visualize where the extension system fits overall, a prior description of the government organization scheme and the interrelationship will follow. The programme has evolved from a highly centralized planned and organized system to one in which continental Portugal has been organized into seven regional services (planning and implementation organizations) with relative autonomy for their region. The seven Direcíçes Regionais have within each a director/coordinator who is directly linked to the national Minister of Agriculture, Fisheries and Food. The director in each region oversees the offices of regional agrarian planning, administration, staff and farmer training, rural extension, protection and production of animal and plant, agricultural marketing, rural infrastructure and other offices with specific functions. The integrated rural development strategy includes the above components. There is a sub-director responsible for rural extension in each region who has responsibility to administer and promote extension education through and with the Directors of Agrarian Zones. The present system is under discussion and might be changed. The agrarian zones are made up of freguesias and concelhos which are political government units within each region. The agrarian zones represent relatively homogenous geopolitcal/farming areas and its numbers differs from region to region.

Population

The national descriptive study was aimed at Directors of Agrarian Zones in continental Portugal, and has assisted in the identification and weighing of the functions and activities of extensionists involved in the development of the agricultural sector. The group that rated the competencies plays a role in communicating new ideas and technologies to the rural population. They also assist to communicate concerns and needs from the freguesias and concelhos to regional and national developmental agencies. The directors in this group are attempting to assist the rural population to increase their agricultural production and income and to improve the quality of life of the rural family. The daily tasks include the management and supervision of the work of their staff (rural extensionists, sanitation and animal health officers, and support staff), preparation of financial budgets, the planning and implementation of educational programmes and campaigns, and the maintenance of positive relationships with other rural development agencies.

What are the characteristics of these Directors of Agrarian Zones? What are the competencies in extension administration, planning, and evaluation that were perceived as necessary by these Directors of Agrarian Zones for an extensionist? What are the time constraints of these directors for carrying out administration/ supervision, planning and evaluation of their rural development programmes? The paper will present data to answer these questions.

Purpose of the Study

The purpose of the study was to identify necessary competencies through the responses by the Directors of Agrarian Zones within twelve competency categories, but in this paper the authors focus only on the areas of administration, planning, and evaluation. The rating by these administrators can serve as the basis for designing training programmes and curriculum development programmes for change agents within both rural extension and other development agencies. These administrators also estimated their time spent in administration/supervision, programme evaluation, programme planning, and other functions. Secondary attention will be given to the characteristics of the population of these administrators such as educational level, sex, age, and other biographical data.

More specifically, the paper describes the responses of Portuguese Directors of Agrarian Zones to the perceived necessity of 23 distinct individual competencies, using a 4 point scale. The information will be used to alert trainers to the necessary activities to be performed by extensionists. The identification of necessary competencies by the sample will assist in designing and reformulating educational and training programmes. It can also serve to delineate the individual job description for an extensionist in Portugal. An assumption in the study is that the population of Portuguese administrators has both administrative and extension experience to rate the necessity of various competencies.

Methodology

The population for the study consisted of all Directors of Agrarian Zones in continental Portugal. The population is located in seven regions: Entre Douro e Minho, Trçs-os-Montes, Beira Litoral, Beira Interior, Ribatejo e Oeste, Alentejo, and Algarve. The response rate for the study was 79 per cent of the population of 64 administrators for 66 Zonas Agrçrias. It occurred that two directors had to manage two agrarian zones at the time of the study (Entre Douro e Minho and Beiro Interior). This self-selected sample will be used to describe the responses from the 52 respondents.

The complete questionnaire was (a) developed through a review of literature in rural development and extension, which identified specific duties and tasks and also used competencies from similar survey research studies, (b) translated from English to Portuguese, (c) validated and field tested through Master's degree students at UTAD, in Rural Development and Extension, as well as proofed and edited by two Portuguese extension specialists, (d) mailed to the population of administrators and (e) coded and the data inputted into a desk-top computer and the responses analyzed by a statistical programme.

The mail-out packet consisted of a letter of introduction, the questionnaire, and a self-addressed envelope with postage. The process included a follow-up reminder letter which was sent after four weeks to those who had not returned the questionnaire. After 9 weeks, the study had a 64 per cent response rate. In order to determine if the group that had not responded was different in any way from the group which had responded to the mailout, a questionnaire was sent again to the non-responding group and an appeal was also made to their supervisors in the regional headquarters to request their participation. By this action, the study received an additional 10 questionnaires, which when analyzed did not differ significantly from the group as a whole. The final response rate was 79 per cent, which was calculated by assuming that each administrator was distinct for the 66 zonas agrçrias. The paper describes the responses to only 3 of the 12 competency categories. The other categories were: programme execution, understanding human behaviour, socio-cultural aspects, teaching, communication, participation, farming systems, appropriate technology and young farmer organizations. The study is related to similar professional competency studies which came out of programmes at the University of Florida, Pennsylvania State, University of Arizona and others.

Characteristics of Directors of Agrarian Zones

The participants in this study were Directors of Agrarian Zones in continental Portugal. What are the characteristics of this group who are administrators and in some cases extensionists? In the group that responded to the questionnaire (79 per cent of the population), the study found, that nationally, 70 per cent passed their infancy or adolescence in rural areas. The proportion of female Directors of Agrarian Zones was 23 per cent. The average age of the group was 41 years. The educational level of the group of administrators was that 18 per cent had achieved the Bacharel degree and 82 per cent had achieved the equivalent to the IngÄnieur Agronome. The group predominately had their majors within the agricultural sciences, while one had a degree in rural sociology. The work experience of the group shows that 21 per cent have 5 or less years of experience, while 79% have 6 or more years of work experience in extension. The average number of staff that are supervised by these zonal heads is 10. With this data, a calculation was made to determine the number of farms per extensionist in Portugal. The rough data indicate an approximate ratio of 1 extensionist to 900 farms. The number of farms was calculated from the 1979 farm census (INE).

Competencies of Change Agents

The paper will now move into the responses by these directors as to the need of various competencies within programme planning, extension administration, and evaluation. The frequencies and means to be presented can assist in the identification of knowledge and skills necessary to carry out the role as a change agent in these categories. The information obtained can also facilitate the process of identifying educational objectives for extension education curriculum and training programs for extensionist.

The responses of the Directors of Agrarian Zones were tabulated using a 4 point scale, with degree four coinciding with absolutely necessary, degree three necessary, degree two seldom necessary and degree one not necessary. Some directors refused to rate the competency and for this reason the total (N) varies from competency to competency.

Table 10.1 shows the responses to competencies involving the extension administration category. The responses show that the majority of directors rated the various competencies as necessary or absolutely necessary. However, in competencies *f* and *j*, the data reflect that over 30 per cent of the directors rated the competencies as seldom or not necessary. Competency *f* might reflect that directors perceive this role to be under their influence rather than a role for an extensionist. Also, the authors find it quite unbelievable that 30 per cent of the Directors perceive computer skills to be seldom or not necessary in the age of the computer.

TABLE 10.1: National Proportional Responses by Directors of Agrarian Zones and Means on the Necessity of Competencies Associated with Extension Administration

Extension Administration	Percentages Degree of Necessity					
The extensionist should be able:	4	3	2	1	MEAN	N
(a) to outline procedures for resolving conflicts and maintain staff morale	50	40	6	4	3.4	50
(b) to outline appropriate staff recruitment	31	49	8	12	3.0	51
(c) to select and supervise staff	36	42	8	14	3.0	50
(d) to conduct a needs assessment evaluation for project planning	22	60	16	2	3.0	49
(e) to outline conditions under which a project programme may need to be adjusted	27	67	6	0	3.2	5
(f) to determine alternative strategies for overcoming the lack of political power on the part of project administrators.	16	48	20	16	2.6	50
(g) to identify both the private and public institutions involved in the agricultural knowledge system, devoted to technology development, transfer, and utilization of technology	43	49	6	2	3.4	51
(h) to revise programmes when necessary to adjust to an emergency situation	35	61	4	0	3.3	51
(i) to collabourate in budget preparation and elabouration	16	62	14	8	2.9	51
(j) to utilize micro computer for word processing and other functions	13	57	20	10	2.7	51

Table 10.2 which shows the responses to the competencies related to programme planning in Portugal. The majority of directors perceived that the programme planning competencies were necessary for an extensionist. However, competencies *d* and *g* were perceived by over 30 per cent to 50 per cent of the directors as seldom necessary or not necessary. They do not agree to the necessity of advisory councils or the historical and philosophical understanding of rural extension by the extension agent. In some respect, it might be necessary to sensitize these directors as to the important role the advisory council can play in identifying community problems and needs as well as in the process of legitimizing the extension programme.

TABLE 10.2: National Proportional Responses by Directors of Agrarian Zones and Means on the Necessity of Competencies Associated with Program Planning

Programme Planning	Percentages Degree of Necessity					
The extensionist should be able:	4	3	2	1	MEAN	N
(a) to formulate realistic goals for the extension programme	76	20	4	0	3.7	51
(b) to consider agricultural policy in preparing programmes	54	42	4	0	2.9	50
(c) to conduct a needs assessment based on clientele needs, interests, and problems	82	16	0	2	3.8	51
(d) to organize and use an advisory committee	20	50	28	2	62.9	50
(e) to prepare an annual and long range plan of work	45	49	6	0	3.4	51
(f) to develop a calendar of events	69	31	0	0	3.7	51
(g) to outline the history, philosophy, and objectives of the extension organization in Portugal/region	2	48	36	14	2.4	50

Table 10.3 shows that there is a high consistency in the response by these directors. The majority rate all the competencies within evaluation at least necessary for extensionists. One concern from the data deals with the directors' perceptions concerning the necessity to interpret research results to the farmer. In competency *d*, 34 per cent of the directors perceived this as seldom necessary for the role of the extensionist. This indicator normally is considered to be important in the necessary institutional interfacing roles between research and extension

(Swanson,1982). It might be important to question further the reason for not perceiving this as necessary by some zonal heads. The role of a research linker or communicator of research results to the producers has been acknowledged as important in the transfer of technology which is one aspect of extension. Are these directors concerned more with the role of an extensionist as a process facilitator rather than a agency linker? The literature points out that the extensionist needs to perform multi-roles in the rural extension agency.

TABLE 10.3: National Proportional Responses by Directors of Agrarian Zones and Means on the Necessity of Competencies Associated with Extension Evaluation

Evaluation	Percentages Degree of Necessity					
The extensionist should be able:	4	3	2	1	MEAN	N
(a) to carry out inquiries to understand the needs of the clientele	41	43	12	4	3.2	51
(b) to interpret the impact of change upon the clientele served	63	31	2	4	3.5	51
(c) to use research findings when making recommendations to farmers	67	31	2	0	3.6	51
(d) to interpret and evaluate research findings reported by research institutions for extension clientele	30	36	26	8	2.9	50
(e) to evaluate the performance of the extension staff	38	40	16	6	3.1	50
(f) to use questionnaires to seek information	18	53	25	4	2.8	51
(g) to analyze and interpret results derived from a questionnaire	31	49	14	6	3.1	51

Time Spent Performing Functions by the Directors of Agrarian Zones

What is the time necessary for Directors of Agrarian Zones to plan and execute the rural development programmes? In Table 10.4, the reader can observe the average time Directors of Agrarian Zones spend performing tasks within administration/supervision, programme planning, programme evaluation and other functions (52 directors responded to this question). The data present the average time of all directors in performing these broad functions. In the analysis of the functions, the data verifies that these administrators spend over half their time in administration/supervision while devoting only 14 per cent of their time to planning and evaluation. In contrast, the data show that they spend 30 per cent of their time in functions outside of that of an administrator. It should be noted that the lack of time spent within planning and evaluation raises important issues and should be studied further. The cycle of planning and evaluation is weak for reasons that might be linked to a dependency situation with regional and national planning organizations.

TABLE 10.4: Estimates in Percentages by Directors of Agrarian Zones for their time spent Performing Specific Functions

Functions	Percent of time devoted to Functions
Administration/Supervision	57
Programme Planning	8
Programme Evaluation	6
Field Demonstrations/Farm Visits	9
Teaching/Training	7
Non-Programmed Extension Activities	7
Other Activities	7

Conclusions from Curriculum Research

The purpose of the research study was to identify professional competencies through the perceptions of Directors of Agrarian Zones for an extensionist in Portugal. In this particular paper, the authors selected three major extension areas (administration, planning, and evaluation) to investigate. The selection was based upon the interest in obtaining a mini-profile for an extensionist, but also to show the reader a contradiction in our results between the perceptions of the Directors of Agrarian Zones for an extensionist and the time directors spent performing various functions in these three areas.

On the whole, the respondents were quite uniform in their appraisal of the necessity for the professional competencies. This consistency in rating competencies as necessary or absolutely necessary should be seen as a positive first step in the curriculum development process. However, a cautionary note is based on two factors: (1) the data show that administrators spend only 14 per cent of their time in programme planning and evaluation, while consistently rating the pre-selected listing of competencies of the survey research instrument positively. These respondents rated competencies without an in teractive interview process that did not allow for triangulation of the questionnaire responses with probing interviews which might change the results. (2) the alternative factor is that the administrative and policy structure of the Direcìçes Regionais allows for minimum time for these functions by Directors of Agrarian Zones. The respondent perceive the importance of the professional competencies, but has no time or there are time management constraints to perform these essential functions by the directors. These zonal heads might be constrained by regional or national policies that interfere in the actual time required for programme planning and evaluation at the level of the agrarian zones.

This study has assisted to develop a profile for an extensionist in Portugal and the information can be utilized to develop training programmes as well as analyze and adjust on-going educational programmes in rural development and extension education within Portugal. The profile itself might serve to develop a national job description for entering extensionist in agrarian zones or other extension services. An additional question needs to be answered and that is which competencies need to be attained and when by the extensionist to determine curriculum programmes for their pre or in-service training. The perceptions of extensionist, specialist and the curriculum developers must also play a role in this job description process.

The study can be used to confirm the necessity to prepare multi-purpose extensionists who can perform as dynamic facilitators and educators in the rural development process. The study determined a profile for an extensionist linked to their performance in the three areas. These educational and/or professional competencies that were identified as necessary can serve as a preliminary point for further discussion in the role of a non-formal educator in Portugal.

The curriculum development process has been established in Portugal through a bilateral cooperative action. The formula for the interactive group process established in this particular situation can be used as a starting point to establish similar joint ventures in Africa to improve agricultural knowledge system. The actions can consider institutional development within agricultural knowledge systems which establishes the bridge for inter-institutional communication in the system.

Summary and Recommendations

In light of the above experience, what should be the future cooperative effort in Africa within agricultural and extension education with Portugal? The analysis of past interventions by donors in a gricultural and extension education programmes point to the importance of improving the communication network with established government programmes and community-based groups. The projects cannot be a isolated success story without linkages to the present system. We need from the beginning to integrate in order to avoid institutional duplication within various regions. The programmes should be an expansion or improvement in the present agricultural knowledge system.

The generation, proliferation and implementation of a new development project without the intra or inter institutional communication linkages spawn pockets or islands of development projects without the necessary integration into the national agricultural knowledge system. All proposed interventions should involve the various governmental and community institutions in the process. We need to avoid establishing unnecessary projects of alternative extension or research institutional systems which do not integrate with existing development institutions and their staff.

Indigenous knowledge assessment and community participation also prevails as an essential component for the assessment process. It serves to enhance the identification of endogenous needs and assists in relevant policy development for food security. The appropriate understanding of the agricultural food system enhances the institutional development process in which the educational curriculum and research agenda link to the global system. In any intervention we need to ask ourselves, what has to happen and who participates within the coordination of policy, organization, and management within the agricultural research, extension and training system to improve food production and consumption. The total assessment process should be interactive with government agencies and key elements in the community and the "limited resource" agricultural population. The development worker must be oriented to listen and maintain an interactive dialogue with the essential and relevant contacts in the agricultural system.

In order to begin with these assumptions bilateral and multilateral projects should be developed, United States universities can form partnerships with Portuguese agricultural universities to enhance the needs assessment process and the following project implementation stage. The partnership can facilitate the development of luso-phone Africa. The synergistic partnership can speed-up the improvement in food production, processing and consumption for the limited resource agricultural population.

The partnership can improve human capital by expanding educational and employment opportunities through joint efforts at a more rapid pace. The process can also facilitate the training of luso-phone Africans. Higher educational opportunities for motivated young staff can be enhanced through access to both Portuguese and U.S. universities. Those that are not bilingual can enter Portuguese universities which remain more familiar to the African students. The common language allows for a reduced time limit in the training of technicians. The student is not required to learn English prior to entry into a U.S. undergraduate programme. The amount of time in training is reduced and the individual can return to the work place earlier to assist the limited resource farmers. The alternative for more advanced African students is that U.S. Ph.D. educational programmes allows them greater flexibility in the type and number of programmes to enter. The selection process must consider early on key people to be involved in the training of the trainers.

At the present time, English and French languages dominate the agricultural knowledge system literature. The donor and recipient nations must begin to identify and translate scientific papers and key texts, for example, to Portuguese. One of the limitations in development for luso-phone Africa is the scarcity of agricultural instructional materials to facilitate the teaching-learning process. The world needs greater cooperation between the luso-phone, anglo-phone and franco-phone nations in identifying, translating and distributing extension and educational instructional materials for developing nations. The materials should be up-to-date and relevant for the socio-cultural situation in which the front-line agricultural workers attempt to decrease the disadvantages for the limited resource farmer.

The bottom line for greater potential in the development process for Africa will be cooperation by multilateral agencies to improve global food security. These types of programmes should be similar to the past cooperation by nations in the security and reconstruction of Europe and North America during and prior to the cold war. The time is at hand that greater international effort be forthcoming in agricultural extension and education development projects in Africa. The multilateral effort requires the same enthusiasm, sacrifice, investment and cooperation to assist in the development of Africa. The globalization of these types of development projects to improve food security for the limited resource farmer is at the crossroads of the so called world order.

REFERENCES

Ban A. W. V. D. and Hawkins H. S., (1988), *Agricultural extension*. Essex, England: Longman Scientific & Technical.

Blackburn, D. J. (ed.), (1984), *Extension handbook*. Canada: University of Guelph.

Boyle, P. G., (1981), *Planning better programmes*. USA: McGraw-Hill Book Company.

Casley, D. J., Kumar K., (1987), *Project monitoring and evaluation in agriculture*. London: World Bank Publication.

Chiavenato, I., (1987), Administraîïo, teoria, processo e prçtica. Lisboa: McGraw-Hill, Ltda.

Fenerstein, M. T., (1986), *Partners in evaluation, evaluating development and community programmes with participants*. Hong Kong: MacMillan Publishers.

INE, (1979), Recenseamento agrÆcola. Lisboa: Instituto Nacional de EstatÆstica.

Isaac, S. and Michael, W.B., (1985), *Handbook in research and evaluation*. San Diego: EDITS Publishers.

Johnston, B. F. and Kilby, P., (1974), The design and implementation of strategies for agricultural development. *Agricultural Administration*. I(3), 165-197.

Jones, G. E. and Rolls, M., (1982), *Progress in rural extension and community development*. Toronto: John Wiley and Sons.

Kaimowitz, D., Snyder, M. and Engel, P., (1989), A conceptual framework for studying the links between agricultural research and technology transfer in developing countries. The Hague: ISNAR.

Koehnen, T.L. and Gaspar, L., (1990), Levantamento Nacional Sobre Administraîïo e Extensïo dentro das Zonas Agrçrias. Proceedings of 1 Jornadas Sobre o Mundo Rural, Braganma, Portugal.

Little, I. M. D., Mirrlees, J. A., (1974), *Project appraisal and planning for developing countries*. Sydney: Gower.

Ministério da Agricultura, Florestase Alimentaïïo, (1984), Os serviîos de extensïo rural nas zonas agrçrias. Lisboa: MinistÄrio da Agricultura Florestas e Alimentaïïo.

Moris, J., (1981), Managing induced rural development. Bloomington, Indiana: International Development Institute.

Ongondo, W. N., (1985), The professional competencies needed by intermediate agricultural extension personnel in the Kenya agricultural extension service. (Doctoral dissertation. Pennsylvania State University at Penns ylvania, (1984). Dissertation Abstracts International.

Roling, N., (1988), *Extension science: Information systems in agricultural development*. London: Cambridge University Press.

Schmiel, A. A. and Faas, R. C., (1975), A research approach to institutional alternatives in the administration of agrarian development programmes. *Agricultural Administration*. 2(4), 285-365.

Sims, H. and Leonard, D., (1989), *The political economy of the development and transfer of agricultural technologies*. The Hague: ISNAR.

Swanson, B. E., (1982), Analyzing agricultural technology systems: A research report. Illinois: Office of International Agriculture, University of Illinois at Urbana-Champaign.

11

INTERNATIONALIZATION OF THE POST-SECONDARY AGRICULTURAL CURRICULUM

DON R. KING and ROBERT A. MARTIN

> "America's young face a set of new national and international circumstances about which they have only the faintest of notions. They are, globally speaking, blind, deaf, and dumb; and thus handicapped, they will soon determine the future directions of this nation."

Examination of the changes in agriculture and the entire educational system indicates great interest in internationalization. Bonham (1986:6) called for a major review of international education at colleges and universities across the U.S.A. A number of factors seem to be driving this movement. These factors include economics and economic competitiveness; interest of students, advances in agribusiness; relevance of educational programmes in terms of the global nature of many problems; current and future market and job opportunities; and the need to interact with colleagues in other countries to gain access to information being generated elsewhere (Henson and Noel, 1989:19-25). These factors and others indicate the need for internationalization of the college curriculum if our agriculture is to remain competitive in today's global marketplace.

Many universities and colleges have been examining the international dimensions of their programmes and have found that the process of internationalization of the curriculum is a priority, and that the environment has never been better for action directed to international education. Americans are beginning not only to understand, but to appreciate the critical relevance of an internationalized educational system. According to Whiteford (1990:5), to internationalize the post-secondary agricultural curriculum means first and foremost to recognize that "they" are "we" and that diversity is a catalyst for the process of growth.

The purpose here is to explain what it means to internationalize the curriculum, why the college curriculum needs to be internationalized, what specifically needs to be internationalized, and how this internationalization process can be accomplished. A related issue focuses on the implications that this process of internationalization has for post-secondary institutions around the world.

What Does It Mean?

Internationalization, global education and other related terms may mean different things to different people. Hanvey (1976, as quoted by Tye, 1990:5) provided a definition that set the stage for the discussion of the issue:

> Global education involves learning about those problems and issues that cut across national boundaries, and about the interconnectedness of systems – ecological, cultural, economic, political and technological. Global education involves perspective taking – seeing things through the eyes and minds of others – and it means the realization that while individuals and groups may view life differently, they also have common needs and wants.

This definition of internationalization helps us put the issue into perspective. It also helps us begin the process of developing a systematic approach for infusing the study of international agricultural systems into the agriculture curriculum. The perspective gained from this definition is that students and educators begin to focus on the concept of awareness, inter-relationships, understanding, broadening perceptions, enhancing knowledge and skills, and cultural enlightenment. Any systematic approach to internationalization of the curriculum will mean that institutions of higher learning around the world must learn to collabourate. This collabouration would take the form of research, teaching, exchanges of teachers and students and scholarly activity.

Why Internationalize?

The role of the U.S.A. as a leader among nations is certainly changing. Despite the position of leadership provided by the U.S.A. among nations of the world for over 50 years, Americans seem ill-prepared for the changes in business, manufacturing, diplomacy, science and technology that have come with an interdependent world. Effectiveness in such a world requires a citizenry and workforce whose knowledge is sufficiently international in scope to cope with global interdependence.

Thus, "education" must serve to develop an awareness of the global nature of the agriculture industry, as it has become increasingly apparent that if a person is to be considered educated in agriculture, he/she must be cognizant of the inter-relationships of various agricultural systems and the governments, cultures and societies in which they function (Martin, 1989:4-5). In the U.S.A., a large number of studies carried out at the national, regional, and local levels have indicated a dismaying lack of knowledge of geography, languages, cultures, political and economic systems, and other intenationally related topics among university students and the public (Lambert, 1989:1-8).

Fundamental forces in the global economy over the last 20 years have resulted in changes to the present structure of the international economy. Chief among these forces are the significant technological breakthroughs in transportation and communication services. An equally important factor is the computer revolution. These three developments have given us a truly global village, and agriculture is no exception to this technological movement. These technological phenomena could play a significant role in bringing institutions of higher learning closer together. Students and faculty at related institutions around the world could link to expand knowledge and understanding. Developing countries have much to gain from these linkages in terms of enhancing research and teaching. More advanced countries have much to gain in terms of understanding of cultures and testing of agricultural principles and theories.

These technological breakthroughs appear to be driven by two basic forces: (1) increased education to the so-called developing countries of the world, and (2) the growing capacity for agricultural research to be conducted all over the world (Schuh, 1989:1-8). These developments in the international economy and their implications, according to Dorner (1989:85-90), require nothing less than a major change in the education we provide for our young people in the United States of America.

It is estimated that during the next decade more than 50 per cent of agriculture college graduates will be employed by companies directly involved in international trade (Henson and Noel, 1989:19-25). Our students will be at a serious disadvantage, as will our nation as a whole, if they are not properly prepared to compete in the international economy (Schuh, 1989:1-8). Having a global perspective positions us to take advantage of new economic realities, and to better prepare our students as world citizens (Purdue Report, 1990:1).

According to Martin (1987:2-4) the mission of agricultural education in the United States of America (U.S.A.) is to foster the development of knowledge and skills related to the industry of agriculture. Pursuant to this mission is a growing need for students and educators to develop an understanding of world agriculture and its impact on U.S. agriculture as well as its effect on local production and marketing of food and fiber. To address this need requires the development of a systematic approach for infusing various aspects of international agriculture systems into the study of agriculture at all levels of the U.S.A. agricultural education programme.

Specifically, the following major concepts provide the rationale for the development of a systematic approach to the study of international agriculture systems:

* There is a need for students and educators to develp a global awareness of agriculture.
* There is a need to understand the importance of agriculture in international trade.
* There is a need for a better understanding of international agricultural marketing systems, economics and agricultural production and management systems.
* There is a need for a better understanding of different cultures and their political systems and how they relate to the food production and education systems.
* There is a need for students and educators to be aware of internationally oriented career opportunities.
* There is a need for students and educators to find ways to enhance problems solving and creative thinking skills.
* There is a need for students and educators to develop an ap-

preciation for different language skills and develop means to build cultural linkages.

* There is a need for students and educators to develop an understanding of the inter-relationships between education, the scientific support base and the total food and agricultural system (Martin, 1987:2-4).

What to Internationalize?

"Internationalization" has been defined as "the incorporation of international dimensions, content and considerations into the teaching, research, extension and public service functions of the university to enhance their relevance in an interdependent world" (Internationalization of U.S. Universities Conference Proceedings, 1990:2). The internationalization of colleges of agriculture is a logical outgrowth of the mission of all land grant universities, and is an essential element of any world-class educational institution.

What to internationalize in a college or university will encompass several important spheres in the institution. The more obvious ones include administrative leadership, organization, faculty development, curriculum, resources and programme activities (Klassen, 1984:8). Post-seconday institutions around the world should give serious consideration to broadening the curriculum through linkages with institutions in other parts of the world. Collabourative teaching and research via telecommunication networks would enrich the curriculum of all institutions.

Most importantly, the curriculum content requires close evaluation. According to Martin (1987:2-4) the curriculum related to agriculture should emphasize, at the very least, the following international subject matter:

* Compare and contrast the marketing systems of the U.S. and at least one other country.
* Compare and contrast the trade policies of the U.S. and at least one other country.
* Describe the general geographical and environmental characteristics of a country other than the U.S.A.
* Identify and explain water use and management in selected countries.
* Define the term "green revolution" and explain its impact on

agriculture.

* Identify various soil types and conditions in at least one country other than the U.S.A.
* Explain the food distribution system in a given country.
* Describe the extension education system in a given country.
* Explain the extent of mechanization in a given country.
* Describe how food is processed and handled in a given country.
* Identify and describe major crops and livestock enterprises of a selected country.
* Explain the uses, management and marketing of crops and livestock enterprises.
* Describe the culture and lifestyles of people in another country and explain their impact on agriculture.
* Identify major historical and cultural events and explain their significance to agriculture.
* Describe the leadership, management and work styles of the participants in the given country and explain their significance to agriculture.
* Describe the types of products imported to the country from U.S.A. and exported out of the country to the U.S.A.

How to Internationalize?

The key to the process of internationalizing a university or college rests on the development of a plan and a strategy that is consistent with the mission of the institution (Whiteford, 1990:5). To bring about internationalization, a high proportion of faculty members with a world view are also needed. Library resources should be available and supportive of an international view. Good communication linkages are necessary as interaction with faculty, students and visitors from other nations must take place. Travel courses, internships, and independent study arrangements can also provide students and faculty members with these types of experiences (Acker, 1989:13-14).

Additionally, leadership by deans, instructional leaders and department heads is also necessary. The administration should hire faculty members who can see the world from several perspectives, recognize faculty members who internationalize their course work, who work internationally, or who maintain international contact and contribute to the international literature. They must also see that college and department curriculum committees include faculty members, and students dedicated to a world perspective, and devise and support summer experiences that send individuals to developed or developing countries.

A more specific or immediate approach towards internationalizing an institution is to infuse international concepts directly into the existing subject matter. Infusion of international knowledge, skills and attitudes should take place at all levels and within all courses in the curriculum. Courses in the curriculum from outside the college also need to be taught from the world perspective, and it is the role of faculty members to see that this happens.

Therefore, is essential that faculty members not only know their discipline but know it from several perspectives. Acker (1989:13-14) proposed that each faculty member pursue his or her discipline from three perspectives: the United States, another developed country, and a developing or low-middle income country. For example, does the French class focus on simply getting along in Paris, or also on negotiating wheat sales in French speaking West Africa? Are the middle east religions viewed from the American perspective with the religions only described, or does the instructor lead the student toward viewing the U.S. through the eyes and mind of the religious person of the Middle East?

Some faculty members will not have had international experiences from which they can draw when teaching their courses. In these cases, "internationalization" may be used as an overarching umbrella for discussion. For example, what possible effects will this have on U.S. agriculture? The effects include more competitive global markets (thus, the need to learn about other cultures, other people's desires and needs); increased market areas and profits to seed and chemical companies (thus, the need to learn better sales and marketing tactics); and the need for quality products to be more competitive.

From an environmental perspective, Brazilian soybeans are indirectly causing Brazilian cattle numbers to rise because of the increased need for soybeans for livestock feeds. The increase in cattle numbers has led to a need for more crop and range land, thus the deforestation of thousands of acres of rainforest vegetation and habitat (loss of plant and animal species) has occurred. It is believed that this situation in turn, has a direct effect on the depletion of the ozone layer, which some scientists hold responsible for global climatic weather changes. It is easy to see how one topic leads to the discussion of others, directly or indirectly related to what we do in the United States.

Conclusion

As Martin (1989:1-8) indicated, the need for developing an awareness of the global nature of the agricultural industry has become one of the major issues of our time. It has become increasingly apparent that if a person is to be considered educated in agriculture, he/she must be cognizant of the inter-relationships of various agricultural systems and the governments, cultures and societies in which they function. It is no longer sufficient to know how to produce food and fiber and conduct or manage the many tasks in today's agricultural industry. Development and enhancement of one nation's agricultural system is unavoidably inter-woven with those of other nations. If these developments and inter-relationships are to be successful, it is critical that students of agriculture learn as much as possible about systems of agriculture in cultures and societies around the world.

One can conclude that faculty members serve as the key to successful internationalization of the curriculum. Henson and Noel (1990:1-14) found that the two most important factors stimulating faculty interest in this area were overseas experience and capability in a second language. Once these types of international experiences are acquired, faculty members become tremendous resevoirs of talent and experience, and thus are in a position to globalize their students' educational experiences.

The key to the process of internationalizing a curriculum rests on the development of a plan and a strategy. The development of this strategy should involve an appropriate participatory process which will promote ownership, define opportunities, benefits, and the current status of international efforts. The formulation of an overall plan provides direction and reduces the possibility of fragmentation and loss of opportunities as well as resources.

The international dimension of agriculture needs to be fully integrated into our course offerings, and additional experiences and programmes (exchange, training, etc.) are needed to provide administration, faculty, and students with the skills and knowledge to have at least an awareness, and preferably, an understanding of the world in which we live and work.

REFERENCES

Acker, D., (1989), "Internationalizing agricultural curricula: who will get it done? Educating for a global perspective." Pp. 13-14 in Curricular Innovation for 2005 – Planning for the Future of our Food and Agricultural Sciences. The North Central Curricular Committee Project. University of Wisconsin-Madison and USDA Higher Education Programmes.

Bonham, G.W., (1986), "Education and the world view". Change Magazine Press, *Council on Learning*, Vol. 4:1-10.

Dorner, P., (1989), "Internationalizing university programs to meet the challenges of the 21st century – Educating for a global perspective." Pp. 16-24 in the North Central Region Curricular Committee Project. U niversity of Wisconsin-Madison and USDA Higher Education Programmes.

Hanvey, R., (1976), "An attainable global perspective", Denver, Colorado: Center for Teaching International Relations, in Tye, K.A. Editor (1990:5), "Introduction: the world at a crossroads", Global Education: From Thought to Action, The, 1991 ASCD Yearbook. Alexandria, VA.

Henson, J.B. and J.C. Noel, (1989), "Faculty and the internationalization of the agricultural education." Curriculum for the Year 2005 – Education for a Global Perspective. The North Central Region Curricular Committee Project. University of Wisconsin-Madison and USDA Higher Education Programmes.

Henson, J.B. and J.C. Noel, (1990), "Internationalizing U.S. universities and colleges of agriculture." Pp. 1-14 in Proceedings: Conference on Internationalizing U.S. Universities: A Time for Leadership, Spokane, Washington.

Internationalizing U.S. Universities, (1990), "A time for leadership: summary of conference." International Program Development Office, Washington State University, Pullman, WA.

Klassen, F. H., (1984), Guidelines for Internationalizing Colleges and Universities. Washington: American Association of State Colleges and Universities.

Lambert, R.D., (1989), International Studies and the Undergraduate. Washington D.C.: American Council on Education.

Martin, R., (1987), Project to Infuse an International Perspective into the Agricultural Education Curriculum. The National Council on Agricultural Education, Alexandria, VA.

Martin, R., (1989), "A global perspective for agricultural education." *The Agricultural Education Magazine*, Vol.61(10):4-5.

Purdue Report, (1990), "School of agriculture internationalization committee report." Unpublished manuscript, Purdue University, West Lafayette, IN.

Schuh, G.E., (1989), "The rationale for international agricultural education for the 21st century – educating for a global perspective," in the North Central Region Curricular Committee Project. University of Wisconsin-Madison and USDA Higher Education Programs.

Whiteford, M., (1990), "Ad hoc committee report on the internationalization of Iowa State university." Unpublished manuscript, Iowa State University, Ames, IA.

Smith, D.C. (1989). "The rationale for international agricultural education for the 21st century", educating for a global perspective" in the North Central Region Curricular Committee Project. University of Wisconsin-Madison and USDA Higher Education Program.

12

THE ROLE OF INTERNATIONAL SEMINARS IN THE GLOBALIZATION PROCESS

GARY A. WHITE

"A healthy economy can only be based on an adequate supply of food. Hunger is a distress which tortures mankind worse than any other form of deprivation. People who have to go hungry cannot work effectively . . . . Anyone in favour of peace must give priority to the fight against hunger."

– Ignaz Kiechle

In the remaining years of this century and beyond, it will be necessary to have a collabourative effort to solve the problems of hunger as well as agricultural overproduction in other parts of the world. Only comprehensive general education and training, such as that uniquely offered through international seminars, will allow us to face these new agricultural challenges of globalizatio n (Kiechle, 1986: 2).

The participation in and study of international seminars offer unique opportunities for anyone interested in the globalization process. It is only through international seminars that many citizens from throughout the world meet to share professional and cultural experiences, research findings and work-related dilemmas through group and one-to-one contact.

International seminars are, quite simply, organized gatherings of people from several countries to share the experiences of work and life in their countries in an effort to learn from one another. During seminars about rural youth and specifically rural development, participants often share information about youth development programmes, transportation networks, financial limitations, and support services and programmes.

Youth and Globalization

> "Investment in training and education is rewarding because the young people of today are the decision-makers of tomorrow. If the young people of this world can develop an understanding for each other's particular problems, then I am sure that we shall be able to improve international cooperation and achieve peaceful development."
>
> – German Minister Kiechle (Kiechle, 1986: 4)

Professionals who provide information to and for youth have the opportunity to create change that lasts a lifetime. Youth are, after all, often prepared to try a new approach and tackle jobs that are worthwhile. If rural youth leaders attend a seminar, and become more effective when communicating with youth, the seminar reaches far beyond the first-person scenario.

An important goal of rural youth seminars is to have participants return to their home country and use what they have learned; thus, seminar sponsors and leaders would hope, becoming more effective and efficient in their rural youth leadership roles (Buermann, 1986: 3). Such was the goal of the 13th International Seminar for the Promotion of Rural Youth Work, July 6-25, 1986, in Herrsching, Germany.

The 13th International Seminar for the Promotion of Rural Youth Work

Specifically, as stated in the programme, the seminar had four central themes:

I. *Problem Analysis*. The sharing of experiences and ideas between those representing the developing and industrialized countries. Topics included rural development, vocational training and the role of youth for the development of rural areas.

II. *Planning Organization and Leadership of Rural Youth Groups*. Subjects such as methods used to form groups, techniques of public relations, and evaluating the work done by youth clubs were discussed.

III. *Methods of Working in Groups*. Topics included improving group dynamics, working creatively in groups, and fostering team work.

IV. *Planning and Organization of Rural Youth*. Subjects such as checklists, new planning techniques, and functions were discussed.

The three-week seminar attracted 24 female and 56 male rural youth leaders from 42 countries. Twenty-three participants were from Africa, 24 from Asia, six from America, one from Australia and 26 from Europe. The biannual conference is organized by the Federal Republic of Germany and sponsored by the Food and Agriculture Organization (FAO) of the United Nations.

The 13th international seminar was divided into two stages:

* During the first 12 days, participants discussed topics such as motivation and attitude, expectations and fears, risk creativity, and cooperation during both small and large group discussions. Trips to German farms and rural youth clubs were meant to give participants a better understanding of agriculture and family life on German farms.
* During the second stage (the final nine days of the seminar), participants created 18 projects. They analyzed their country's specific rural problems, surveyed local project conditions, and determined goals that should be achieved with each project. After the projects were completed, small groups formulated a public relations plan to help the projects become a reality.

Cost Versus Results

Few, if any studies have been completed that evaluate the effectiveness of international seminars, thus providing very little supporting information for comparing seminar cost with benefit to participants. If a government or special interest group is interested in sponsoring international conferences, research evaluating the effectiveness of the seminars may help these organizers plan the seminar – financially and otherwise.

The German government did not provide specific information about the cost of the 13th International Seminar for the Promotion of

Rural Youth Work. However, the expense is certainly greater than the cost of hosting a local or national seminar. Transportation, food and housing arrangements for international participants and speakers is more expensive than travel arrangements and room and board for those attending local conferences. The lack of a common language among participants creates further costs – an expense, perhaps, unique to international seminars. During the 13th international seminar, English, French and German language groups gathered, and translators were hired to be available throughout the entire three week period.

Cost and Participants from Developing Nations

Participants were required to finance personal travel expenses. This cost could have been a considerable burden for participants – especially those from the developing nations. However, the Food and Agricultural Organization (FAO) of the United Nations, the German government, and other funding sponsors were called upon for support. The generosity of these organizations allowed many participants from the developing countries to attend the seminar. Participants from developing nations especially appreciated the support, and, therefore, were serious about learning as much as they could during the seminar.

Purpose of the Research

The purpose of the study was to assess the effectiveness of the 13th biannual seminar. More specifically, the objectives were to determine:

* if the exchange of experience between participants improved their understanding of rural youth problems;
* if the seminar improved planning, organizational and leadership skills of participants;
* if the participants' experiences during the seminar improved their ability to work in groups and with supervisors; and
* if the seminar improved participants' planning and organizational skills in developing projects and programmes.

The Questionnaire

A questionnaire was mailed to the 80 seminar participants one year after the seminar was completed. The one year wait allowed the participants to evaluate the seminar more objectively: They had time to readjust to their own surroundings and use some of their new-found skills and knowledge with rural youth in their own country. The initial excitement of experiencing a new culture probably had worn off by the time the questionnaire was received.

The original questionnaire was translated from English into German and French, and divided into two parts: Part I asked general questions about the country the participant represented, the respondent's professional responsibilities, and their future plans in international work. In Part II, respondents were asked to evaluate the effectiveness of the international seminar in meeting its goals. A scale of 1 to 99 was used to rate 40 seminar activities; 1 being least effective, and 99 being very effective. A score of 50 indicated "somewhat effective."

After three months, a follow-up questionnaire was mailed to participants who did not return the first questionnaire. After six months, 50 questionnaires were returned. Specifically:

* 13 respondents were living in Africa;
* 1 was living in Australia;
* 11 were in Asia;
* 4 were living in North America;
* 20 were residing in Europe; and
* 1 was living in South America.

Sixteen questionnaires were returned by government officials, 21 from rural youth officers and 13 from educators.

The cost of conducting the study was approximately $2,500. Personal time, language translations, photocopying, international mailings, and return postage were the greatest expenses.

Findings

Analysis of the data collected suggests international seminars had helped participants gain a better understanding of world cultures and the education of rural youth.

". . . . the primary goal of this seminar is, through intensive cooperation, to put to the test different possibilities for motivating and communicating with our partners, and to examine their applicability for planning and carrying out rural youth programs."

– Karl Gross, 1986: 5

If a major objective of the seminar was, as Dr. Gross stated in his opening speech, to increase international cooperation and encourage interest in international rural youth work, then the seminar was extremely effective: Every person responding stated that they planned to participate in additional international seminars. This finding was particularly relevant since 72 per cent of the respondents reported that this seminar was the first international conference they had attended. In addition, 96 per cent stated that the 13th international seminar was well-organized. Specifically, respondents reported:

* The seminar helped rural youth leaders gain a greater understanding of rural youth problems in other countries. The participants believed activities such as reports from participants of other countries, informal one-on-one talks, and small group discussions as well as projects developed in small groups were the most helpful activities (See Table 12.1). Visits to rural youth clubs and farms garnered the least amount of interest.

TABLE 12.1: Effectiveness of Seminar in Broadening Participants' Understanding of Rural Youth Problems in Countries

Activity	Mean
	N=50
Country Exhibits	68.0
Individual Country Reports	80.2
Informal One-on-One Sharing	80.1
Small Group Activities	74.9
Small Group Discussions	77.0
Rural Youth Club Visits	52.7
Farm Visits	60.6
Projects Developed in Small Groups 76.0	
Informal Evening Recreation	73.1
Formal Social Functions	63.9
Overall Mean	70.7

Scale = 1-99. (A rank of 1 is least effective, and a rank of 99 is very effective. A score of 50 indicates "somewhat effective.")

* The international seminar also improved participants' planning and organizational skills. The respondents indicated that small group activities and the development of a rural youth programme were particularly effective activities that help them improve their organizational skills (See Table 12.2). Large groups meetings and the selection of a small group representative contributed the least.

TABLE 12.2: Effectiveness of Seminar in Improving Participant Planning and Organizational Skills

Activity	Mean N=50
Small Group Formulation	71.7
Small Group Introductions	72.0
Small Group Activities	79.0
Selection of Small Group Representatives	64.3
Evaluation of Methods Used	72.6
Large Group Informal Meetings	62.2
Material Presented and Handed Out	69.9
Organization of Evening Activities	68.5
Preparing Country Reports	68.7
Planning a Rural Youth Programme	78.3
Overall Mean	70.7

Scale = 1-99. (A rank of 1 is least effective, and a rank of 99 is very effective. A score of 50 indicates "somewhat effective.")

* The seminar improved youth leaders' group project skills and their abilities to work in a group. Respondents indicated that they gained a greater understanding of fostering creativity in groups, as well as the social differences between countries (See Table 12.3). The participants ranked the selection of project leaders and a question-and-answer session as the least effective activities designed to meet this objective.
* The biannual seminar also helped participants manage their professional responsibilities in their own countries. However, the ten activities designed to meet this fourth objective were evaluated as least effective, with a mean score of 63.2. Respondents indicated that a discussion of techniques contributing to effective teamwork was the most effective exercise, and another activity, the identification of funding strategies to support rural

youth, was rated the least effective (See Table 12.4).

TABLE 12.3: Effectiveness of Seminar in Improving Effectiveness as Team Members Working on Group Projects

Activity	Mean N=50
Understanding Social Differences	79.0
Choosing Project Leaders	65.5
Motivating Other Team Members	71.9
Improving Your Perception of Other Individuals	77.6
Methods of Directing Creative Group Work	81.7
Improving Your Cooperating Skills	76.9
Evaluating Individual Group Member's Skills	72.7
Improving Your Communication Skills	77.9
Question and Answer Session in Small Groups	66.0
Evaluating Your Own Strengths and Weaknesses	77.8
Overall Mean	74.7

Scale = 1-99. (A rank of 1 is least effective, and a rank of 99 is very effective. A score of 50 indicates "somewhat effective.")

TABLE 12.4. Effectiveness of Seminar in Assisting Participants with Rural Youth Work in their Countries

Activity	Maean N=50
Identifying Strategies for Seeking Funds to Support Rural Youth Work	45.6
Suggesting Techniques that Contribute to Effective Teamwork	77.0
Suggesting Specific Activities that Contribute to Cooperation	73.7
Identifying Strategies to Solve Technical and Economic Problems	61.8
Identifying Strategies to Solve Communication Problems	64.9
Improving Your Work with Governmental Agencies	55.9
Identifying Strategies to Slow Rural Youth Exodus	58.0
Identifying Ways to Increase Rural Youth Employment	54.6
Identifying Ways to Improve Educational Opportunity	64.2
Contributing to Your Effectiveness in Your Work	76.2
Overall Mean	63.2

Scale = 1-99. (A rank of 1 is least effective, and a rank of 99 is very effective. A score of 50 indicates "somewhat effective.")

Results by Continent, Professional Experience

Rural youth leaders from Africa ranked 30 of the 40 activities more effective than did other participants grouped by continent. Through this finding, organizations that sponsor participants from developing nations may find the positive results of generosity. Participants from the developing nations were particularly eager to learn and appreciated the ideas and concepts presented during the international seminar (See Table 12.5).

The European group ranked seminar activities lowest on the scale. When comparing participants' opinions as grouped by years of experience in rural youth work or by professional responsibility, no significant differences among mean scores were noted.

Seminars, Education and GlobalizationThe Benefits

> "I have never attended a seminar before, but this one changed my life. Recently, I was promoted, and (also) declared Field Officer of the Year . . . (these things happened) all because of the skills I learned and applied from the seminar. Things will never be the same again."
>
> – William Salaon Ole Yiaile

Overall, the respondents rated the 40 seminar activities at 69.8 on the 99 – point scale. While a mean of 69.8 signaled room for improvement, participants obviously believed the seminar was effective in satisfying its objectives as well as their own expectations.

The most moving and often most revealing portion of the questionnaire was the "personal comments" section. Annemieke Korten, an advisor/teacher from Holland, wrote:

> "The 13th seminar in Herrsching was unforgettable for me. Before this seminar, when I watched TV and saw people from other countries (black or white), I saw them as strangers. But, now, when I see those people on TV, I identify them with the people I met in Herrsching. They are not strangers anymore, but friends, people who have their own problems and feelings . . . .
>
> The feeling that everybody is equal has become stronger. The world has become smaller, and there are less borders. The experience we had together will always be in my heart, and I will keep it there as a great treasure."

TABLE 12.5: Means, Standard deviation, F-value and F-probability from composite response to ten seminar activites as related to each seminar objective

Seminar Objective	Participants from Africa	Participants from Asia	Participants from America & Australia	Participants from Europe	Total	F-Value	F Prob.
	(N=13)	(N=11)	(N=6)	(N=20)	(N=50)		
Objective 1: Improved understanding of rural youth problems	79.2 (a) 15.5 (b)	69.9 10.7	72.5 9.1	64.9 9.5	70.7 12.9	4.03*	.013
Objective 2: Improved planning, organizational, leadership skills	82.2 12.9	75.6 8.5	67.7 3.1	61.5 10.9	70.7 13.4	11.39**	.000
Objective 3: Improved ability to work in groups and with supervisors	86.3 7.1	76.6 9.2	81.0 7.3	64.2 13.8	74.7 13.9	12.23**	.000
Objective 4: Improved planning, organizational skills in developing projects, programs	75.3 16.2	68.9 6.0	72.1 7.8	49.4 13.9	63.2 16.9	13.35**	.000

* group mean
** standard deviation

Conclusions

The strengths of the 13th international seminar include:

* *The exposure and experience of different cultures*. Participants enjoyed learning about the differences and similarities of their cultures. They found that cultural differences certainly do exist, but the differences really are not so great. Rural youth leaders throughout the world often have the same goals, the same responsibilities, and the same problems.
* *The creation of a network of rural youth leaders from throughout the world*. Seminar participants found that they could contact each other, thus making rural development training programmes much easier to develop. We are now learning just how important worldwide cooperation and globalization is to our interests and wellbeing.
* *The creation of unity*. Seminar participants learned the benefit of team building, and enjoyed a feeling of camaraderie. They saw a need to draw on the expertise of fellow rural leaders for help.

Recommendations

* "(The seminar) was very useful for my development in relating to others and understanding the situation in global relations. The programme enabled me to make personal and professional contacts throughout the world. I fully support and recommend the continuation and increase of this type of professional exchange . . . .
* People should have more opportunities to repeat this experience. I know myself I could get 100 times more out of another programme because I would be more personally prepared. I feel others woul d be in a similar situation, especially if it was their first overseas experience."

– Lib McClure

As mentioned, a mean of 69.8 signals room for improvement. The seminar was not without drawbacks and limitations.

Additional Follow-up Support

During a follow-up meeting in 1988 with 13 seminar participants, many said they needed more support upon return to their home countries. They suggested additional support training, and followup meetings and services.

Many questionnaire respondents also wrote about the lack of adequate follow-up support. Many participants stated that they discovered and addressed some important problems during the seminar, but once they returned home, nothing had changed, and some coworkers were not receptive to their initiatives. Rural youth leaders did not want to be staff trainers – they wanted to be educators of young people.

One rural youth leader compared the seminar's lack of follow-up support to sending a high-tech irrigation system to a developing country without directions and guidance. "If you don't have the help you need to learn the machine's daily needs," he said, "soon you'll be right back where you started from."

Training Done Annually, On Different Continents

Sponsors should consider hosting the seminar annually, instead of biannually, and in various continents on a rotating basis. European participants found the seminar least effective. Sponsors need to consider hosting the seminar annually, moving the seminar to another part of the world every other year. Germany will still reserve its place as the primary sponsor. However, European participants may gain more from visiting another continent every other year, experiencing the culture, and being in a new environment.

Opportunities for Further Research

Governmental Roles within Globalization Process

Participants' benefit versus governmental benefit is an intriguing issue to be addressed by those interested in governmental priorities within the globalization process. Public relations plays a major role in the sponsorship of the International Seminar for the Promotion of Rural Youth Work, and governments may or may not consider the participants' best interests when planning the event. By hosting the seminar, Germany certainly gained good relations – and ultimately agricultural dollars – with governments throughout the world.

Financial Investment of International Seminars

According to this study, the expense of conducting an international rural youth seminar is justified, for it provides great benefits to participants. However, more detailed research comparing f inancial investment and seminars' effects on participants is needed.

Research exploring the benefits of specific activities offered at international seminars may also be useful. What do seminar participants particularly enjoy and find interesting? Small group and one-to-one interaction was particularly helpful to participants of this study. What do participants find least enjoyable or helpful? This study suggested that the selection of project leaders and visits to rural youth clubs were not wise uses of conference time.

In addition, an analysis of the structure of international seminars and the amount of time necessary to satisfy seminar goals would help seminar organizers plan the most interesting and efficient use of conference time.

Summary

International rural youth seminars are effective tools that catalyze and further the globalization process. Agriculture globalization and our efforts to achieve an understanding of world cultures and food systems through international seminars is becoming increasingly important. As Dr. Gross stated in his opening speech to the rural youth leaders attending the 13th international seminar (Gross, 1986: 2):

> "The agricultural situation has not significantly improved, but rather has worsened. This holds just as true for the highly developed agriculture of America as for the agricultures of Europe, Africa, or Asia. Five billion people now populate our planet, and we can count on over six billion by the year 2000. But, already today about 500 million people suffer from hunger, for each day the world's population grows by the size of one large city. All the related problems can only be solved with solidarity and collective responsibility."

REFERENCES

Buermann, Helmut, (1986), "Aims of the 13th International Seminar for the Promotion of Rural Youth Work." Unpublished paper, Rural Youth Institute, Herrsching, Germany.

Gross, Karl, (1986), "Opening of the 13th International Seminar for the Promotion of Rural Youth Work in Herrsching on July 8, 1986." Summary of the 13th International Seminar for the Promotion of Rural Youth Work. Federal Ministry of Food, Agriculture, and Forestry, Bonn, Germany.

Kiechle, Ignaz, (1986), "Closing address by Ignaz Kiechle." Summary of the 13th International Seminar for the Promotion of Rural Youth Work. Federal Ministry of Food, Agriculture, and Forestry, Bonn, Germany.

INDEX